By Bread Alone

By Bread Alone

LESTER R. BROWN

with

ERIK P. ECKHOLM

PUBLISHED FOR THE OVERSEAS DEVELOPMENT COUNCIL

PRAEGER PUBLISHERS

New York

Published in the United States of America in 1974
by Praeger Publishers
A Division of Holt, Rinehart and Winston
200 Park Avenue, New York, N. Y. 10017

Library of Congress Cataloging in Publication Data

Brown, Lester Russell, 1934-
  By bread alone.
  Bibliography: p.
  1. Food supply. 2. Population. I. Eckholm, Erik P., joint author.
II. Title
HD9000.6.B77   338.1'9   74-16477
ISBN 0-275-33540-2
ISBN 0-275-63640-2 (pbk.)

Printed in the United States of America

789 039 9876

CONTENTS

Part Three. AREAS OF CONCERN AND HOPE

Part Four. RESPONSES

Part Five. TOWARD CENTURY'S END

FOREWORD

by JAMES P. GRANT

President, Overseas Development Council

Lester Brown and Erik Eckholm break important new ground in their timely analysis of the changing food situation. Soaring world food prices in early 1973 apparently symbolized the emergence of a new economic era and a new international order. Dramatic rises in food prices were followed by jolting developments on several fronts. Most conspicuous were the Arab oil embargo, the raising of oil prices, and sharply rising fertilizer prices, accompanied by severe cutbacks in fertilizer exports to developing countries as the industrial nations pre-empted scarce supplies.

Viewed from the perspective of the 1980's, the crises of scarcity of the mid-'seventies will probably appear as essentially the product of continuing rapid economic and population growth within the constraints of a finite physical system and relatively inflexible political and economic structures. Global increases in population and in affluence have together doubled the annual increase in demand for food in the last twenty years. The current demand for some 30 million tons, strains the capacity of the world agricultural system. Skyrocketing world demand for other commodities, most notably oil, is converting traditional buyers' markets into sellers' markets.

Global economic shifts of this magnitude rarely take place smoothly, and the world now faces very difficult policy choices. Will governments respond by making the structural changes required through international negotiations and cooperation? Or will the world become locked into a pattern of chaos and conflict analogous to that of the 1930's, sentencing whole nations and much of mankind to massive suffering?

By Bread Alone is a case study of the world's most essential commodity, illustrating both the problems posed by the new international order and the policy alternatives open to mankind. As the authors show, the United States, the world's breadbasket, has special responsibilities in this area. By skillfully handling its approach to this basic commodity, the United States can help to shape the new "rules of the game" for access to raw materials, for expanding production, for establishing global reserves, and for changing lifestyles—new approaches needed for successful global management of *many* essential global resources.

Two of the policy recommendations in *By Bread Alone* warrant highlighting. First, a cooperative effort to promote rapid agricultural development in the poorer nations of the world—with particular attention to increasing the production of smaller farms—is urgently needed. The developed countries have reached the point where large-scale increases in agricultural production over the next decade will be possible only at substantially higher costs. Readily cultivable land and water resources have already been utilized, and fertilizer use is already so intensive that in many cases additional applications bring negligible returns. In other words, if the one-third increase in world grain production that will be required ten years hence is to come primarily from the developed countries, food prices will necessarily be much higher and will add to inflation everywhere.

If, on the other hand, the bulk of the increase in production comes from the developing countries, as the authors recommend, the cost of food will be less likely to increase. The limitations of organization, financing, and applying technology have kept the use of inputs low in most of the poorer countries. As one consequence, an additional ton of fertilizer will produce twice as much additional rice or wheat in South Asia as in Japan, Europe, or North America. Moreover, the developing countries have large pools of underemployed labor which can be put to use in lieu of mechanical power. Increased production in the developing countries, relying primarily on small farmers, results not only in maximum yields per acre but also in many ancillary benefits—increased rural employment, improved income distribution, reduced rural-urban migration, and, by increasing the motivation for smaller families, lower birth rates.

Of equal importance is the authors' emphasis on slowing the

growth in demand for food. This requires bringing population growth to a halt sooner than is now contemplated by most demographers and political leaders. The world must find means of stabilizing population far below the presently projected 10–16 billion, and the authors suggest possible means for doing so. But the need to slow the growth in demand for food also calls for a reduction in grain use by the world's affluent minority. (Grain consumption in North America, for example, is now approaching one ton annually per person.) This can be accomplished in part through a modest change in diets, reducing consumption of grain-intensive livestock products.

By Bread Alone is unique in its interdisciplinary analysis of future world food-production prospects. As world leaders consider the challenges brought by global food scarcity, it should serve as an exceedingly useful resource.

ACKNOWLEDGMENTS

This book owes much to our many Overseas Development Council colleagues who participated in its production. Blondeen Duhaney typed numerous drafts with skill and efficiency. Georgia Shelton, Deborah Everett, and Margaret Koch helped with the typing. Valeriana Kallab provided valuable editorial assistance, aided by Carol Hoban. The office management of Michael O'Hare helped make it possible to meet tight deadlines. John Tidd's research support made writing the book much easier.

Gladys Topkis, our editor at Praeger, was a delight to work with. All or parts of the manuscript were usefully reviewed by Raymond Ewell, James Grant, George Harrar, Nathan Koffsky, John Sewell, Davidson Sommers, and Sterling Wortman, but the conclusions remain the responsibility of the authors alone.

About the Overseas Development Council

The Overseas Development Council is an independent, non-profit organization established in 1969 to increase American understanding of the economic and social problems confronting the developing countries, and of the importance of these countries to the United States in an increasingly interdependent world. The ODC seeks to promote consideration of development issues by the American public, policymakers, specialists, educators, and the media through its research, conferences, publications, and laison with U.S. mass-membership organizations interested in U.S. relations with the developing world. The ODC's program is funded by foundations, corporations, and private individuals; its policies are determined by its Board of Directors under the Chairmanship of Theodore M. Hesburgh, C.S.C. The Council's President is James P. Grant.

ODC Board of Directors

By Bread Alone

1.

OVERVIEW: THE CHANGING FACE OF FOOD SCARCITY

In the early 'seventies the soaring demand for food, spurred by both continuing population growth and rising affluence, has begun to outrun the productive capacity of the world's farmers and fishermen. The result has been declining food reserves, skyrocketing food prices, and intense competition among countries for available food supplies. Fundamental changes in the world food situation have left governments, institutions, and individuals everywhere unprepared and vulnerable.

Growing global insecurity on the food front is directly related to the precipitous decline in world food reserves. Since World War II, the world has relied on two major food reserves: carryover stocks of grain in the principal exporting countries and cropland held idle in the United States under government farm programs. Together they provided a substantial buffer against the vagaries of weather and the whims of the market place. In 1961 these reserves amounted to 222 million tons of grain, or 95 days' worth of world consumption. By 1974, however, they had declined to a level representing global needs for only 26 days.

Thus in mid-1974 the world food supply-demand equation was precariously balanced. A poor harvest in any major producing country—the United States, the Soviet Union, India, or China—would send economic shock waves not only throughout the food sector of the world economy but, as it fueled the fires of inflation, throughout its other sectors as well. The vulnerability of the supply-demand balance to the weather suggested that the climate itself might well replace pollution as the dominant global environmental concern.

In this situation, national governments have resorted to a variety of techniques to obtain or ensure adequate food supplies for their people. Their actions have given rise to a new phenomenon: a global politics of food scarcity. During the summer of 1972, the Soviet Union employed secrecy to corner the world's wheat market by buying a large share of the exportable supplies of wheat before even the American government knew what was happening. The following summer, the United States—the source of 85 per cent of all the soybeans entering the world market—abruptly announced an export embargo on soybeans in an effort to curb soaring soybean and food prices at home. This action, taken without warning or consultation with other countries, triggered a wave of diplomatic protests from Europe and Asia. For the billion people in East Asia for whom soybeans are a vital food staple and an essential source of scarce protein, the U.S. decision posed an ominous threat.

A similar situation developed with rice when Thailand, a leading world supplier, banned rice exports for several months in order to prevent politically costly price rises at home. This move was successful in its objective, but it wreaked havoc with efforts to prevent runaway food prices in other Southeast Asian countries. And in a similar spirit Brazil, despite its widely proclaimed food-producing potential, imposed export restrictions on both soybeans and beef.

The abrupt transition of the world food economy from a buyer's market to a seller's market that these national moves signaled in the early 'seventies, as well as the consequent rise in food prices, was not widely anticipated. Between late 1972 and the end of 1973, the world price of wheat tripled, and the price of rice followed. Soybean prices doubled in a twenty-four month period.

The sudden increase in wheat prices was followed in a matter of months by an equally dramatic rise in petroleum prices. From 1960 to 1972 the world price of a bushel of wheat and that of a barrel of oil were nearly equal, ranging from $1.35 to slightly over $2.00. A bushel of wheat could be traded for a barrel of oil in the world marketplace. In late 1973, the price of wheat soared past $5.00. For a brief period a bushel of wheat could be exchanged for two barrels of oil. Then came the Christmas Eve, 1973, oil price increase by the oil-exporting countries—the second doubling in price within the year—and the price of oil soared above that of wheat, reaching $8.00 per barrel.

These dramatic price increases raised one of the oldest questions with which economists have wrestled: What is the true value of a commodity? What is a fair and reasonable price? There are no obvious answers. In trying to shed light on this issue, several points need to be kept in mind. Wheat is a renewable resource, oil is not. Most of the world's exportable supplies of each are controlled by a single geographic region: North America in the case of wheat, the Middle East in the case of oil. Countries exporting oil or wheat stand to benefit from the price rises. No country exports both, but a great number import both. The poorer countries importing both wheat and oil suffered the greatest damage. The many countries having no valuable raw materials of their own to export exhausted their limited foreign-exchange reserves in a matter of months, and several were on the verge of international bankruptcy.

Short supplies of food and energy dramatize the extent of global interdependence. No country is entirely isolated from the effects of these scarcities—or from their trade and monetary repercussions. The capacity of U.S. agriculture to supply low-cost food to American consumers was thought to be inexhaustible, yet in 1973 Americans suddenly discovered that they were sharing food scarcity with consumers throughout the world. The United States was paying its rapidly rising oil-import bill with food exports. Indeed, the share of world food and energy consumption crossing national boundaries is climbing steadily. Japan imports well over half of its total cereal supplies, Egypt nearly 40 per cent. The countries of the European Economic Community import nearly all their petroleum, as well as four fifths of the high-protein feeds for their livestock industries. The United States already depends on imports for one third of its petroleum supplies; if its recent demand trend persists, it is expected to import half by 1985.

These events of the early 'seventies signal a fundamental shift in the structure of the world food economy. Throughout most of the period since World War II, the world food economy has been plagued by chronic excess capacity, surplus stocks, and low food prices. But emerging conditions suggest that this era is ending and is being replaced by a period of more or less chronic scarcity and higher prices, with little if any land held out of production. Short-term price fluctuations and temporary commercial surpluses should not obscure the more basic long-term forces at work.

Changing conditions on both the demand and supply sides of the world food equation are contributing to this shift. Throughout most of history, increases in the demand for food derived from growth in population. Since the time of Malthus, the food problem has been viewed as a food/population problem. World population growth continues to be rapid, but rising affluence now has emerged as another major claimant on the world's food-producing resources.

The impact of population growth on the demand for food is easy to understand. A 3 per cent increase in population generates a 3 per cent increase in the demand for food. But the impact of rising affluence is not so readily understood. One way to visualize it is in terms of per capita grain requirements. In the less developed countries, only about 400 pounds of grain per year is available to the average person. Almost all of this quantity must be consumed directly merely to meet minimal food-energy needs; very little can be converted into livestock products. By contrast, the average North American uses nearly a ton of grain per year. Of this, only 200 pounds is consumed directly as bread, pastries, or breakfast cereal. The remainder is consumed indirectly in the form of meat, milk, and eggs. Thus the average North American currently uses up *five times* as many agricultural resources as the average Indian, Nigerian, or Colombian.

The combined effect of population growth and rising affluence is expanding the world demand for food at a rate without precedent. At the turn of the century, the annual growth in global demand for cereals was probably about 4 million tons per year. By 1950 it was about 12 million tons per year. As of 1970, only twenty years later, the world demand for cereals was expanding by 30 million tons per year—the equivalent of the annual wheat crop of Canada, Australia, and Argentina combined. And this increase in demand is incessant, occurring in years of good and bad weather alike.

On the supply side, three sets of factors are beginning to affect efforts to augment world food output as rapidly as is necessary. Serious technological constraints are limiting the rapid expansion of food, particularly beef and soybeans; all four of the major resources used to produce food—land, water, energy, and fertilizer —are now in tight supply; and in a growing number of situations the pressures of growing demand for food are beginning to undermine the ecology of major food-producing systems.

The inability to achieve technological breakthroughs in critical areas is a significant limitation on the expansion of food supplies. In the case of beef, agricultural scientists have not been able to devise any commercially viable means of producing more than one calf per cow per year. For every animal entering the beef-production process, one adult animal must be fed and otherwise maintained for a full year. No breakthrough in this area appears to be imminent. This would not pose a serious problem if there were a great deal of unused grazing capacity in the world, but unfortunately much of the world's pastureland is already overgrazed, and much more is fully utilized.

Another technological limitation on efforts to expand supplies of high-quality protein is the inability of scientists to dramatically increase per-acre yields of soybeans. As we have noted, soybeans are a major source of high-quality protein for livestock and poultry throughout the world, and in East Asia they are consumed directly as food by perhaps a billion people. Soybeans are therefore extremely important in economic terms. They have become the leading export of the United States, surpassing not only more traditional farm exports, such as wheat and corn, but also high-technology items, such as electronic computers and jet aircraft. Yet since 1950 soybean yields per acre have increased less than 30 per cent while corn yields have increased a remarkable 140 per cent. Thus the world gets more soybeans essentially by planting more soybeans. As of 1973, one of every six acres of U.S. farmland was planted to soybeans. As idled cropland disappears in the United States, the inability to achieve a soybean-yield breakthrough may create serious global supply problems.

The world is now facing, for the first time, shortages in each of the four basic agricultural resources—land, water, energy, and fertilizer.

From the beginning of agriculture until about 1950, most of the year-to-year increases in world food output came from expansion of the area under cultivation. Since 1950, however, the major increases—probably four fifths of the current gains in output— are attributable to intensification of cultivation on existing land area. Most of the good cropland in the world is already under cultivation. Additional opportunities for expanding the world's cultivated area still exist, but they are mainly limited to the interior of Latin America and parts of sub-Saharan Africa. And even in these regions, the cost of food produced on the new land may be much higher than that of food grown in cultivated areas. Brazil, which occupies much of the interior of Latin America, now has the largest grain deficit in the Western Hemisphere.

But the principal constraint on efforts to expand world food supplies during the final years of this century may well be water rather than land. In many regions of the world, fertile agricultural land is still available—provided that water can be found to make it productive. But most of the rivers that lend themselves to damming and to irrigation have already been developed. The expansion of irrigated area is slowing as the more attractive sites are exhausted. Future efforts to increase fresh-water supplies for agricultural purposes will focus increasingly on such techniques as the diversion of rivers (as in the Soviet Union today), the desalting of seawater, and the manipulation of rainfall patterns to increase the share of rain falling over moisture-deficient agricultural areas. Indeed, such initiatives as Rhodesia's recently announced plan to systematically seed clouds to increase rainfall by 10 per cent— possibly at the expense of neighboring African countries—raises the prospect that meteorological warfare soon may emerge from the province of science fiction.

Increasing world food production also requires a substantial increase in the amount of energy available for doing so. The recent quadrupling of the world price of energy is certain to affect future food-production prospects adversely, but no one can yet foresee exactly how. In more modern agricultural systems, such as that of the United States, the amount of energy now used to produce food greatly exceeds the amount of food energy the crops themselves yield. But as energy-intensive as farm production is, it consumes less than one fourth of the energy used in the U.S. food system. The rest is used to transport, process, preserve, and distribute the food. Perhaps the grossest inefficiency in the entire process is the usual means of transporting food from market to home. The average American shopper drives a two-ton automobile several miles to a supermarket at least once a week to transport perhaps thirty pounds of food. In the developing countries, the future availability of energy will have a profound effect on efforts to provide adequate nutrition, for large increases in energy inputs will be necessary if food production in these nations is to increase rapidly.

The fourth major agricultural resource—fertilizer—is also in very short supply. The outlook in this case, too, is for generally higher prices in the future. One reason for the fertilizer shortage is a lag in the construction of new production facilities, but even when supply catches up with demand, the rising cost of energy will undoubtedly keep fertilizer prices well above the historical level. The production of nearly all of the world's nitrogen fertilizer (which accounts for roughly half of all fertilizer used) utilizes natural gas or naphtha as a raw material. In addition, the manufacturing process is energy-intensive, requiring large amounts of electrical power. The combination of soaring energy prices, the enormous capital requirements needed to create new production facilities, and the time required to bring new facilities into production means that nitrogen fertilizer will be in critically short supply for many years at least.

Finally, the ecological undermining of major food-producing systems also is beginning to have an adverse effect on the prospects of increasing world food production. Until recently, the oceans were viewed as an almost limitless source of protein, but the outlook has been sharply altered in the past few years. From 1950 to 1970, the world fish catch climbed steadily, more than tripling over this period from 21 million to 70 million tons. Since then, the catch declined for three consecutive years—even while the capital and effort expended to bring in the catch continues to rise. Many marine biologists now feel that the global catch of table-grade fish is at or near the maximum sustainable (i.e., self-regenerating) level. Overfishing, depleted stocks, and declining catches are affecting the haddock fishery of the northwest Atlantic and the anchovy

fishery along the western coast of Latin America. The Peruvian
anchovy fishery, the world's richest, yielded as much as 12 million
tons—or one fifth of the world fish catch—during the late 'sixties.
Largely because of overfishing, in 1973 the catch fell precipitously,
to scarcely 2 million tons, and is now being rebuilt. As growth in
marine protein supplies lags behind the global growth in demand,
additional pressure will be shifted to land-based protein resources.

The tragedy unfolding in the African countries south of the
Sahara Desert is an example of another type of ecological overstress that is diminishing the earth's food-producing capacity, although the problem exists elsewhere as well. Over the past thirty-
five years, human and livestock populations along the sub-Saharan
fringe have increased rapidly, nearly doubling in some areas. As
these populations have multiplied, they have put more pressure on
the ecosystem than it can withstand. The result has been overgrazing and deforestation, encouraging the advancement of the
Sahara Desert at rates up to thirty miles per year along the desert's
3,500-mile southern fringe, stretching from Senegal to northern
Ethiopia. As the desert expands southward, human and livestock
populations retreat before it. The result is ever greater pressure on
the fringe area, which in turn contributes to further denudation and
deforestation, setting in process a self-reinforcing cycle.

Several consecutive years of drought have brought this deteriorating situation to a disastrous climax. If, as some meteorologists
believe, the life-giving belt of monsoon rains is shifting southward,
then ecological overstress and climatic changes are reinforcing
each other with catastrophic human consequences. If the process of
desertification is not reversed, then Africa—which has one of the
highest population growth rates of all the continents—may lose a
sizable slice of its food-producing capacity.

The Indian subcontinent provides a third dramatic example of
ecological overstress. Over the past generation, as human and
livestock populations have grown, the subcontinent has been progressively deforested. This trend has increased the incidence and
severity of floods. The situation is most serious in the Himalayas
and the surrounding foothills, for this is where nearly all of the
subcontinent's major river systems—the Indus, the Ganges, and
the Brahmaputra—originate. The long-term dangers inherent in

continuing deforestation could have been predicted several years ago, yet many were surprised when Pakistan's August, 1973, flood —the worst in its history—washed away entire communities and, in some regions, destroyed the recently harvested wheat crop in storage as well as the summer crop standing in the fields. Since the deforestation trend has not been checked, one can only predict that the incidence and severity of flooding in Pakistan, India, and Bangladesh will be much greater in the future than it is at present. In effect, deforestation, particularly in Nepal, may be gradually undermining the subcontinent's food-producing capacity—to the grave detriment of the nearly three quarters of a billion people who now depend on it.

Clearly, the food-producing ecosystems in many parts of the world are being threatened by the pressures of a continuously growing demand for food. The examples given above are only three of the many that could be cited. The time has come to inventory these ecological stresses and assess their impact on future world food-production prospects.

The changing world food situation is forcing us to redefine the problem and rethink our response to it. Traditionally most analysts have viewed the projected demand or need for food against the technological potential for expanding world food production. It is relatively easy to envisage a doubling or tripling of world food output based on known reserves of land and water, achieved through vastly increased inputs of energy and fertilizer. Some even suggest the possibility of a severalfold increase, assuming the uniform application of advanced technology and of the most sophisticated management techniques available. That there is a vast technological opportunity for expanding food supplies is not debatable, but this is not the real problem. The critical issue is *at what price* the additional resources will be brought into use. We know that most good land in the world is already under cultivation. We know that, with a few exceptions, the most desirable irrigation sites already have been developed. We know that energy, and therefore fertilizer, will be more costly in the future than in the past. We know that in the more advanced countries, where yields are already high, further increases in production will be far more costly than those of the past.

In order to bring these marginal resources into use, those world prices for food must rise above their historic levels. Unfortunately, however, recent food-price rises have already far exceeded growth in income among several hundred million of the world's poorest people. As a result, the food-intake level of millions of low-income people is being pushed below the survival level—in many regions reversing the long-term trend of improved nutrition, lengthening life expectancy, and declining infant mortality.

Historically, famine has been limited to relatively small geographic areas, as in Ireland in 1847 and in West Bengal in 1943. But advances in global and national food distribution and transportation systems now ensure that food scarcity is allocated according to *income* levels, with scarcity concentrated among the world's poor, wherever they are. Today, even while the threat of traditional famine persists in some areas, a less visible crisis of hunger and malnutrition is emerging among the world's lowest income groups—whether in the Philippines, Bangladesh, sub-Saharan Africa, northeastern Brazil, or among the Andean Indians. The silent crisis of malnutrition may be denying close to a billion human beings the basic right to realize their full genetic potential, their full humanity.

The prospect of a long-term steady climb in food prices, outstripping the purchasing power of a large segment of mankind, presents the international community with a formidable challenge, necessitating a radical shift in the traditional approach to food scarcity. Unless an effort is made to slow the growth in world *demand* for food, the world will be forced farther and farther up the cost curve in order to bring ever more marginal resources into use.

The deterioration of the world food situation during the first half of the current decade, together with currently foreseeable trends, also makes it quite clear that the world cannot remain long on its present demographic path. The choice is between famine and family planning, for future population growth clearly will be reduced by rising death rates, as is already occurring in some African and Asian countries, if it is not reduced by declining birth rates. An effort of unprecedented proportions is required to reduce birth rates among the more affluent—who exert such a disproportionately large per capita claim on the earth's scarce resources —as well as among the poor, where birth rates tend to be so high. Programs must be launched immediately to make family-planning services available to everyone, to meet the basic social needs of the poor that affect motivation for smaller families, to encourage new social roles for women, and to reorient national economic and social policies so as to promote low fertility.

A simultaneous effort is needed to simplify diets among the more affluent, to reduce, not their nutritional value, but their wasteful per capita claim on the earth's scarce agricultural resources. Important economic, ecological, and health considerations—all involving self-interest—now join the basic moral question of the distribution of scarce resources to argue for the simplification of diets among the rich, particularly for the substitution of high-quality vegetable protein for animal protein. The widespread substitution of vegetable oils for animal fats, such as margarine for butter, in the United States during the past generation provides both an example of the kind of change required and proof of its feasibility.

The changing nature of the food problem also calls for a major shift in geographic emphasis. The opportunity for easily expanding production in the developed countries has diminished sharply now that idled cropland in the United States has been returned to production. There is little prospect of quick, easy gains in the United States, Western Europe, the Soviet Union, or Japan, although substantial gains still are possible in all but Japan.

The world's principal unrealized potential for expanding food production is now concentrated in the developing countries. Although soil quality in Bangladesh is as good as in Japan, rice yields are only one third of those attained in Japan. India's area of cropland is roughly comparable to that of the United States, yet it harvests only 100 millions tons of grain, while the United States harvests 250 million tons. And corn yields in Brazil and Thailand are still less than one third those of the United States.

As resources become scarce, the comparative advantage in additional food production shifts toward those areas where conditions offer the highest returns. Today, the increase in food output that can be produced with an additional ton of fertilizer or gallon of fuel is far higher in the developing countries than in the industrial countries. Since fertilizers are already used very heavily in the agriculturally advanced nations of Europe, in Japan, and in the United States, an additional pound of fertilizer applied in these nations may return no more than five additional pounds of grain. But in countries such as India, Indonesia, or Brazil, another pound of fertilizer can yield at least ten additional pounds of grain. It is unfortunate and ironic that, when world fertilizer shortages emerged in 1973, the more advanced nations acted to restrict their fertilizer exports to the poor nations, where the fertilizer could have produced much more food.

A similar situation exists with respect to energy. Additional inputs of energy to agriculture in countries like the United States and Japan are bringing rapidly diminishing returns in food production. In most developing countries, by contrast, additional energy inputs to operate irrigation pumps and in the form of fertilizers are an essential key to tapping vast unexploited food-production potential.

Although all these factors indicate that the greatest unrealized agronomic potential now resides in the developing world, this potential will not materialize easily. Agricultural development in the poor nations involves complex social, political, and economic changes; and without a strong commitment to these changes on the part of the governments of these countries, the needed agricultural progress will not occur. But in most cases the modernization process can be greatly facilitated by appropriate kinds of technical and economic assistance from the more prosperous nations.

For a variety of reasons, special attention in the developing countries needs to be focused on farmers with small landholdings. Growing evidence suggests that, where small farmers have access to needed inputs, credit, and supporting services, they engage in labor-intensive cultivation and produce considerably higher yields of food per acre than do farmers on larger estates. The recent shifts in emphasis by the World Bank, the U.S. Agency for International Development, and other development agencies to give greater attention to small farms and rural development are an important step in the right direction, but government agencies *within* the developing countries have often failed to reorient their own programs to encourage progress among the poorer small farmers. In most developing nations, small-farm progress can contribute simultaneously to the solution of several acute problems. It can help to improve income-distribution patterns, reduce unemployment, check the swelling flow of people from the countryside to the cities, and greatly expand national and world food supplies. This approach has a further important benefit; evidence from developing countries in many parts of the world indicates that a rural development strategy centered on small farms, by spreading the benefits of economic progress among the poorest groups, can create a social environment that greatly increases the motivation to limit family size.

Over the past two decades, nations have devised numerous means for managing commercial *abundance*—including special farm-subsidy programs and the withholding of cropland from production. It has now become essential to develop the policies and institutions, both national and international, for managing *scarcity*. Foremost among the new institutions needed is a new world food-reserve system. Cooperative international management of food reserves would reintroduce some measure of stability to the world food economy and also help to ensure that the capacity of the international community to respond to food emergencies is maintained. The extreme price volatility that is likely in the absence of an effective reserve system will not serve the interests of producers, consumers, or government policy-makers attempting to cope with inflation.

The rapid integration of the world food economy and the changing nature of global food scarcity raise difficult moral issues. In an interdependent world plagued with scarcity, if some of us consume more, others must of necessity consume less. For example, should the Soviet Union again unexpectedly purchase a substantial share of the world's exportable wheat supplies, then consumers in low-income countries will be deprived of supplies that they need merely to maintain their minimum food requirements. If an affluent minority throughout the world continues to expand its consumption of livestock products, grain prices may be pulled out of reach of the poorest quarter of mankind. And if Americans continue to drive large automobiles, consuming a disproportionately large share of the world's available energy supplies, then world energy supplies will become more scarce, and farmers in India and elsewhere in the developing world may be unable to obtain fuel to operate their irrigation pumps. The world food problem has many new dimensions, but none is more complex or difficult to deal with than the moral one.

PART ONE

Dimensions of the Problem

2.

HISTORY AND GEOGRAPHY OF MALNUTRITION

In the late twentieth century, an era of unprecedented affluence, hunger is still the common lot of much of mankind. For this group the quality of life is influenced more by the lack of food than by any other single factor. For them, the hope for assured food suplies that came with the discovery of agriculture has never been realized. Daily existence is still circumscribed by the quest for food, reducing life to very fundamental biological terms.

THE EVOLUTION OF AGRICULTURE

Throughout most of his 2-million-year existence, man survived as a predatory hunter and a gatherer of fruits, nuts, and berries. Life was largely a quest for food under the constant threat of starvation—a quest whose difficulty checked the growth in human numbers. Then, perhaps as recently as 10,000 years ago, man learned to domesticate animals and plants and began the great transition from hunter to tiller. Although there are still a few bands of hunters scattered about the earth, this transition is virtually complete. Man has substituted the vicissitudes of weather for the uncertainty of the hunt.

When man first turned to agriculture, the earth supported no more than 10 million people—fewer than now live in London or Iraq. Since then, a series of technological innovations has brought about an enormous expansion in the earth's food-producing capacity. Six of them stand out: the use of irrigation, the harnessing of draft animals, the exchange of crops between the Old World and the New, the development of chemical fertilizers and pesticides, advances in plant genetics, and the invention of the internal-combustion engine.

After the discovery of agriculture itself, irrigation was man's first major effort to alter his environment in order to produce more food. The emergence of a distinctly irrigated agriculture dates back some 6,000 years to the Tigres-Euphrates flood plain, and quite possibly also to that of the Nile. Irrigated agriculture provided the surplus food and spurred the social organization that gave rise to the earliest civilizations.

The next agricultural innovation that greatly increased the earth's food-producing capacity was the harnessing of animals for tillage purposes. Exactly when this occurred is not certain, although we know it was after man learned to irrigate, and not later than 3000 B.C. This breakthrough enabled man to convert roughage, a form of energy which man could not digest, into a form that could be used to increase his food supply. By augmenting man's limited muscle power, the harnessing of draft animals raised the efficiency of his labor so that a small segment of the population could be spared from food-producing activities. It is probably not a coincidence that the earliest cities emerged about the same time that man learned to harness draft animals.

Christopher Columbus is not customarily credited with a major role in expanding the earth's food-producing capacity, but his contribution was profoundly important. By linking the Old World to the New, he also joined two systems of agriculture that apparently had evolved independently. Crops domesticated in the two regions were quite different. Thus when Columbus established the trans-oceanic link, he set in motion an exchange of crops that continues today. Interestingly, some crops found a more comfortable ecological niche in the world to which they were transferred than in the one of their origin. For example, the introduction of the potato into Europe, the Soviet Union, and China greatly increased food production in those regions. Today potato crops in Europe and the Soviet Union are several times that in the New World, where the potato originated.

TABLE 2-1. AREA OF ORIGIN, MAJOR CROPS.

Old World	New World
wheat	maize
oats	squash
barley	beans
sorghum	pumpkins
rye	white potatoes
sugar cane	sweet potatoes
soybeans	tomatoes
olives	avocados
lemons	cocoa
oranges	cassava
peaches	strawberries
pears	papaya
walnuts	sunflowers
	tobacco
	yams

Of the three principal grains consumed by man—wheat, rice, and corn—only corn (or maize) was indigenous to the New World. Today, however, corn is produced on every continent; it has become a leading feed grain in many countries and a dietary staple in others. Wheat, rye, barley, oats, and grain sorghum were all introduced from the Old World into the New, where the environment proved to be highly receptive. Without these small grains, much of the vast land area of the low-rainfall region of the United States might have remained in grass, for corn requires more moisture than is commonly available over much of the Great Plains. The soybean, now the leading U.S. export product, was introduced to North America from China.

The movement of crops between the New World and the Old has been very much a two-way exchange, but this was not the case with livestock and poultry. Except for the turkey, all members of the New World farmyard—including horses, cattle, hogs, sheep, and chickens—came from Europe.

A dominant factor in efforts to expand the world's food supply, particularly since 1950, has been the use of agricultural chemicals to improve soil fertility and to control pests. A German chemist, Justus Von Liebig, is considered the father of modern soil chemistry. In the 1840's Von Liebig demonstrated that all the nutrients that crops remove from the soil can be replaced by man. Although this discovery laid the foundations for the modern chemical fertilizer industry, it did not become commercially important until well into the twentieth century, largely because the frontiers offered the traditional alternative of bringing new land under the plow. Today, however, fertilizer is increasingly being substituted for land in efforts to expand food production.

Closely paralleling growth in the use of fertilizer by the world's farmers has been growth in the use of chemical pesticides. As crop varieties have been improved to become larger and more lush, they have become exceedingly attractive to pests. The use of chemicals toxic to the pests endangering a particular crop is the most effective way yet developed of combating those pests. One of the difficulties, of course, is that the chemicals may be harmful to other species of plants and animals as well.

The invention of the internal-combustion engine greatly augmented the energy resources available for expanding man's food supply. Some 5,000 years after draft animals were first harnessed for agricultural purposes, man achieved a quantum jump in the energy per person available for food production. Today, perhaps two thirds of the world's cropland is tilled with mechanical power.

Since Gregor Mendel's discovery of the fundamental principles of heredity, our ability to alter the genetic composition of domesticated species of plants and animals has led to a series of advances that have greatly increased the earth's food-producing capacity. Plant breeders have been able to select, classify, and combine various genetic traits in order to alter literally dozens of plant characteristics. For example, they can make plants shorter or taller, more responsive to fertilizer, more resistant to drought and disease, more tolerant of cold; they also can change the quantity and quality of protein content and the cooking characteristics of various foodstuffs.

A particularly impressive achievement has been the advance made in cereal productivity as the result of genetic breakthroughs. This process began with the hybridization of corn in the United

States, a discovery that contributed importantly to the tripling of U.S. corn yields over the past generation. Later advances in cereal breeding, embodied in the discovery of the high-yielding dwarf varieties of wheat and rice, have given rise to the so-called Green Revolution within the past decade.

Improvements in cereal productivity have been at least matched by advances in livestock and poultry. The first domesticated cow probably yielded no more than 600 pounds of milk per year, barely enough to support a calf to the point where it could forage for itself. In India, milk production remains at about that level today. By contrast, in 1973 the average milk cow in the United States yielded over 10,000 pounds of milk annually. The world's record is held by a cow in the state of Washington, "Skagvale Graceful Hattie," which recently produced more than 44,000 pounds of milk in a single year—55 quarts daily—thus outperforming its early ancestors by a factor of more than 70 to 1.

The first domesticated hens did not lay more than about fifteen eggs (or one "clutch") per year. In 1973, however, the average American hen produced 228 eggs. For some times, U.S. hens held the world egg-laying title, but a few years ago an industrious Japanese hen set a new record by laying 365 eggs in 365 days. U.S. agricultural analysts project continuing gains in productivity for cows and hens, although the rates of increase have already begun to taper off as biological limits are approached.

What Man Eats

What man eats depends on many factors, most importantly on where he lives. Since most food is produced in the area of the world in which it is consumed, local climate (particularly rainfall level), soil type, and prevailing vegetation have a strong influence on dietary habits. Beyond these factors, income level is a major determinant of dietary patterns. Religious and social taboos also influence diets, but they are comparatively minor factors.

In his efforts to survive over the millennia, man has learned to eat the seeds of many plants, roots and tubers, stems and leaves, and fruits. In the animal world, he has learned to consume other mammals, including cattle, horses, sheep, and goats, as well as poultry and fish. The human diet is dominated by cereals, the starchy food staples that provide just over half the total human food-energy intake. Actually this figure greatly underestimates the importance of cereals, since it does not include the sizable share consumed indirectly in the form of meat, milk, and eggs. Among the cereals consumed, rice and wheat dominate, with each supplying about one fifth of the total.

Four other food groups each account for about one tenth of man's food-energy supply: fruits, nuts, and vegetables; sugar; animal fats and vegetable oils; and livestock products and fish. If food intake were measured in protein instead of calories, livestock products and fish would be much more significant.

TABLE 2–2. SOURCES OF MAN'S FOOD ENERGY.

Food	Percentage of Energy Supplied
Cereals	56
Rice	21
Wheat	20
Corn	5
Other cereals	10
Roots and tubers	7
Potatoes and yams	5
Cassava	2
Fruits, nuts, and vegetables	10
Sugar	7
Fats and oils	9
Livestock products and fish	11
Total	100

In every society in the world for which data are available, as income rises, the share of calories provided by cereal declines and that provided by livestock products rises. The share coming from cereals varies widely among geographic regions, from a low of 24 per cent in North America to a high of 74 per cent in Asia. In high-income regions, such as the United States, Australia, and New Zealand, the share of calories in the diet derived from livestock products exceeds that derived from cereals.

In some regions of the world, roots and tubers are more important than cereals. This is true of large areas of Africa south of the Sahara and of parts of tropical Latin America, including much of northeastern Brazil. In these parts of the world malnutrition is especially acute among children in the post-weaning stage, who are not able to consume enough of the low-protein cassava, for example, to meet their minimal protein needs.

The specific starchy staple consumed in a given region is dictated largely by local growing conditions. Wheat is the principal food staple in 45 countries, including those of Western and Eastern Europe, North America, and Oceania. It is also an increasingly important food in many other countries. Rice is the principal food staple in only about 25 countries, but this group includes many of the world's most populous nations. Corn dominates diets in sixteen countries in Latin America and sub-Saharan Africa. In many tropical countries, cassava or yams are the principal food staple, and in some Central American countries, plantains and bananas provide more calories than any other food.

A hierarchy of preferences applies even to the world's starchy food staples. As incomes rise, preferences shift from roots and tubers to cereals. Among the cereals, wheat and rice are generally preferred over sorghum, barley, and corn. Within the principal rice-consuming countries, wheat consumption is rising steadily as incomes rise.

FAMINE IN HUMAN HISTORY

The discovery of agriculture permitted man to initiate a steady expansion of the earth's food-producing capacity. Since agriculture began, food production has increased several hundredfold. Unfortunately, man's numbers have also expanded to absorb the additional food, always pressing against the limits of supply.

Under these circumstances, a sudden, sharp reduction in the food supply in any particular geographic locale has usually resulted in widespread hunger and famine. (Famine as we discuss it here may be distinguished from the long-term problems of hunger and malnutrition, which chronically afflict a sizable portion of mankind.) We have no accurate or complete record of the number of famines affecting agricultural man over the millennia, but what evidence is available indicates that they must number in the hundreds if not the thousands.

Whether it results from natural disasters or from man-made causes, notably war, civil or international, severe famine is always a horror. Humans not only suffer and die in large numbers, but many are pushed to extreme behavior by starvation. In addition to hoarding and stealing food, starving people have been known to resort to murder and cannibalism as well as to selling children to obtain money for food. Rather than slowly starve to death, thousands of Romans allegedly threw themselves into the Tiber during the famine of 436 B.C. Whole families are reported to have drowned themselves in the Indian famine of A.D. 1291. Cannibalism was reported in pre–twentieth-century famines in England, Scotland, Ireland, Italy, Egypt, India, and China. It has been linked with famine in the twentieth century as well; cemeteries in many parts of Russia had to be guarded in 1921 and 1922 to prevent the exhumation of freshly buried corpses.

Famines in Asia are in a class by themselves because of their frequency and the scale of the loss of life. Asia's rice-growing areas, supporting the earth's largest and densest populations, are especially susceptible because they lie within the monsoon belt, where rainfall is unreliable—sometimes failing altogether, sometimes coming in excess. Over the millennia, numerous famines in China have taken a toll of human life in the tens of millions. Modern Asia, with more than half the world's people, continues to be the part of the planet most vulnerable to massive famine due to natural catastrophe.

To many Westerners, however, perhaps, the best-known famine occurred in Ireland in 1846. The Irish population grew rapidly during the late eighteenth and early nineteenth centuries as a result of the expanded food supply made possible by the introduction and highly successful cultivation of the potato. In the summer of 1846, potato blight suddenly struck the country. An estimated 1.5 million of Ireland's 8 million people starved to death in the wake of that crop failure. Large-scale emigration to the United States followed in the ensuing decades; many Americans today can count refugees from the Irish potato blight among their ancestors. Famine, emigration, delayed marriages, and low birth rates in the century and a quarter since the famine have combined to reduce Ireland's current population to 3 million, less than half what it was prior to the potato blight.

Recent decades have witnessed several famines or near-famines due to war—more often than not, civil war. The last major European famine was the Soviet famine of the early 'thirties, in which an estimated 3 million to 10 million starved as a result of the large-scale social displacement and reorganization during the farm-collectivization period. Vast numbers of people in the Netherlands were close to starvation at the end of World War II; high mortality was averted only by an immediate postwar relief effort led by the United States. In 1943, a major famine occurred in West Bengal, India, when floods destroyed the rice crop, costing some 2 million to 4 million lives. Relief measures were slow to be introduced because of the difficulty of wartime supply and communications.

At the end of World War II, the United States provided large quantities of food in postwar relief for Western Europe and Japan, helping to prevent what might have been major famines in these two regions. Following this effort, the United States decided that it had the agricultural technology and the food-production capacity to assume unilaterally a global famine-relief role on a continuing basis in cases of natural calamity.

Largely as a result of U.S. initiative, the world has been spared most famines due to natural causes since 1943. (Those caused by war are often less susceptible to international assistance.) In the mid-'sixties, for example, after a crop failure in India that might have resulted in one of the largest famines in history, food-aid shipments of nearly 10 million tons for two successive years prevented major disaster.

Yet mankind is far from having eliminated the threat of starvation. Famines resulting from civil war have occurred in the last five years. Several hundred thousand people may have died of starvation in Biafra in 1969–70 during the Nigerian civil war, when political and military constraints restricted external aid to the stricken region. During the Pakistani civil war of 1972, which resulted in the establishment of Bangladesh, thousands of Bengalis starved to death, and many more, weakened by hunger, died of diseases. The loss of life due to hunger and malnutrition would have been much greater, however, had not the international community, led by India, provided several million tons of food for wartime refugees and for the population of war-ravaged, newly independent Bangladesh.

As of the summer of 1974, several hundred thousand people had perished in the Sahelian zone just south of the Sahara Desert in West Africa and Ethiopia in a famine of disastrous proportions, which has been spreading since the early 'seventies as a result of several years of drought and the accelerating southward spread of the desert. Although a substantial international food-relief effort has been launched, the fact that reserve stocks of grains in the United States and other principal producing nations are at their lowest point since the postwar era is to some extent hampering the capacity of the traditional disaster-relief institutions to respond to the emergency. Seemingly insurmountable problems of transportation and communications in this vast underdeveloped region have also limited the effectiveness of disaster-relief operations.

The urgent need for a new international approach to food stockpiling and food aid is all too evident. The current capacity of the international community to respond adequately to major food emergencies is ominously uncertain.

Nutritional Needs

Man's food-energy, or calorie, requirements vary with individual physique, level of physical activity, and climate. Standards for an adequate daily diet range from an average of 2,300 calories per capita in the Far East to 2,700 per capita in Canada and the Soviet Union. People in most of the rich countries of North America, Northern and Eastern Europe, and parts of South America and Oceania consume 3,000 to 3,300 calories daily.

Caloric intake is a good quantitative indicator of diet adequacy, but protein intake, essential to body growth and maintenance, is the key quality indicator. Most people suffering from calorie deficiencies and many with adequate caloric intake suffer from protein malnutrition, which is taking an enormous toll of the mental and the physical development of children in the poorer nations today.

The problem is not just a lack of protein but a lack of protein of high quality, such as that found in animal products (meat, milk, and eggs) or pulses (peas, beans, soybeans, and other legumes). Protein quality—or protein usefulness to the human body—is determined by the combination of amino acids found in the food. If one or more of the key amino acids is missing, as it is in cereals, then the protein is of much less value to the body. Conversely, when amino acids are added in the right proportion—as when beans are added to a diet of grains—the result is much more usable protein than if either food is consumed without the other. Adequate dietary planning requires that calorie and protein needs be considered together, for when energy intake is inadequate, the body converts part of the protein consumed into energy instead of using it for tissue building.

A U.N. committee of experts has recently calculated the minimum protein requirement of an adult male weighing 65 kilograms (143 lbs.) as ranging from 37 to 62 grams per day, depending on the quality of the protein consumed. Some experts would place the requirement for an active, healthy life much higher. In the early sixties, nutritionists in the U.S. Department of Agriculture recommended 60 grams per day, including at least 10 grams of animal protein, as the minimum level of protein intake for the average adult.

National averages, which do not take into account variations within a given country, indicate that daily protein intake ranges from more than 90 grams per day in many affluent countries to about 40 grams per day in some of the poorest nations. Average per capita consumption of animal protein—a useful indicator of the quality of available protein—varies even more, ranging from 40–70 grams per day in the developed nations to 5–20 grams in most developing nations.

EFFECTS OF MALNUTRITION

In his book *The Nutrition Factor,* Alan Berg provides a graphic description of the effects of malnutrition:

The light of curiosity absent from children's eyes. Twelve-year-olds with the physical stature of eight-year-olds. Youngsters who lack the energy to brush aside flies collecting about the sores on their faces.

Agonizingly slow reflexes of adults crossing traffic. Thirty-year-old mothers who look sixty. All are common images in developing countries; all reflect inadequate nutrition: all have societal consequences.*

Most children in the poor countries suffer from protein malnutrition at one time or another. Even children who received adequate protein while being breast-fed often experience protein deficiencies after weaning because of the changeover from mother's milk to a diet of cheap, starchy, easily digestible foods, like cassava, yams, and bananas. The stomachs of young children will not hold enough of these bulky staples to provide an adequate supply of protein.

The advanced symptoms of protein malnutrition are well known: swollen bodies, peeling skin, brittle, reddish-brown hair. What is less immediately visible is the enormous toll protein malnutrition takes on the physical and mental development of the young. Where death certificates are issued, the death of preschool children in the poor countries is generally attributed to measles, pneumonia, dysentery, or some other disease, but in fact, these children are often victims of malnutrition. Severely malnourished infants or children have low resistance and frequently die of routine childhood diseases. According to the Food and Agriculture Organization, malnutrition is the biggest single contributor to child mortality in the developing countries. This contention is supported by studies in Latin America showing malnutrition to be the primary cause, or a major contributing factor, in 50 to 75 per cent of the deaths of children aged one to four years. In many of the poor countries of Asia, Africa, and Latin America, children under six years of age account for half of all the deaths that occur. In Nigeria, for example, 180 of every 1,000 babies die before their first birthday. In India and Pakistan the number is 130, and in Peru it is 110. Many other children die before reaching school age, and more die during early school years.

The pervasive impact of undernourishment was dramatically illustrated during the summer of 1968, when India held trials in

* Alan Berg, *The Nutrition Factor* (Washington, D.C.: The Brookings Institution, 1973), p. 9.

New Delhi to select a track and field team to go to the Olympics in Mexico City. Although the Indian population then numbered 525 million, not one contestant could meet Olympic qualifying standards in any of the thirty-two track and field events. Outdated training techniques and the lack of public support were partly responsible, but widespread undernourishment undoubtedly contributed to this poor showing. By contrast, the youth of Japan today are conspicuous examples of the positive physical changes improved nutrition can bring. Well-nourished from infancy as a result of Japan's postwar affluence, teenagers on the streets of Tokyo average perhaps two inches taller than their elders.

Protein is as important for mental development as for physical growth. Protein shortages in the early years of life impair the growth of the brain and the central nervous system, thus preventing the realization of genetic potential and permanently reducing learning capacity. The relationship between nutrition and mental development was strikingly shown in a study recently completed in Mexico. An experimental group of thirty-seven children who had been hospitalized for severe protein malnutrition before the age of five was found to average 13 points lower in IQ than a carefully selected control group that had not experienced severe malnutrition.

Unfortunately, some of the effects of malnutrition in the early years of life are lasting and irreversible. No amount of compensatory feeding, education, or environmental improvement in later life can repair the damage to the central nervous system. Protein shortages today are depreciating the stock of human resources for at least a generation to come.

NUTRITION TODAY

There has been substantial progress in improving the nutritional state of the world over the last two decades. Estimates in the 'fifties showed that a majority of people in most African, Latin American, and Asian nations (including Japan) were not consuming adequate amounts of calories or protein or both. Today, most of the countries of East Asia—Japan, China, South Korea, Taiwan, Hong Kong, Singapore, Malaysia—have achieved an adequate average food-intake level, largely eliminating malnutrition. In West Asia, Israel and Lebanon are among the countries adequately nourished today. Argentina, Uruguay, Chile, Brazil, and Mexico have also achieved adequate *average* consumption levels, although in almost every case the distribution of food is very uneven, and the poorest fraction of the population continues to be malnourished.

Perhaps the most impressive gain among the developing countries has been China's apparent achievement of an adequate diet for its 800 million people. None of the scores of scientists, journalists, economists, and doctors who visited China in the past few years has reported observing any of the obvious clinical signs of malnutrition that were prevalent in China less than a generation ago and that still exist in so many other developing countries. China's success appears to have been gained not so much by increases in per capita food production as by a more equitable distribution system and by the frugal use of available resources to produce the needed foodstuffs.

By far the most extensive remaining area of nutritional deficiency today is South Asia—mainly India, Pakistan, and Bangladesh. In Latin America, the remaining severe malnutrition is concentrated in northeastern Brazil, among the Andean Indians, among Mexico's landless laborers, and in parts of Central America. Malnutrition persists in scattered pockets throughout Africa, but it is currently most prevalent in the Sahelian countries, where outright starvation as well as severe malnutrition is now threatening the lives of many.

Probably a billion or more people suffer from serious hunger or malnutrition, at least during part of the year. Infants, growing children, and pregnant women—the groups with the highest protein requirements—generally are the most malnourished elements of societies. Available evidence suggests that such vitamin-deficiency diseases as rickets, scurvy, and beri-beri are major problems in only a few areas of the world today. However, vitamin A deficiency and iron-deficiency anemia continue to be significant nutrition problems throughout much of the world. Inadequate levels of vitamin A cause blindness or eye diseases for many millions in the developing nations. Anemia, which results in sluggishness, fatigue, and generally poor health, has been found to affect important portions of the population in many nations, rich and poor. Expectant mothers are especially susceptible to anemia, which increases the chances of death or disease as a result of pregnancy and childbirth and also impairs the health of newborn infants.

The problem of malnutrition is inseparable from the problem of poverty. Traditional food habits and lack of nutritional education, internal parasites, and ecological constraints contribute to malnutrition: but these are in many ways simply additional manifestations of poverty. Even in the United States, malnutrition is often found where there is poverty—among migrant workers, in parts of the rural South and Appalachia, and in urban slums. The Select Committee on Nutrition of the U.S. Senate recently estimated, on the basis of U.S. nutrition standards, that 6 per cent of the national population suffer from malnutrition. Only the provision of food assistance by the federal government to tens of millions keeps the number from being much higher.

The connection between poverty and malnutrition is impossible to ignore in the poor countries. Where income is low, cheap energy foods such as cassava, potatoes, and cereals dominate the diet, often accounting for 60 to 80 per cent of the total calorie intake. Protein-rich livestock products or pulses are usually sparsely available in these circumstances, and protein deficiencies are commonplace.

Ironically, while much of mankind is hungry, obesity is today a leading health problem in rich countries such as the United States. If the number of people suffering from nutritional problems resulting from overconsumption were included, the poorly nourished proportion of the population of the affluent countries would multiply severalfold.

What is most alarming about recent trends in the world food economy is the prospect that in many nations the major nutritional gains of the past two decades are now being reversed. The tripling of world wheat and rice prices during the 1972–74 period is having a disastrous effect on consumption levels among the world's poorest people. If reliable data were available, they would doubtless show a rise in infant mortality rates and nutrition-related diseases in many poor countries. By mid-1974, a rising rate of malnutrition—representing a step backward in the struggle to reduce global hunger—was being reported in such diverse areas as Guatemala and India.

Most ominous is the real possibility that a long-term upward shift is taking place in world food prices, far outpacing the growth in income among at least several hundred million of the world's poorest people and driving their purchasing power even farther below the level necessary to obtain an adequate amount of food. The international community has not yet confronted this question in a meaningful way, nor has it systematically examined the alternatives available to help soften the impact of these trends. A deterioration in the nutritional outlook for much of the human race not only will be a moral outrage but will inevitably contribute to a deterioration in social and political systems as well, undermining mankind's efforts to create a workable world order.

3.

POPULATION AND AFFLUENCE

From the beginning of agriculture until quite recently, nearly all of the growth in demand for food stemmed from population growth, for everyone except a select few lived at the subsistence level. Only in modern times has rising individual consumption begun to contribute importantly to the global growth in food demand. Indeed, the failure of analysts to anticipate the emergence of rising affluence as an important claimant on world food resources in recent years is one reason growth in supply has lagged behind demand.

IMPACT OF POPULATION GROWTH

The arithmetic of population growth is familiar to many. The current world population growth rate of nearly 2 per cent annually —which brings a doubling every 35 years—is unprecedented. It took 2 million years for man's numbers to reach 1 billion, but the second billion came in only 100 years, and successive billions are coming even faster. At the present rate of increase, the sixth billion will require less than a decade. If the present growth rate were to be maintained for a century, it would then take only a year to add one billion to the population and only three years to add a number equal to the entire population of the world today.

In the year 1972, world population increased by 71 million—the difference between 120 million births and 49 million deaths. The annual addition to the world population occurs primarily in Asia (see Table 3–1). Two countries, China and India, contribute nearly 40 per cent of the annual world increase. Although its population is substantially larger than that of India, China adds only a little more to world population than India, since its birth rate has begun to decline more rapidly than India's.

TABLE 3-1. NATIONAL SOURCES OF WORLD POPULATION INCREASE, 1972.

	Millions
China	13.3
India	12.8
Indonesia	3.4
Brazil	2.8
U.S.S.R.	2.2
Bangladesh	1.9
Mexico	1.8
Pakistan	1.7
Japan	1.4
Nigeria	1.4
United States	1.3
Philippines	1.3
Thailand	1.1
Iran	1.0
Turkey	1.0
Egypt	.7
Colombia	.7
Ethiopia	.7
Burma	.7
South Korea	.7
All other countries	19.1
Total	71.0

SOURCE: U.S. Agency for International Development.

Some of the comparatively small and poor countries add more to the world's annual population gain than some of the larger, rich ones. Mexico, for example, now contributes more to world population growth than the United States and Canada combined. The Philippines now adds more people each year than does Japan. Brazil adds 2.8 million additional people in a year while the Soviet Union adds only 2.2 million.

Assuming constant per-capita food-consumption levels, population growth translates directly into additional demand for food. A

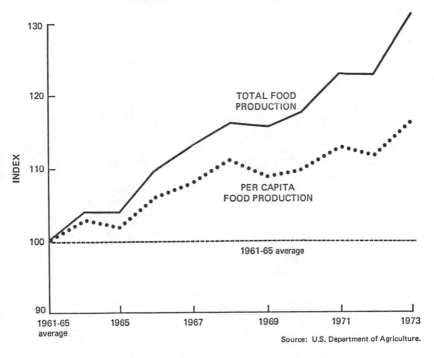

Figure 3-1. Total and Per Capita Food Production in More Developed Countries, 1961-73

population that doubles in 35 years means a doubled demand for food during the same period. Where population increases 3 per cent yearly, as is today the case in several countries, it multiplies nineteenfold in a century. This means that food supplies likewise must be expanded nineteenfold in the same time period.

The relationship between population growth and the success, or lack of success, of efforts to improve diets is dramatically evident in Figures 3–1 and 3–2. Over the past decade, food production in both the developed and the developing countries has expanded about 30 per cent. This expansion has resulted in a substantial (15 per cent) increase in per capita food production in the developed countries.

In the less developed countries, however, a similarly impressive growth in food production has been almost wholly absorbed by

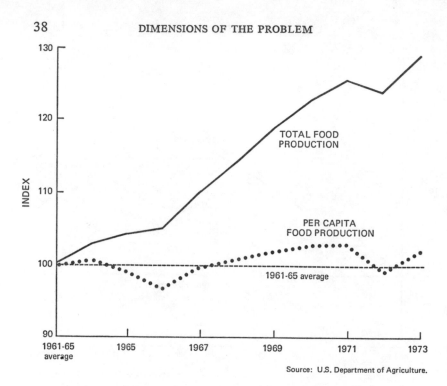

Figure 3-2. Total and Per Capita Food Production in Less Developed Countries, 1961-73

increases in population. The result is virtually no improvement in per-capita food production. Furthermore, given the growing scarcity of the basic inputs of land, water, energy, and fertilizer, it is becoming increasingly unlikely that the less developed countries will be able to improve diets significantly in the foreseeable future unless they can quickly reduce birth rates. Indeed, it appears very possible that per capita food production will even decline in the years ahead.

If the population growth rate of a country continues to be high for an extended period, the descendants of the present population will be doomed to unbelievably miserable conditions of existence. The demand for food will outrun all available indigenous supplies of land and water, creating severe and chronic scarcity. If population growth were the only source of additional demand the world's farmers had to contend with, it would be more than enough, but they must also attempt to meet the demands of rising affluence.

IMPACT OF RISING AFFLUENCE

The relationship between changes in income and changes in per capita food consumption is generally described by economists in terms of the "income elasticity coefficient of demand." Simply stated, this is a numerical expression of the percentage increase in income that is spent on food. The relationship is perhaps easiest to understand when it is expressed in terms of grain requirements. Since grain dominates food-energy supplies in most societies, whether it is consumed directly or indirectly in the form of livestock products, it is a useful indicator of consumption patterns. Another advantage of using grain as an indicator is that data on grain consumption are available for many parts of the world, but they are not available for all foodstuffs considered collectively. Since the various cereals —principally wheat, rice, corn, and sorghum—are rather homogeneous, it is valid to group them into a single category. Once the demand has been established for a given amount of cereal, it can readily be converted into resource requirements—land, fertilizer, water, etc.

In the developing countries of Asia, Africa, and Latin America, the per capita availability of grain is only about 400 pounds per year, or about a pound per day. When only this much grain is available, nearly all of it must be consumed directly to meet minimal energy needs In North America, by contrast, the average person consumes nearly one ton of grain per year (Table 3–2). Of this, about 200 pounds is consumed directly in the form of bread, pastries, and breakfast cereals. Most of the remainder is consumed indirectly, in the form of meat, milk, and eggs. Also included in indirect per capita consumption is 35 pounds of grain in the form of domestically produced alcoholic beverages, principally beer and bourbon.

Thus the average North American requires roughly five times the agricultural resources needed by an Indian, a Colombian, or a Nigerian. This ratio is not likely to widen appreciably. The lower limit on the consumption range is established by the survival level;

if consumption drops much below 400 pounds of grain per year, survival is in question. At the other extreme, the physical capacity of the human stomach limits the average person's claims on agricultural resources.

TABLE 3–2. ANNUAL PER CAPITA GRAIN CONSUMPTION IN SELECTED NATIONS, 1964–66 AVERAGE.

	Grain Consumed Directly (pounds)	Grain Consumed Indirectly (pounds)	Total Grain Consumed (pounds)	Grain Consumed as Multiple of Indian Consumption
Canada	202	1,791	1,993	5
United States	200	1,441	1,641	5
U.S.S.R.	344	883	1,227	4
United Kingdom	169	856	1,025	3
Argentina	223	625	848	2
West Germany	160	588	748	2
Mexico	305	242	547	2
Japan	320	211	531	2
China	312	118	430	1
India	288	60	348	1

SOURCE: FAO, *Food Balance Sheets, 1964–66 Average,* and U.S. Department of Agriculture.

AFFLUENCE AND LIVESTOCK PRODUCTS

Because of their relatively high cost, the growing consumption of livestock products—meat, milk, and eggs—is perhaps the single most pronounced change in dietary habits as incomes rise. This phenomenon may be assessed by looking at the changes occurring within a given country as income rises over time or by comparing consumption patterns in countries at various income levels.

In the case of the United States, reasonably detailed and accurate data on consumption patterns are available for the past sixty years (Figure 3–3). Between 1910 and 1950, there was relatively little change in dietary habits; per capita beef consumption fluctuated around 60 pounds per year. After 1950, however, it began to climb rather steadily. From 1950 to 1972 it virtually doubled, increasing

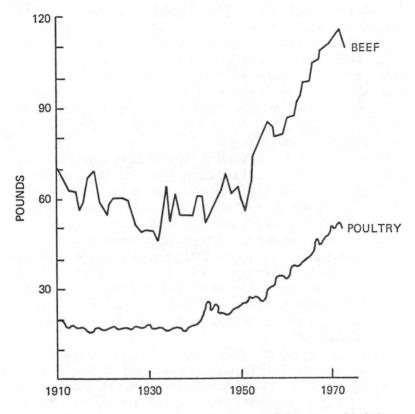

Source: U.S. Department of Agriculture.

Figure 3-3. U.S. Per Capita Consumption of Poultry and Beef, 1910-73

from 63 to 116 pounds, but in 1973 it fell to 109 pounds as exceptionally high prices and even occasional beef shortages appeared in the United States.

Pork consumption, on the other hand, remained rather static, fluctuating around 65 pounds, although it began to dip somewhat in the mid-seventies. The recent decline in pork consumption is apparently a result of growing consumer sensitivity to the dangers of its high fat content.

Poultry consumption in the United States was relatively constant at about 16 pounds per person per year between 1910 and 1940. Since 1940, however, it has climbed steadily, reaching 50 pounds per person in the early 'seventies. This marked increase in consumption over the past generation mostly reflects the increased production efficiency and sharply reduced costs that have made poultry attractive to price-conscious shoppers. The rise in poultry consumption may also reflect public apprehension regarding the high fat content of beef and pork.

In the case of beef and poultry, the rises in consumption since 1950 have been dramatic. Pork consumption has remained essentially constant. This trend in meats contrasts sharply with the trend in the consumption of milk and eggs, which peaked during or shortly after World War II and has declined ever since. In the United States, for example, per capita milk consumption reached 900 pounds per year during the final years of World War II. By 1973, however, it had dropped to 555 pounds, a very substantial decline reflecting such factors as the shift to a lower-calorie diet, the substitution of margarine for butter and of sherbet for ice cream, and the growing use of coffee lighteners and whipped toppings of nondairy origin.

Similarly, the per capita consumption of eggs peaked at nearly 400 per year around 1950, but since the early 'sixties has been dropping steadily; by 1973 it had fallen below 300, and it is still declining sharply. The transition of the labor force from a predominantly blue-collar to a largely white-collar one and the associated substitution of the "coffee break" for breakfast is one factor in this decline. The warning of the medical community that high egg consumption means a high intake of cholesterol, and hence an increased risk of heart disease, is another significant cause of the decline in egg consumption.

Consumption of livestock products varies widely among countries. In the United States, Argentina, and Australia, the average person consumes close to 250 pounds of meat annually, or about five pounds a week. In France, Canada, and West Germany, per capita meat consumption is about 200 pounds per year. Citizens of the United Kingdom consume 170 pounds of meat per year. At the opposite end of the scale are the low-income countries, most of them in tropical or subtropical regions, in which the average person consumes less than 20 pounds of meat per year. There is a middle group of countries, including the Soviet Union, Sweden, and Spain, in which meat consumption is about 100 pounds per year. Where incomes permit, per capita consumption of meat appears to increase until it reaches somewhere between 200 and 250 pounds per year, after which it may stabilize.

In the countries that consume large quantities of meat, there is a wide diversity in the types of meat favored. The more populous countries in the European Economic Community—Germany, France, and the United Kingdom—and Japan consume somewhat more pork than beef. In the United States and the U.S.S.R., consumers prefer beef. In Australia, beef displaced mutton, historically the principal source of meat consumed there, during the late 'sixties. Poultry consumption has risen rapidly in almost all industrial countries, reaching its highest level in the United States.

Per capita consumption of milk and eggs likewise varies widely among countries. In a number of countries, mainly in Europe, consumers use a quart or more of milk per day. In other countries, particularly in East Asia, very little milk is consumed, largely because of the inherited lactose intolerance among people of Chinese descent. Consumption of eggs also varies among countries, but not quite so widely as milk consumption. In some countries, the average person consumes more than one egg per day. In the lowest-income countries, the figure is less than two per month.

GLOBAL DEMAND TRENDS

World grain production in 1974 will total more than 1,200 million tons, or close to a third of a ton for each of the world's 3.9 billion people. The world grain supply now grows at an annual average of about 30 million tons, or about 2.5 per cent per year. Of this annual growth in supply, roughly 22 million tons are required to meet the demands of population growth and about 8 million tons to meet the demands of rising affluence. Thus the annual increase in global demand for food generated by rising affluence is well over one third that required to meet population growth.

Only recently has a large segment of humanity begun to increase its level of food intake systematically and steadily. This trend has been most pronounced in the United States, where consumption of some livestock products has more than doubled over the past generation. In the northern tier of industrial countries, stretching eastward from Britain and Ireland and including Scandinavia, Western Europe, Eastern Europe, the Soviet Union, and Japan, dietary patterns are now more or less comparable to those of the United States a generation ago. Rising income in these countries is being translated into additional demand for livestock products, but few can respond to this growth in demand entirely out of indigenous resources. Most must import either some livestock products or the feed grains and soybeans to produce them. By 1974, at least one third of the grains produced in the world—over 400 million tons—were being fed to livestock. The global use of grains for animal feed grew by more than 6 per cent annually throughout the 'sixties.

Given what is known about the relationship among population growth, rising affluence, and the demand for food, we can project future food demands on the basis of various assumptions concerning population growth and individual consumption levels. If, for purposes of discussion, we accept the U.N. medium projection of a population of 6.5 billion by the end of the century, and if we assume an average global food-consumption level approximating that currently prevailing in Western Europe (nearly a half ton of grain per person each year), we can project a need for almost 3 billion tons of grain annually, or roughly 2.5 times current output, by the year 2000. World population growth alone—with no increase in per capita food intake—would require an increase of nearly one billion tons of grain per year, or roughly four times the current production of North America. But if we assume, for purposes of speculation, that the world will reach the current North American level of food consumption by the end of the century, world grain requirements would be 5.5 billion tons per year, or well over four times the current global production level. Perhaps it would be better to recognize and acknowledge forthrightly that the rest of mankind will probably never consume as much food as the average North American.

4.

ECOLOGICAL UNDERMINING OF
FOOD SYSTEMS

In many areas of the world, the pressure of the growing demand for food is now ecologically undermining major food-producing systems. This is not a new development. What is new is the scale and acceleration of the process, which is now adversely affecting world food-production prospects.

The most conspicuous examples of such ecological damage result from the expansion of human and livestock populations beyond the basic carrying capacity of the land, and from land mismanagement. The massive destruction of vegetative cover and the erosion of topsoil are apparent in the spreading deserts of Africa, Asia, and Latin America; in increasingly frequent and severe floods in some regions; in the silting of irrigation reservoirs and canals; and in the abandonment of millions of acres of arable land to erosion. The decline in fish catches as a result of overfishing provides another disturbing example of the loss of productive capacity as a result of excessive pressures to expand food supplies. The catch of a growing number of fish species has been endangered as the world scramble for marine protein has intensified.

The endangerment of food-producing systems is the most immediately serious ecological consequence of spreading agricultural activities, but by no means the only one. Even where food-producing capacity is not being adversely affected, efforts to increase the food supply—either by expanding the area under cultivation or by intensifying cultivation through the use of agricultural chemicals and irrigation—may cause ecological disasters, such as the inadvertent modification of climate, the eutrophication of fresh-water lakes and streams, the rapidly rising incidence of environmentally induced illnesses, and the threat of extinction of a growing number of wildlife species. New signs of agricultural stress on the earth's ecosystem appear almost daily, as the growing demand for food presses against our ecosystem's limited capacities.

THE ADVANCING SAHARA

A striking example of the diminution of the earth's food-producing capacity through ecological overstress is today evident in the Sahelian zone south of the Sahara Desert, where several consecutive years of drought have brought a deteriorating situation into sharp focus. Over the past thirty-five years, human and livestock populations along the desert's fringe have increased rapidly, nearly doubling in some areas. The result has been overgrazing, deforestation, and over-all denudation of the land. According to some experts, by the early 'seventies the number of animals maintained in the region was more than twice the ecosystem's carrying capacity.

Overgrazing and deforestation have caused the desert to move southward at an accelerated rate all along its 3,500-mile southern fringe, from Senegal in the west to northern Ethiopia in the east. A U.S. government study indicates that the desert is expanding at up to 30 miles per year in the more devastated areas. As human and livestock populations retreat before the encroaching desert, they put ever greater pressure on the receding fringe area. This in turn contributes to more overgrazing and deforestation, setting in process a self-reinforcing cycle.

The threat of massive famine in six West African nations first caught international attention in 1973. Roughly 600,000 tons of grain were dispatched in international relief efforts that year and again in 1974. By late 1973, it had become apparent that a major relief effort would be necessary in Ethiopia as well. But this situation requires far more than the temporary panacea of food relief, which deals only with symptoms. What is needed above all is a large-scale program to arrest and reverse the southward movement of the desert. This will require a concerted, cooperative effort by the tier of countries most immediately affected, by the next tier of countries to the south, which will shortly be affected, and by a large number of donor countries, which must provide extensive economic resources and technical know-how in desert reclamation and land management. Above all, the Sahelian situation calls for the immediate launching of a major effort to slow and stabilize population growth in the region. Such a long-term cooperative international program will have to be comparable in scope to the program that launched the Green Revolution in the late 'sixties. Anything less will not suffice. Already the second tier of countries below the Sahara is being affected as people and livestock retreat southward across national boundaries. Within a matter of years, the desert will begin to encroach upon these countries as well.

At this writing, the Food and Agriculture Organization of the United Nations has just launched a program involving aid from many nations and private organizations to promote the ecological, economic, and human recovery of the Sahel. With proper soil, water, and range management, both grain and livestock productivity in parts of the region could be increased over predrought levels. Massive efforts will be needed to stabilize shifting sand dunes, revegetate denuded rangelands, and design appropriate new cultivation systems. However, the vastness of the Sahel and the delicate social problems involved in any attempts to alter the living habits of the proud nomadic peoples inhabiting much of the region will make progress on a significant scale exceedingly difficult.

The process of desertification afflicting the Sahara region in Africa is also occurring in Asia, Latin America, and southern Africa. Both Chile and Peru are losing arable land to spreading deserts as is India. In most cases, a blend of human and natural factors is encouraging the spread of the deserts.

DEFORESTATION, FLOODING, AND SILTING

Ecological overstress is very much in evidence today in the Indian subcontinent. Over the past twenty-five years, as human and livestock populations have expanded, the subcontinent has been progressively deforested. Pressure on the fringe of the Thar

Desert, in the Indian state of Rajasthan, is forcing 30,000 acres of fertile land out of cultivation each year and has already claimed half the state's area. Robert Brooks has vividly described the problem:

A classic illustration of large-scale destruction is afforded by the spectacle of wind erosion in Rajasthan. Overgrazing by goats destroys the desert plants which might otherwise hold the soil in place. Goatherds equipped with sickles attached to 20-foot poles strip the leaves off trees to float downward into the waiting mouths of famished goats and sheep. The trees die and the soil blows away two hundred miles to New Delhi, where it comes to rest in the lungs of its inhabitants and on the shiny cars of foreign diplomats.*

A massive reclamation project in Rajasthan is being attempted by the Indian government and U.N. agencies, which plan to rechannel the waters of the Sutlej River to the desert and eventually bring 4 million acres under irrigation.

Even several years ago, one did not need much training in soil and water management to predict with alarm the long-term consequences of the accelerating deforestation of the subcontinent. The problem is most serious in the Himalayas and the surrounding foothills, for this is where nearly all the major river systems of the Indian subcontinent—the Indus, the Ganges, and the Brahmaputra —originate. Anyone who observed the subcontinent over the past fifteen or twenty years should not have been surprised in the late summer of 1973 by the worst flood in Pakistan's history—a flood so severe that it destroyed a sizable share of the spring wheat crop in storage on farms as well as much of the standing crop in some areas. Since deforestation is continuing, the incidence and severity of flooding in Pakistan, India, and Bangladesh seem certain to worsen in the future and to undermine further the food-producing capability of a region that faces the awesome task of feeding nearly three quarters of a billion people.

Where land denudation is occurring, the problems associated with the loss of topsoil often do not end with abandonment of the

* Robert R. Brooks, "People Versus Food," *Saturday Review*, September 5, 1970, p. 10

severely eroded land. Much of the topsoil finds its way into streams and rivers and eventually into irrigation reservoirs and canals. A dramatic and unfortunate example of this indirect loss of productive capacity is provided by the $600 million Mangla reservoir, recently constructed in the foothills of the Himalayas in Pakistan. Feasibility studies undertaken in the late 'fifties assumed the reservoir's life expectancy to be 100 years. But as the population in the watershed feeding the Mangla reservoir has grown rapidly, so has the rate of denudation and soil erosion. As a result the reservoir's life expectancy is now believed to be 75 years or less.

Efforts to expand the area of farmland in one locale may reduce the water available for irrigation in another. Thus farmers moving up the hillsides in Java are causing irrigation canals to silt at an alarming rate, necessitating rural public-works efforts to restore lost irrigation capability. In Egypt, damming the Nile at Aswan expanded the irrigated area of producing cereals, but at the same time it largely eliminated the annual deposits of rich alluvial silt on fields in the Nile Valley, forcing farmers to rely more on chemical fertilizers. In addition, interrupting the flow of nutrients into the Nile estuary probably caused the precipitous decline in the fish catch there.

EUTROPHICATION OF LAKES AND STREAMS

One response to the steadily growing demand for food has been a great increase in the use of chemical fertilizers since mid-century. This expansion has benefited mankind enormously, but not all the effects have been positive. The runoff of chemical fertilizers from farmlands into rivers and lakes is contributing to the eutrophication, or overfertilization, of fresh-water bodies. Where livestock populations are concentrated, nutrients in the manure produced also tend to wash into waterways, contributing to eutrophication.

How much agricultural factors have to do with the eutrophication problem and how much is attributable to other causes remains an open question; certainly the answer varies from region to region. The contributions of industries or sewage plants to water pollution are far easier to pinpoint and study. Whatever the cause, the process itself is clear enough. Nitrates and phosphates introduced into fresh water through the runoff process serve as nutrients for algae and other aquatic plant life. Algae in particular thrive and multiply rapidly. As the vast numbers of algae that are produced die and decompose, the free oxygen supply in lakes and streams is depleted. Thus fish life, beginning with those species having the highest oxygen requirements, is destroyed. Apart from its impact on marine life, decomposition of the massive population of algae produces foul odors, making the water unfit for recreational uses. Unarrested eutrophication usually brings about the death of a fresh-water body, converting it into a putrid swamp.

Thousands of fresh-water lakes are threatened throughout North America and Europe and, to a lesser extent, also in many poor countries where fertilizer use is increasing. Filipino villagers are finding that the use of fertilizer in rice paddies is resulting in the eutrophication of local lakes and ponds, depriving the populace of fish, a traditional source of animal protein. The cost to mankind of losing these fresh-water lakes is staggering.

Recent studies have suggested that fertilizer and livestock wastes in many European countries account for over 50 per cent of all nitrogen runoff entering lakes and streams. European livestock alone may be contributing eight times more nitrogen and eleven times more phosphorous to waterways than does the human population. The nature and extent of agriculture's role in water pollution in the United States are just beginning to be studied, but it is clearly significant. With each cow and steer producing 3.6 tons of waste annually—equal to the amount produced by ten to sixteen humans—feedlot operations ranging up to 150,000 head obviously create a major runoff problem.

ENVIRONMENTALLY INDUCED ILLNESSES

The growing use of chemical fertilizers is causing another more localized but hazardous problem: the chemical pollution of drinking water. Nitrates are the main worry, since they have risen to toxic levels in some communities in the United States. Both children and livestock have become ill, and some have died, from drinking water that contained high levels of nitrates. Excessive nitrates can cause metahemoglobanemia, a physiological disorder affecting the blood's oxygen-carrying capacity. Since the problem is generally local, it can be countered effectively by finding alternative (usually more costly) sources of drinking water. Bottled water is being used in some California communities. Groundwater nitrates in southern Illinois rose above the FDA tolerance levels in the early 'seventies, creating enough of a health threat for the state government to hold hearings on the possibility of limiting the use of nitrogen fertilizer. This proposal, which would have limited the level of fertilizer applied by many Illinois farmers to a level below that used by many progressive farmers, was eventually rejected.

Both agricultural pesticides and industrial wastes are adding growing amounts of highly toxic mercury to the biosphere. Concentrations in some localities have reached a point where they adversely affect human well-being, causing not only discomfort but sickness and death. It is a known fact that when the mercury content of water, fish, and other foods reaches a certain level, the central nervous system of more complex organisms, particularly man, begins to be affected. Known deaths from mercury poisoning have occurred in such widely dispersed areas as Japan (89 deaths), West Pakistan (4), Iraq (300), and Guatemala (20). In Japan, twenty-two brain-damaged children were born to mothers who did not have enough mercury in their bodies to exhibit symptoms of mercury poisoning themselves, but did have enough to affect their vulnerable fetuses.

The mercury content of 89 per cent of the swordfish on sale in U.S. markets in 1971 was above the tolerance level established by the Food and Drug Administration, causing the agency to advise Americans against further swordfish consumption. For similar reasons, the government of Sweden has recommended that Swedes limit consumption of fish from indigenous fresh-water lakes to one serving per week. The Japanese Ministry of Health has urged the Japanese people to restrict their intake of fish, a staple of the Japanese diet, to reduce their bodily accumulation of toxic chemicals.

Throughout the poorer countries of tropical regions, an even greater threat to human well-being is the snail-borne disease known as schistosomiasis, or bilharzia. Now that malaria has been largely eradicated, schistosomiasis is the world's leading infectious disease, affecting some 200 million people in North Africa, the Middle East, sub-Saharan Africa, South Asia, East Asia, the Caribbean, and the northeast coast of Latin America. Although the disease is seldom immediately fatal, its victims are debilitated by recurrent fever and diarrhea.

Labeled by some the "poor man's emphysema" because, like emphysema, it is induced by conditions created by man, schistosomiasis is a persistent disease that thrives in areas under continuous irrigation. The disease has spread rapidly where the expansion of irrigation systems has created an ideal environment for the alternate host of the parasites, a fresh-water snail. The disease is most often contracted in flooded rice fields by barefoot workers whose skin is penetrated by the aquatic parasite. The schistosomes, or tiny worms, then migrate through the bloodstream and lodge in the liver, where they reproduce. The eggs are excreted with body wastes, often ending up in irrigation canals, open sewers, and drainage ditches, where they are hatched and are once again taken up by the snail, thus completing their life cycle. The disease is most prevalent where human excrement is used as fertilizer, as in China, and where there is frequent flooding or where a lagoon serves as a source of community water for everything from washing clothes to bathing.

ENDANGERED SPECIES

Man is not the only species threatened by expanding agricultural activities. Indeed, many animals have a much lower tolerance for environmental changes than man does. Thus far during this century, an average of one animal species per year has quietly made its exit in some part of the world. The U.S. Department of the Interior's list of endangered species of mammals, birds, and fish within the United States now totals more than 100. One recent worldwide list of endangered animal species, though obviously far from complete, includes 982 mammals, birds, reptiles, amphibians and fish. As we move upward along the steeply inclined curve of population growth, newly endangered species are added to the list almost weekly.

Expansion of the area under cultivation poses a threat to many animal species because it destroys their natural habitat. Numerous species of Asia's mammals, most notably the Bengal tiger and the Indian rhinoceros, are being endangered by the spread of agricultural activity. Recent reports indicate that fewer than twenty clouded leopards remain in Bangladesh's Chittagong hill tracts. Fewer than 4,000 of man's close kin, the orangutan, remain in Indonesia. The Anatolian panther in Turkey, the largest leopard species in the world, is expected to become completely extinct within the next few years. Today there are no more than 2,500 wild elephants in Sri Lanka, fewer than half the number twenty years ago. Their source of subsistence is diminishing steadily as their forest and jungle habitat is cleared to produce food for the island's population, which is now doubling every thirty-two years. The spread of agriculture associated with continuing rapid population growth in East Africa is beginning to encroach upon the region's game reserves, which contain some of the world's most diverse and abundant forms of wildlife.

The use of chemicals to protect crops from disease, weeds, and various pests has become widespread, contributing greatly to man's expanded food supply. Pesticides are by definition toxic to at least some species of life. If taken in sufficient dosage, many can be debilitating or lethal to humans as well. Indeed, the misuse of most major pesticides has fatally poisoned humans at one time or another. What sets DDT and other chlorinated hydrocarbons apart from the more traditional pesticides, consisting of compounds of arsenic, lead, mercury, and copper, is their persistence. The synthetic pesticides do not break down or decompose readily in nature: thus, as long as use continues, the amount in the environment keeps mounting and circulating widely in water and air currents. DDT and many related fat-soluble pesticides accumulate in aquatic organisms, and the levels present multiply rapidly as one moves up the food chain.

Pravda has reported that in the Soviet Union the reckless use of chemical pesticides in agriculture is decimating many forms of wildlife, causing many species to become zoological rarities. The duck-hunting season was reportedly canceled in 1970 because of the declining number of ducks. *Pravda,* now beginning to sound increasingly like Rachel Carson, claims that the extinction of species "is worrying us more and more every year. Why do we see almost no flocks of geese and cranes in April? Almost all the partridges are gone. Our woods, gardens, and fields are becoming quieter and quieter."*

In Denmark, the return of the storks from wintering in North Africa has long been a national event celebrated by young and old alike. At one time, 10,000 storks arrived each year; in 1970, only seventy pairs came. The use of pesticides by farmers to control the locust in East Africa and the Nile River Valley is apparently eliminating the storks as well. In the United States, the bald eagle, the national symbol, is now threatened with extinction by an intolerable level of non-biodegradable pesticides, particularly dieldrin, in the biosphere.

Many new approaches to the nonchemical control of pests are being explored under the general heading of "integrated pest management." These include such biological controls as pest sterilization and the development of bacterial, viral, and insect predators and parasites, as well as preventive measures such as changes in cultivation practices and the breeding of pest-resistant crop varieties. While the science of integrated pest management is still in its infancy, the nonchemical control of pests could be practiced—on the basis of present knowledge—far more widely than it is currently. The U.S. Council on Environmental Quality summarized the situation in the United States in 1972:

> In spite of its many benefits, integrated pest management is still not in widespread use—proably because of a variety of attitudinal factors as well as economic and personnel constraints. Some of the reasons include the farmers' lack of incentive to change pest-control practices, the complexity of these new management techniques, fear of crop loss. inadequate information on economic threshhold levels. an inadequate supply of trained professionals, and a limited number of fully developed nonchemical or selective chemical control methods.†

In most poor countries, of course, the economic and scientific obstacles to effective biological or environmental control of pests

---

* *New York Times,* April 27, 1970.
† Council on Environmental Quality. *Integrated Pest Management* Washington. D.C., 1972. p. viii.

are much greater than in the United States. Unfortunately, despite some efforts by the FAO to promote effective and ecologically sound pest management, in major areas of the world for many years to come there will be no alternative to increasing the application of chemical pesticides and herbicides—including DDT—if food-production and malaria-control needs are to be satisfied. Agricultural modernization in the developing world is bringing an escalating need for pest control. A stepped-up international effort to ensure ecologically viable pest-control practices is essential in order to avoid or minimize the potential for environmental disaster in many developing countries.

Swedish zoologist Kai Curry-Lindahl estimates that more than 300 species and subspecies of animals have already vanished from the face of the earth as a result of man's activities. Plant as well as animal species are disappearing as a result of the spread of agriculture and other human activities. Observing the rapid encroachment of agriculture on the vast tropical forests, Paul W. Richards recently wrote:

> Much of the plant and animal life of the tropics may thus become extinct before we have even begun to explore it. If we believe that all living creatures should be a source of wonder, enjoyment and instruction to man, a vast realm of potential human experience may disappear before there is even a bare record of its existence.*

Once destroyed, these species cannot be re-created by man. The trend can be reversed only by cooperation on a global scale.

INADVERTENT CLIMATE MODIFICATION

Efforts to meet man's expanding needs for food, energy, and material goods are creating seemingly endless possibilities for altering the earth's climate, either intentionally or unintentionally. The list of ways in which man may inadvertently be affecting the earth's climate, at least locally, is already long. It includes the consumption of energy—which can either warm local areas (as in

* Paul W. Richards, "The Tropical Rain Forest," *Scientific American* No. 299 (December, 1973). p. 67.

urban heat centers, which are measurably warmer than surrounding areas) or contribute to a cooling of the earth (by discharging dust particles into the atmosphere and thus reducing the inflow of solar energy). Agricultural activity, especially bringing marginal land under the plow, can result in dustbowl conditions, with similarly depressing effects on the flow of solar energy.

Climatological data show that the earth's average temperature rose by about 0.5 degrees Centigrade between 1880 and 1940. Since 1940, however, it has dropped 0.3 degrees Centigrade. No one can say whether this observed decline was due to long-term natural cyclical changes, to increased particulate matter in the upper atmosphere as a result of volcanic activity, to the expansion of agricultural dustbowls in parts of Africa and Asia, to increased industrial activity, or to some other factor. What is significant is that man's activities are now on a scale that can affect, and may already be affecting, the earth's climate.

One prominent climatologist, Reid Bryson of the University of Wisconsin, has presented considerable evidence that windblown dust from agricultural activities, denuded lands, industrial pollution, and natural sources is responsible for a recent global cooling trend and for potentially disastrous shifts in global climatic patterns (see Chapter 5). Other experts, however, ascribe these climatic changes to such causes as sunspots or astronomical movements. A report prepared for the United Nations in the summer of 1971 summed up the state of knowledge on the subject: "There can be little doubt that man, in the process of reshaping his environment, in many ways has changed the climate of large regions of the earth, and he has probably had some influences on global climate as well—exactly how much, we do not know."*

COUNTING THE COSTS

The market price of food represents only one of the costs associated with its production. Resistance to some of the less easily calculable environmental costs of indefinitely expanding the food supply is beginning to be reflected in constraints on food production. Thus many countries have banned or drastically limited the

* *New York Times*, September 23, 1971.

application of DDT, dieldrin, and other chlorinated hydrocarbons used as pesticides. In some parts of the world, conservationists are objecting to the construction of new irrigation reservoirs.

In the United States, a growing number of local and state governments are banning the use of phosphates in detergents because of eutrophication, and the regulation of phosphate fertilizer in some communities is now only a matter of time. The conflicts between economic efficiency and ecological soundness are myriad, and societies are increasingly forced to make unpleasant trade-offs between the two values. Many potent, low-cost pesticides threaten some species of wildlife with extinction. Chemical fertilizer is far cheaper than organic fertilizer, but runoff is a more serious problem. Beef finished in large commercial feedlots is cheaper than that finished in family-farm feedlots, but waste disposal is much more problematic.

We do not know how many species of birds, fish, and mammals must be sacrificed in order to achieve a 5 per cent increase in the world's food supply. We do know that as the number of people in the world goes up, the number of extant species goes down. Over time, willingness to pay all the costs involved in indefinitely expanding the world food supply surely will diminish.

5.

GROWING GLOBAL FOOD INSECURITY

The period since World War II has been characterized by excess capacity in world agriculture, much of it concentrated in the United States. The world was fortunate to have, in effect, two major food reserves during this period—one in the form of grain reserves in the principal exporting countries, the other in the form of reserve cropland, virtually all of it land idled under farm programs in the United States. These two reserves have provided a valuable degree of price stability, since their size could be adjusted to compensate for production fluctuation. Most important, they have provided a cushion when crop failures or droughts, as in India or the Soviet Union, created major unexpected import needs.

INDEX OF WORLD FOOD SECURITY

Grain reserves, including both food grains and feed grains, are most commonly measured in terms of carryover stocks—the amount in storage at the time the new crop begins to come in. World carryover stocks are concentrated in a few of the principal exporting countries—namely, the United States, Canada, Australia, and Argentina. Since 1960, world grain reserves have fluctuated from a high of 155 million metric tons to a low of about 100 million metric tons. When these reserves drop to 100 million tons, severe shortages and strong upward price pressures develop. Although 100 million tons appears to be an enormous quantity of grain, it represents a mere 8 per cent of annual world grain consumption, or less than one month's global needs—clearly an uncomfortably small working reserve and a perilously thin buffer against the vagaries of weather and plant disease. As world consumption expands by some 2.5 per cent annually, so should the size of working reserves; yet over the past two decades reserves have dwindled while consumption has continued to climb.

For the past dozen years or so, the U.S. government has paid its farmers to keep roughly 50 million acres idle. Although this source of supply cannot be tapped so quickly as grain reserves, most of the acreage can be brought back into production within twelve to eighteen months once the decision to do so has been made.

In recent years, the need to draw down grain reserves and to utilize reserve cropland has arisen with increasing frequency. During the food crisis years of 1966 and 1967, when world grain reserves were at a dangerously low level, the United States brought back into production a small portion of its 50 million idle acres. This happened again in 1971 as a result of a corn blight in the United States. In 1973, in response to growing food scarcities, world grain reserves once more declined, and the United States again resorted to cultivating its idle cropland, but to a much greater extent than on previous occasions. Government decisions in early 1973 permitted much of the idled cropland to come back into production, and in 1974 no government payments were made for keeping cropland idle.

Global reserve stocks fell to close to 100 million tons in 1973 and still further in 1974. Thus world grain reserves have dropped to their lowest level in more than two decades, although the world's population has increased by half in this period. The sum of global reserve stocks and the potential grain production of idle cropland gives a good indication of the total reserve capability in the world food economy in any given year. Taking this total as a percentage of world grain consumption provides a rough estimate of global food security for the year. As Table 5–1 demonstrates, the world is now in a highly vulnerable position. In 1973 and 1974, world reserve capabilities in relation to consumption needs fell far below any previous level in the postwar era, to the equivalent of only twenty-six days' worth of world consumption. In 1961, reserves represented 95 days' worth of world consumption.

TABLE 5–1. INDEX OF WORLD FOOD SECURITY, 1961–74.

Year	Reserve Stocks of Grain	Grain Equivalent of Idled U.S. Cropland	Total Reserves	Reserves as Days of Annual Grain Consumption
	(millions metric tons)			
1961	154	68	222	95
1962	131	81	212	88
1963	125	70	195	77
1964	128	70	198	77
1965	113	71	184	69
1966	99	79	178	66
1967	100	51	151	55
1968	116	61	177	62
1969	136	73	209	69
1970	146	71	217	69
1971	120	41	161	51
1972	131	78	209	66
1973	106	24	130	40
1974[a]	90	0	90	26

[a] Preliminary.

SOURCE: Prepared on the basis of U. S. Department of Agriculture data.

From the end of World War II until quite recently, world prices for the principal temperate-zone farm commodities, such as wheat, feed grains, and soybeans, have been remarkably stable. Since in the years ahead world food reserves may be chronically low, and the idled crop acreage in the United States may be consistently low or even disappear entirely, very volatile world prices for the important food commodities can be expected.

DEPENDENCE ON THE NORTH AMERICAN BREADBASKET

The extent of global vulnerability is demonstrated by the degree of the world's dependence on one region—North America—for exportable food supplies. Over the past generation, the United States has achieved a unique position as a supplier of food to the rest of the world. Before World War II, both Latin America (especially Argentina) and North America (the United States and Canada) were major grain exporters. During the late 'thirties, net grain exports from Latin America were substantially higher than those from North America. Since then, however, the combination of the population explosion and the slowness of most Latin American governments to reform and modernize agriculture has eliminated the region's net export surplus. With few exceptions, Latin American countries are now food importers.

As Table 5-2 illustrates, over the past three decades North America—particularly the United States, which accounts for three fourths of the continent's grain exports—has emerged as the world's breadbasket. The exports of Australia, the only other net exporter of importance, are only a fraction of North America's. Moreover, the United States is now not only the world's major exporter of wheat and feed grains but also the world's leading exporter of rice. Indeed, North America today controls a larger share of the world's exportable surplus of grains than the Middle East does of current world oil exports.

Exportable supplies of the crucial soybean are even more con-

TABLE 5-2. The Changing Pattern of World Grain Trade.

Region	1934–38	1948–52	1960	1966	1973[a]
	(millions metric tons)				
North America	+5[a]	+23	+39	+59	+91
Latin America	+9	+1	0	+5	−3
Western Europe	−24	−22	−25	−27	−19
Eastern Europe and U.S.S.R.	+5	—	0	−4	−27
Africa	+1	0	−2	−7	−5
Asia	+2	−6	−17	−34	−43
Australia and New Zealand	+3	+3	+6	+8	+6

[a] Preliminary, fiscal year.
[b] Plus sign indicates net exports; minus sign, net imports.
Source: Based on U. S. Department of Agriculture data.

centrated than those of grains. Although as recently as the 'thirties China supplied nearly all the soybeans entering world markets, continuing population growth has gradually absorbed its exportable surplus. As of 1973, China was importing small quantities from the United States. The position of principal supplier has been taken over by the United States, which provided over 90 per cent of the world soybean exports in the 'sixties and early 'seventies. With world demand for high-quality protein surging upward, Brazil, virtually the only other nation exporting soybeans on a large scale, has recently boosted its soybean production and exports. For the foreseeable future, however, the United States is likely to continue supplying three fourths or more of the world's soybean exports.

REDEFINING FAMINE

Between late 1972 and early 1974, international food prices escalated rapidly in response to the growing excess of world demand over available supplies and the decline of world food reserves. Wheat and rice prices tripled, and soybean prices more than doubled. Soon after the soaring food prices began to have an impact, the exercise of new-found bargaining power by the oil-exporting nations brought a similar escalation in world petroleum prices (Figure 5–1). Simultaneously, phosphate and nitrogen-fertilizer prices also soared. For those nations that must import food, fuel, *and* fertilizer, these price increases had a disastrous effect on foreign-exchange reserves, the terms of trade, and future development prospects.

High food prices and shortages are an inconvenience for affluent societies and individuals, but they place poor nations, and the poor within all nations, in a dangerous predicament. When global food reserves are low, the capacity of the international community to provide relief in response to emergencies such as droughts or crop failures is greatly diminished. At the same time, high prices may keep needed food out of the reach of poor nations and individuals. For the sizeable segment of mankind that spends 80 per cent of its income on food, a doubling in the price of wheat or rice cannot possibly be offset by increased expenditures. It can only drive a subsistence diet below the survival level.

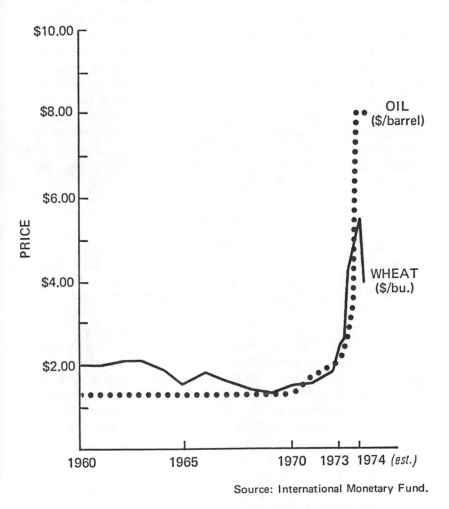

Source: International Monetary Fund.

Figure 5-1. World Oil and Wheat Prices, 1960-74

One factor that today makes it possible for the world's affluent to ignore such tragedies is the change in the way in which famine manifests itself. In earlier periods, famine was largely a geographical phenomenon. Whole nations or regions—for example, Ireland or West Bengal—experienced dramatically high rates of starvation and death. As mentioned earlier, famine today is generally more evenly spread among the world's poor rather than concentrated in specific locales. (The current tragedy in the Sahel region south of the Sahara desert is an obvious exception.) The modern version of famine does not usually confront the world with dramatic photographs, such as those of the morning ritual of collecting bodies in Calcutta during the Bengal famine of 1943, but it is no less real in the human toll it takes. Reports in 1974 of rising rates of nutrition-related deaths in several poor countries underscore the need for closer attention to this ominous trend.

DECLINING FOOD ASSISTANCE

As food prices soar, seriously limiting the ability of the poor countries (and of the poor within all countries) to *buy* needed food, sources of food *aid* are drying up as well. Over the last two decades, the only large-scale perennial food-aid program has been that of the United States under Public Law 480. This landmark measure, passed in 1954, made it "the policy of the United States to use [its] abundant productivity to combat hunger and malnutrition and to encourage economic development in the developing countries" through concessional sales and humanitarian grants. For nearly two decades, the PL 480 program satisfied many goals simultaneously—providing an outlet for U.S. commercial surpluses, building future commercial markets, aiding the economic development of recipient countries, supplying U.N. and voluntary-agency nutrition programs, and forestalling massive famine in situations of natural disaster.

At a time of record international food prices, shrinking reserve stocks of grain, and increased rates of malnutrition among the world's poor—in short, the very time when the world need for food aid is at its highest—the quantities of food supplied by the United States under PL 480 have fallen sharply as a result of tight world supplies, lucrative export markets, and government fears of contributing to domestic food-price inflation. Although the decline in the PL 480 program has not been great in dollar terms, when it is examined according to the quantity of food shipped and the distribution among recipient countries, the shrinkage is quite dramatic.

In analyzing the recent decline in PL 480 aid, it is necessary to distinguish between Titles I and II of the program, since aid under the two titles is disbursed differently for different purposes. Under Title I, most food is sold, for convertible currencies or dollars, under long-term loans, with interest rates set below commercial levels. Since 1971, in contrast to past practice, only small amounts of food have been sold for local currencies, and only where there exists a genuine U.S. need for these currencies. The dollar value of Title I food-commodity exports increased slightly, from $549 million to $640 million, between FY 1972 and FY 1974. However, the total quantity of grains and high-protein products shipped in 1974 fell to less than a third of 1972 levels and less than one tenth the large volume of the mid-'sixties. Milk shipments were eliminated entirely. Even these figures are deceptive, for roughly half of all American food aid in 1974 has been supplied to two countries alone—South Vietnam and Cambodia. Table 5–3 shows the decline in the volume of food shipments under Title I of PL 480 from 1960 to the present.

TABLE 5–3. Food Shipments under PL 480, Title I, 1960–74.[a]

Commodity	1960[b]	1965[b]	1970	1972	1973	1974[c]
	(thousands of metric tons)					
Wheat and products	8,199	13,705	5,765	4,615	2,517	1,005
Milk (dried)	8	42	18	19	2	0
Rice	453	561	884	813	987	620
Corn, sorghum	787	728	1,078	1,217	1,289	454
Vegetable oils	339	364	240	193	107	148

[a] Sales for dollars on credit terms and foreign currencies; all years but 1970 on fiscal-year basis.
[b] Includes aid under Titles I and IV in previous legislation.
[c] Estimate.
Source: U.S. Department of Agriculture.

Under Title II, most food is provided on a grant basis to governments, voluntary agencies, and the U.N. World Food Programme (WFP). The commodities supplied are used in nutritional programs for vulnerable groups such as mothers, infants, and school children; in "food for work" programs to build needed infrastructure such as irrigation and drainage facilities, schools, and roads; and in disaster-relief activities.

Food grants under Title II increased slightly between the mid-'sixties and 1972, but over the last two years even the dollar value of Title II food shipments has fallen (from $380 million to $248 million), and this fact in an era of soaring prices has resulted in a devastating decline in the quantity of food supplied. In 1974 wheat shipments are down one half from 1973, and rice and milk shipments have disappeared altogether. Only the tonnage of coarse grains (corn, oats, sorghum) has risen, reflecting the shipment of 250,000 tons of grain sorghum to the Sahel (Table 5–4).

TABLE 5–4. Food Shipments under PL 480, Title II, 1960–74.[a]

Commodity	1960	1965	1970	1972	1973	1974[b]
Wheat and products	979	1,473	1,464	1,614	1,649	718
Milk, dried	147	199	133	115	26	0
Rice	89	0	7	248	33	0
Corn, oats, sorghum and products	359	498	330	257	246	379
Blended food products	0	0	149	266	195	182
Vegetable oils	0	106	81	187	111	53

[a] Voluntary agency grants, WFP, government-to-government grants for disaster relief and economic development; all years but 1970 on fiscal-year basis.
[b] Estimate.
SOURCE: U.S. Department of Agriculture.

In 1972, some 90 million of the world's poorest people earned or received food originating within the Title II program, including 46 million in maternal, infant, and child-feeding programs; 15 million in food-for-work programs; and 28 million in disaster-relief and refugee programs. An estimated 20 million nutritionally vulnerable people have been cut off from these programs in the past year as a result of the decline in food supplied under Title II.

The shrinking supply of goods provided under Title II over the past year is also having a disastrous effect on many valuable programs of the voluntary agencies (such as CARE, Church World Service, and Catholic Relief Services) as well as on the WFP—all of which depend heavily on U.S. food grants. Ironically, this is happening at a time when the voluntary agencies are putting new emphasis on the very kind of rural and agricultural development projects that may help provide a long-term solution to the present crisis—and even as the U.S. Congress is advocating increasing reliance on the private sector in foreign-aid activities. Similarly, the nutritional and public-works projects of a growing international institution, the WFP, are being curtailed. The WFP, with projects currently under way in eighty-eight nations, has grown rapidly since it was initiated in the early 'sixties. To finance its activities, it depends on pledges of commodities and funds from FAO-member governments. In 1974, because of rising prices of both commodities and freight, many planned development projects were suspended or canceled, and some ongoing projects were cut. According to WFP Executive Director Dr. Francisco Aquino, the tripling of many commodity prices since 1972 resulted in an estimated shrinkage of the WFP's "food basket" by about 40 per cent, seriously affecting the program's ability to meet its commitments. The WFP pledging target for 1975–76 is $440 million, but commitments of at least $650 million will be needed if its planned program is to be implemented.

CLIMATIC VULNERABILITY

No single factor has a greater impact on food production in any country than the weather. When the weather is good, harvests are generally bountiful. When nature is less charitable, harvests fall. Thus in 1972, when rainfall was poor in the Soviet Union and in parts of Asia and Africa, total world food production fell by a few percentage points, even while demand climbed by a comparable amount. In 1973, by contrast, excellent weather in most regions made it possible to attain a new record in world food production.

Although weather has always been a central concern of farmers and agricultural policy-makers, in the past the availability of substantial food reserves provided a vital buffer against the vagaries of climate. But currently, with global reserves dangerously low, the weather in all producing regions is receiving a new degree of international attention and concern. Economic stability in most nations and survival in some are critically linked to the climatic patterns of this and coming years. The climate—and possible interventions to alter it—is becoming an important element in international affairs.

At the same time that world dependence on North American food exports is increasing so dramatically, there is growing awareness that this extreme dependence leaves the world in a very dangerous position in the event of adverse crop years in North America. The United States and Canada are affected by the same climatic cycles. There is now considerable evidence indicating that North America has been subject to clusters of drought years that recur roughly every twenty years. Although meteorologists disagree about the existence of weather cycles, some leading American scientists assert that a cyclical drought phenomenon can be traced as far back as the Civil War period, when data on rainfall were first collected. The most recent drought, which occurred in the early 'fifties, was comparatively mild. The preceding one, twenty years earlier, was far more severe and contributed to the "dustbowl" era in the United States.

If the United States experiences another stretch of drought, quite possibly during the current decade, the impact on production is not likely to be so great as in the 'thirties because of improved soil-management and water-conservation practices. But, given the overwhelming dependence of the entire world on North America's exportable margin of food, *any* decline in production can create a situation of great risk. Moreover, one does not have to accept the drought-cycle theory to realize that years of poor rainfall are inevitable in any case.

Complicating the global climatic outlook are the alarming recent findings of several prominent meteorologists. Among others, Dr. Reid Bryson, Director of the Institute for Environmental Studies at the University of Wisconsin, and Hubert Lamb, an eminent British meteorologist, assert that fundamental changes are occurring in global climatic patterns. Bryson argues that the atmosphere's increasing level of particulate matter—to which man's agricultural and industrial activities are making a growing contribution—is responsible for the global cooling trend in evidence since 1940. He maintains that closely associated changes in the atmospheric wind and water cycles are bringing greater instability to climatic patterns throughout the world.

While there is disagreement about the ultimate causes, many meteorologists agree that the monsoon belt—which customarily provides a vital rainy season for southern Asia and north-central Africa—may be experiencing a gradual southward shift. If this theory is correct, it helps to explain the severity of the recent drought in sub-Saharan Africa; it further suggests that low rainfall years in the densely populated Indian subcontinent and Southeast Asia may become more frequent.

Climatology is still an infant discipline, and dependable predictions of future weather patterns remain out of man's reach. But if one indisputable lesson is to be drawn from recent meteorological findings and debates, it is that climate is an unreliable variable. The margin of safety provided by large reserve stocks of food must be restored and maintained to minimize chances for weather-induced disaster.

GLOBAL POLITICS OF FOOD SCARCITY

As food becomes more scarce, several already apparent and disconcerting modes of international conduct may become more frequent and intense, particularly the use of secrecy to gain special advantages in food markets, competition between rich and poor nations for limited food supplies, and unilateral decisions to withhold food supplies from dependent importing nations.

A special case of the last of these actions occurred in mid-1973, when the United States failed to respond to Chile's request for wheat on credit. Since Chile's foreign-exchange reserves were then exhausted and bread shortages were developing, this American action undoubtedly contributed to the downfall of the Allende government in September, 1973. Although Americans decry the use of petroleum as a political weapon, calling it "political blackmail," the United States has been using food aid for political purposes for twenty years—and describing this as "enlightened diplomacy."

The use of secrecy and its consequences attracted much attention in 1972, when buyers from the Soviet Union covertly managed to corner a sizable share of the U.S. wheat crop. Concealing the size of their domestic grain shortfall, the Soviets quietly arranged contracts to import about 28 million tons of grain, most of it purchased from the United States—the largest commercial transaction in history. By withholding information on the magnitudes of both domestic needs and intended purchases, they were able to make their purchases at an unreasonably low price level, supported by unwarranted U.S. government subsidies. The Soviet gain was largely at the expense of other foreign buyers and U.S. consumers, for the world grain-price spiral was greatly intensified when the shock of the massive Soviet purchase hit the market place. The question arises as to whether countries not sharing information should have unlimited access to supplies. An earlier disclosure of intentions by the Soviet Union would have enabled the United States to expand its grain production earlier and also would have allowed for a more equitable sharing among nations of the inevitably higher prices.

The probable nature and results of more intense global competition for tight food supplies were foreshadowed in 1973. Bangladesh, threatened with famine, pressed with only limited success for the United States and the Soviet Union to direct part of the Soviet-purchased grain to help feed its population. India, confronted with an unanticipated need to import several million tons of grain, found that the extremely high prices resulting from international bidding for available supplies had seriously limited the amount it could buy. Fortunately, the Soviet Union agreed to loan 2 million tons of grain to India, which partially helped India to weather its food crisis in 1973. Growing rice purchases by the increasingly affluent nations of the Middle East and North Africa helped to drive international rice prices still higher, reducing the purchasing power of many poor African and Asian nations that badly needed rice imports.

It is in the context of growing world dependence on the United States for protein and grains that we must view the abrupt and unilateral imposition of export restrictions on soybeans and feedstuffs by the U.S. government in June, 1973. Although these export controls represent an effort to fight food-price inflation within the United States, they had the inevitable result of greatly intensifying inflationary pressures and food shortages in other nations of the world.

By imposing export controls, the United States placed itself in the morally untenable position of denying food to other nations, all of which had relatively less food. The reliability and integrity of the United States as a trading partner was called into serious question; nations that have been urged to depend on the United States for food suddenly found their promised supplies cut severely and without warning. American negotiators at upcoming trade negotiations may not be permitted to forget the U.S. export controls as they press other nations to lower agricultural trade barriers. Attempts to export inflation—like attempts to export depression in an earlier era—may well prove self-defeating in the end. Nor is the United States the only food-exporting country to impose controls. Thailand, Brazil, Argentina, and other nations all imposed food-export controls in 1973.

These trends in international economic conduct reflect a much more basic shift in national trade-policy concerns. Since World War II, the overriding objective of national trade policies has been to secure access to *markets* abroad for exports—whether soybeans or machinery. While this concern remains vital, the emergence of scarcity in many commodities has brought to the fore another important concern: the assurance of access to *supplies* of needed resources. The international community has gradually reduced tariff barriers and evolved guidelines governing restrictions on imports, but no such guidelines have yet been devised to deal with the other side of the international trade coin: restrictions on exports.

The urgent need for new departures in international food policies becomes clear when we consider what might happen if the global grain crop again were to fall by a few percentage points, as it did in 1972—but this time in a situation where neither large reserve stocks nor idled cropland is available to cushion the impact. It is impossible to predict precisely what would ensue, but certain trends seem probable. Governments of the principal exporting nations would come under extremely strong pressure to limit food exports and thus hold down domestic food prices. Although refusal to apply export controls would create domestic political and economic instability, doing so in the cases of crucial commodities would cause great hardship in the importing nations. Political acrimony and a breakdown in cooperative endeavors in nonagricultural areas might well accompany efforts by traditional suppliers to cut off some of those who are dependent on them for food.

Frantic deals, barters, and secret purchases of food supplies by individual nations, presaged in early 1974 by the efforts of oil-importing nations to secure supplies for themselves in the wake of the Arab oil embargo, would also probably develop. Some nations would have the wherewithal to obtain adequate supplies in this fashion, but others—probably including many of the neediest countries—would not. As world prices skyrocketed to new highs, inflation and domestic economic instability would grow even more critical than they already are in most nations. There is little doubt as to who would suffer most. Climbing death rates among the poorest quarter of the world's population would inevitably result as those with the financial capacity to do so outbid each other for limited available exportable supplies.

PART TWO

Four Basic Resources

6.

LAND FOR FOOD

There are essentially two ways of increasing the world food supply from conventional agriculture. One is to expand the area under cultivation. The other is to increase output on the existing cultivated area. From the beginning of agriculture until about 1950, expanding the cultivated area was the major means of increasing the world's food supply. Since that time, raising output on the existing cultivated area has accounted for most of the increase. An estimated four fifths of the annual rise in world food output achieved in the early 'seventies was due to the intensification of cultivation.

As human population growth has continued its steep ascent, the cropland per person has declined until today there is only one acre for each of us. Since most of the economically feasible opportunities for bringing new land under the plow already have been exhausted, further population growth leaves no real alternative to pressing ahead with efforts to raise the productivity of available cropland—and to curb the growth in the demand for food.

THE AREA-TO-YIELD TRANSITION

Prior to the twentieth century, rates of increase in output per acre were so low as to be scarcely perceptible within any given generation. Only in recent decades have some countries succeeded in achieving an increase in output per acre sufficiently sustained and rapid to be considered a yield "takeoff."

The timing of the transition from the area-expanding method of increasing food production to the yield-raising method has been very uneven throughout the world. As population pressures built up in Japan in the late nineteenth and early twentieth centuries. Japanese farmers were forced to intensify cultivation and were probably the first to succeed in making the transition. Several northern European countries in which available farmland was limited also successfully completed the transition early in the twentieth century. In the United States, the frontier had vanished prior to World War I, but a yield-per-acre takeoff was not achieved until mid-century, when economic conditions made the use of the accumulated technologies profitable. Farm output lagged during the intervening period but rose when land used to produce feed for horses was released for food production after World War I as tractors began to displace horses.

A second group of industrial countries, including the United Kingdom, Canada, and Australia, made the area-to-yield transition during the early 'forties, largely as a result of strong wartime economic incentives to expand production. (Interestingly, U.S. corn yields had remained static for eight decades between the Civil War and the outbreak of World War II.)

The grain varieties that have developed indigenously in most of Asia, Latin America, and Africa are usually well adapted to local growing conditions but not highly responsive to the modern inputs —principally chemical fertilizer—that fuel a takeoff in per-acre yields. As a result, by the early 'sixties there were very few examples of sustained, rapid yield increases in the developing countries.

During the first half of the 'sixties, food production in the developing countries as a group began to fall behind population growth, bringing rising food prices, growing food scarcity, and increasing dependence on food aid from the United States. This was a direct result of the fact that many of these countries had virtually exhausted the supply of new land that could readily be brought under cultivation but had not yet achieved a takeoff in yield per acre. It was in this context that the discovery of new seed varieties, combined with production-oriented economic incentives and inputs, brought about the Green Revolution. New breeds of wheat and rice adaptable to a wide range of conditions have permitted a hesitant beginning toward yield-per-acre takeoffs in many developing countries.

EXPANDING THE CULTIVATED AREA

Since the beginning of agriculture, crop cultivation spread from valley to valley and eventually from continent to continent until today some 3.6 billion acres (more than 11 per cent of the earth's total land surface) are under cultivation. Expressed as a percentage of total surface, the area cleared by man seems small, but as a percentage of the land area that is actually supporting vegetation, it is quite large. And it is very large indeed in terms of the limited land area that is suitable for crops useful to man.

Permanent meadow, pasture, and grazing lands supporting wild and domestic animals are almost twice as plentiful as the arable land area of the world. Grazing lands exceed croplands by varying amounts in all parts of the world except Western Europe. Africa, with its vast stretches of savanna, contains the largest portion of the earth's grazing area, but all geographic regions have substantial expanses of grazing land. Compared with the earth's arable land, grazing land tends to be located at higher elevations and to be drier, steeper, and more rocky.

The 70 per cent of the earth's dry surface that is not classified as agricultural land is unsuited to agriculture for a variety of reasons, especially lack of moisture or inclement temperature. Much of the world is too dry to support flourishing plant life. The Sahara Desert covers a significant part of the African continent. The Thar Desert, in the northwestern corner of the Indo-Pakistan subcontinent, is larger than the cultivated areas of Pakistan and Bangladesh combined. Huge areas of China and Mongolia are covered by the vast Gobi Desert. The interior of Australia is largely desert and wasteland. Deserts are somewhat less common in Europe and the Western Hemisphere, although large dry areas do exist in southern Europe, coastal Peru, northeastern Brazil, Central America, and the southwestern United States. Where rainfall is not a limiting factor, land may be nonagricultural because of its location at elevations too high or in regions too cold to support commercial crops—as in the North American Rocky Mountains, the South

American Andes, the European Alps, the vast Asian Himalayan plateau, and the extensive northern latitudes of Canada and the Soviet Union.

If the earth's arable lands were placed end to end around the equator, they would form a belt only 200 miles wide. With the exception of the Argentine Pampas, the great bulk of the world's fertile and well-watered agricultural land—including the American corn belt, the Gangetic plain of India, and the rich farmlands of Western Europe—lies north of the equator.

TABLE 6-1. WORLD ARABLE LAND.

	Arable Land[a] (million acres)	Arable Land per Capita (acres)
Europe	348	.77
U.S.S.R.	575	2.35
North America	583	2.55
Latin America	294	1.00
Asia	1,144	.55
Africa	529	1.50
Oceania	116	5.88
World total	3,600	.98

[a] Includes land under permanent crops. Latest available data.

SOURCE: Food and Agriculture Organization, *Production Yearbook, 1972.*

Estimates of how much additional land can be brought under cultivation vary widely, but they are not very useful because none specifies at what cost the additional land could be made productive or at what food-price levels its cultivation would be profitable. Meaningful estimates must take into account the level of capital inputs and technology required to expand the cultivated area and the relationship of the cost of the food that could be produced on it to the prices that people are able to pay. There is little if any potential for new farmlands in Asia and Europe and relatively little in the Soviet Union. Most of the countries of North Africa and the Middle East, dependent as they are on irrigation or dryland farming, cannot significantly expand the area under cultivation without developing new sources of irrigation water.

Sub-Saharan Africa and the Amazon Basin of Brazil are the only regions with sizable portions of well-watered, potentially arable land, and there is little doubt that cropland will expand there. But it would be a serious error to view Africa and Brazil as vast, unexploited repositories of good farmland. Much of the potentially cultivable land is in the tropics, and experience indicates that the farming of tropical soils is often not economically feasible. The soils (which are not usually very fertile to begin with) and their protective forest cover form a fragile ecological system. Organic materials in the soil decay very rapidly in the tropical climate, and the soils often lose whatever fertility they had once the forest above —the abundant source of new vegetative matter—is removed. Thus farming new soils may require heavy, continuous applications of chemical fertilizer. In addition, when they are fully exposed to sun and oxygen, some tropical soils undergo chemical changes and compaction, becoming too solid to farm.

A critical key to opening large areas to agriculture in sub-Saharan Africa is eradication of the tsetse fly, which carries the cattle-killing disease trypanosomiasis to over a third of the continent. Larger regions would become available for grazing and to a lesser extent for crop production if the fly were eliminated. But progress toward overcoming this extremely difficult problem is likely to be slow and costly.

A long-term international project has been initiated under the leadership of the World Health Organization and the U.N. Development Programme to attempt to eliminate the less widespread problem of onchocerciasis ("river blindness"), a debilitating disease that now afflicts 1 million West Africans. If the two-decade program could control the black fly that transmits this disease, an estimated 16 million acres of fertile river-valley cropland could be restored to production.

Apart from these possibilities, no further significant opportunities to expand farm area are likely to be found unless the cost of desalinization is reduced to make it economically feasible or the technology is developed to shift rainfall from the oceans to arid land masses. At the global level, the record of the past two decades suggests that it is far cheaper and easier to expand the food supply by intensifying cultivation on the existing cropland than by bringing new land under the plow.

RAISING OUTPUT PER ACRE

One of the critical questions associated with future gains in food production is the extent to which the trend of rising per-acre yields of cereals in the more advanced countries can be sustained. In some countries, the growth in per-acre yields is already beginning to slow, and capital investments per additional unit of output are climbing sharply. In Japan, for example, raising rice yields very far above their current level would involve phenomenal costs. In the United States, raising average corn yields from 90 to 100 bushels per acre requires far more fertilizer than was needed to raise yields from 50 to 60 bushels.

It is significant that the main sources of increased agricultural productivity—the use of chemical fertilizer, improved crop varieties (including hybrids), and the use of pesticides and irrigation— have all been known for at least several decades. The key question now is: Are there any other sources of increased productivity, in existence or in the process of development, that are comparable to these traditional ones? If not, can we expect a slowdown in the rate of increase in yields per acre in the more agriculturally advanced countries?

A definitive answer to these questions is not possible, but we can gain some perspective by examining historical cereal-yield trends in some of the more agriculturally advanced countries and by comparing current cereal yields in the principal producing countries. The trends in Japan's rice yields, Britain's wheat yields, and U.S. corn yields since the beginning of the century are especially revealing (Figure 6–1).

Rice yields in Japan rose steadily but slowly during the first half of this century; since then, their upward trend has been a great deal more rapid. But despite their steady progress, *Japanese rice yields have barely doubled* in more than seven decades. This suggests that unless the rice-producing developing countries, such as the Philippines, Indonesia, Thailand, Bangladesh, China, and India —all of which have rapidly growing populations and little or no new land to bring under the plow—can dramatically improve on Japan's exemplary performance, they will be in grave difficulty on

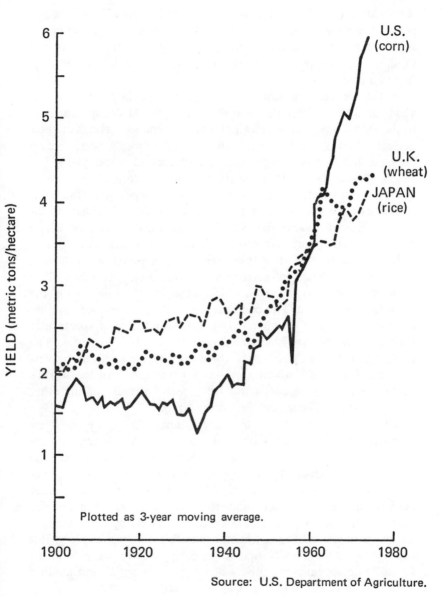

Figure 6-1. Selected Cereal Yields, 1900-1973

the food front. (Remember that a population growing at even 2 per cent per year multiplies sevenfold in a century. And one growing at 3 per cent annually—as, for example, is the case in the Philippines, Thailand, and Bangladesh today—multiplies nineteen-fold in a century!)

In the United Kingdom, little effort was made to raise wheat yields until World War II, when the U-boat threat demonstrated to to the British how vulnerable they had become as a result of their neglect of agriculture. Within two decades, yields were nearly doubled, but in recent years the rate of gain in wheat yields has fallen off sharply. At four metric tons per hectare (1 hectare = 2.471 acres), wheat yields in the United Kingdom in the mid-seventies are more or less representative of those of other north-western European countries, such as France and Germany, which also have made impressive gains over the past generation.

During the first third of this century, corn yields in the United States not only failed to increase but in fact declined slightly. This trend was abruptly reversed during the late 'thirties, with the hybridization of corn. The combination of hybrid corn seed and an abundant supply of cheap nitrogen fertilizer led to a spectacular growth in yields that has continued into the mid-'seventies. The tripling of U.S. corn yields is all the more impressive given the vast acreage of this crop, which accounts for one eighth of the world's cereal harvest and exceeds the total cereal harvest of all other countries except China and the Soviet Union.

There can be no doubt that corn, domesticated by the New World Indians in the pre-Columbian period, is an enormous asset to U.S. agriculture, making an important contribution to the strength and productivity of the U.S. farm economy. Corn production in the United States is expanding far faster than that of other cereals, as well as faster than the over-all world demand for cereals. This has helped to take up the slack left by other cereals, the yields of which have not been expanding nearly so rapidly. But can we expect this rate of increase in corn yields to continue in the future? Further gains will undoubtedly be substantial, but another tripling of corn yields does not appear likely.

Another way of gaining perspective on the question of the future potential increases for yield is to compare yields in the principal grain-exporting countries. Table 6–2 shows the twenty largest national harvests in individual cereals, ranked according to scale of production. The U.S. corn crop leads the list in terms of both scale of production and level of yields, which exceed six metric tons per hectare. The only other cereal harvest to exceed four metric tons

TABLE 6–2. Principal National Cereal Harvests, 1972.

Country	Cereal	Production (thousands of metric tons)	Yield (metric tons per hectare)
U.S.	corn	141,053	6.09
U.S.S.R.	wheat	85,800	1.47
China	rice	69,878	2.07
U.S.	wheat	42,043	2.20
India	rice	39,530	1.08
U.S.S.R.	barley	36,800	1.35
China	wheat	34,502	1.20
China	corn	28,560	2.71
India	wheat	26,477	1.38
China	millet	22,005	.76
U.S.	sorghum	20,874	3.81
China	barley	18,502	1.42
France	wheat	18,123	4.58
Canada	wheat	14,514	1.68
Brazil	corn	14,500	1.38
U.S.S.R.	oats	14,000	1.23
Indonesia	rice	12,640	1.91
Turkey	wheat	12,085	1.29
Canada	barley	11,287	2.23
France	barley	10,426	3.90

Source: FAO, *Production Yearbook, 1972.*

per hectare is wheat in France. The per-hectare yields of the other leading cereal harvests are only a fraction of that of U.S. corn: Soviet wheat yields are one fourth those of U.S. corn; Chinese rice yields, one third; Indian rice yields, scarcely one sixth. Within the United States, the yield of wheat is scarcely one third that of corn.

The cereal yields of different countries vary according to the cereal, the level and seasonal distribution of rainfall, the use of fertilizer, the temperature, soil types, and cultural practices. Rainfall and the level of technology probably explain most of the variations. The effect of rainfall on yields can be illustrated by comparing wheat yields in the United Kingdom and Australia. These two countries have comparable levels of technological sophistication, but wheat yields in the United Kingdom are 4.5 metric tons per hectare, five times the 900 kilograms per hectare obtained in Australia. U.S. corn yields are four times Soviet wheat yields, but that portion of the U.S. wheat crop that is grown under rainfall conditions comparable to those in the Soviet Union achieves yields only half again as great as Soviet wheat yields. Wheat yields in the U.S. corn belt are more than double those achieved in the semi-arid Great Plains wheat-growing area.

Our examination of historical yield trends and comparative contemporary yields in principal cereal-producing countries shows that, under appropriate growing conditions, corn is a highly productive cereal whose yields surpass those of other cereals by nearly one half. Rice, on the other hand, is exceedingly unresponsive to attempts to achieve rapid gains in yields. Both the long-term historical experience in Japan and the more recent contrasts in India between the dramatic gains in wheat yields and the scarcely perceptible gains in rice yields (see Chapter 10) reinforce this basic and troublesome point.

In looking at future prospects for raising yields, it seems inevitable that increases in the more advanced countries—for example, in corn yields in the United States, in wheat yields in the United Kingdom and France, and in rice yields in Japan—will slow down markedly during the remainder of this century. A steadily expanding share of growth in world food supplies must come from developing countries, which have far more unrealized agronomic potential. The difficulties of getting rapid gains in rice yields anywhere and of getting further rapid gains in cereal yields in the more advanced countries do not encourage optimism about the adequacy of future supplies in the absence of a sharp slowdown in the world rate of population growth.

Fortunately, in many regions, particularly in the developing countries, there is still vast potential for exploiting the traditional sources of productivity increases. But with the world demand for food growing by at least 2.5 per cent annually, or twelvefold per century, more and more regions will eventually reach the point where further yield increases will become very costly.

A crop's photosynthetic efficiency, defined as the percentage of solar energy used relative to that available on a given land area, is the ultimate factor limiting crop output per acre. The actual position of leaves on plants, the density of the plant population, the temperature, and plant physiology are key factors regulating photosynthetic efficiency. The upper yield limit can be increased by developing plants with greater photosynthetic efficiency or by improving cultivation practices to improve efficiency per acre. Hybrid corn and sorghum plants as well as new varieties of wheat and rice plants are more efficient users of solar energy in the production of grain, and their smaller size permits a dramatic gain in the number of plants per acre.

It is often assumed that the record yields attained on experimental plots under closely controlled conditions can easily and quickly be translated into higher national average yields. Unfortunately, this is not the case. In the United States, for example, the average yields of wheat today are far below those attained on experimental plots during the late nineteenth century, and the same is true for many other crops. Equally widespread and equally unwarranted is the assumption that all countries eventually will be able to match the average yield in the nation with the highest yield or that the performance of the best farmers can be emulated by all. The yield levels potentially attainable by individual countries vary widely with rainfall, temperature, soil types and topography, production costs, managerial abilities of farmers, and other factors. Per-acre yields may vary even more among individual farmers in the same area than among various nations or regions, as a result of basic differences in the innate capacities or motivations of farmers.

Failure to distinguish between the technical potential for expanding food production and the economically profitable possibilities of doing so has resulted in confusing variations among estimates of future food production. The experience of Japan—where rice

yields seemed to level off in the late 'sixties and early 'seventies—
suggests the importance of the interrelationship of relevant economic factors. Both the prices received by farmers and the costs of
production must be weighed in assessing potential increases in
production. As farmers move up the per-acre-yield curve, a point
of diminishing returns is eventually reached at which additional
costs begin to exceed additional returns. Thus it is unrealistic to
expect farmers to produce up to the full technical potential.

There can be no doubt that further breakthroughs in plant
breeding and agricultural practices will permit further yield increases for many crops. In some regions, the potential of existing
technologies is far from realized. It is also certain that higher food
prices can bring forth greater food production at any given level
of technology. But the prospect that future world food-production
gains will be both slower to come and increasingly costly cannot be
ignored. Man's efforts to increase the future supply of food will
prove futile in the end if they are not accompanied by equally
strong efforts to limit growth in the demand for food.

Loss of Arable Land

As efforts to expand the world's cultivated area are intensified,
it is important to remember that in many regions the cultivated
area is declining. Unfortunately, the paucity of data prevents an
accurate estimate of the extent of this problem. Most countries,
rich and poor, keep detailed records on the additions to their cultivated area resulting from irrigation, land reclamation, and settlement projects, but farmland lost to transportation; to recreational,
residential, and industrial development; to soil erosion; or to the
spread of deserts is not monitored. The fragmentary data available
suggest that millions of acres of cropland are being lost each year
throughout the world.

Few countries have well-defined and enforced land-use policies
to protect agricultural land. In the United States, for example,
farmland has been used indiscriminately for other purposes, with
little thought given to the possible long-term consequences. Spreading cities, airports, shopping centers, and housing developments
are consuming an estimated half-million acres of cropland annually

in the United States. In Japan, the cultivated area was greatest around 1920, and it has declined substantially since then. Some countries in Western Europe—notably Sweden, Norway, Ireland, and Switzerland—have been losing agricultural land to urban growth for the past several decades.

One consequence of the continuous growth in population is the spread of agriculture to lands with thin mantles of topsoil that will not sustain continuous and intensive cultivation. Fuel demands for heating and cooking have long exceeded the replacement capacity of local forests, and in many parts of the world there is little forest land left. In these circumstances, exemplified by India and Pakistan, people are unable to afford fossil fuels and so are reduced to using cow dung for heating and cooking. This expedient, in turn, deprives the soil of badly needed organic matter and nutrients.

Increasing human population in the poor countries is almost always accompanied by a nearly commensurate growth in the livestock population, in order to expand draft power and food supplies. As herds of cattle are increased, they denude the countryside of its natural grass cover. Overgrazing by goats and sheep is even more damaging because it affects trees and shrubs as well. Combined with progressive deforestation, it is resulting in nearly total denudation of the countryside in some poor countries, creating conditions for the rapid spread of soil erosion by wind and water. Literally millions of acres of cropland in Asia, the Middle East, Africa, and the Andean countries are being abandoned each year because severe soil erosion has made them unproductive, or at least incapable of sustaining the local inhabitants with existing agricultural technologies. It takes centuries to form an inch of topsoil through natural processes, but in some areas of the world man is managing to destroy it in only a fraction of that time.

History provides us with many examples of man's abuse of the soil. North Africa, once the fertile granary of the Roman Empire, is now largely a desert or near-desert. Overplowing and overgrazing of the Great Plains during the early decades of this century left that area vulnerable to the wind erosion that culminated in the dustbowl era of the 'thirties. The United States had the resources, the technical know-how, and the will to respond to this crisis by extensive strip cropping, including the "fallowing" of 20 million acres, and by constructing literally thousands of windbreaks in the form of rows of trees across the Great Plains. As a result, today erosion is negligible and land productivity high in the Great Plains. Had the United States not been able to respond in this fashion, much of the Great Plains, like the once-fertile fields of North Africa, by now might have been abandoned.

Many of the world's densely populated regions—such as western India, Pakistan, North Africa, and northern China—face similarly severe wind and water erosion of their soils because of the acute and growing pressure of human and livestock populations on the land, but they do not have enough slack in their food systems to permit the diversion of large acreages to fallow. These areas could be rescued by a massive effort involving reforestation, the controlled grazing of cattle, terracing, and systematic management of watersheds. But all these measures require enormous financial resources, technical know-how, and organizational capacity that are not now available in these regions.

The significance of wind erosion goes far beyond the loss of topsoil. As noted earlier, a continuing buildup of particulate matter in the atmosphere—not only from the industrial activities of the rich countries but also from wind erosion of soil in the poorer countries—could affect the earth's climate by reducing the amount of incoming solar energy. Should this relationship be established, the richer countries would have still another reason to provide substantial capital and technical assistance to the poor countries in their efforts to confront this common threat to mankind. Clearly the poorer countries on their own do not have the resources necessary to arrest and reverse this trend.

MULTIPLE CROPPING AND FALLOWING

One important way to increase agricultural production as land becomes scarce is to harvest more than one crop each year on the same land—a practice known as multiple cropping. Although multiple cropping was practiced in Egypt and Mesopotamia as long as 6,000 years ago, the science is still in its infancy, and its potential is only beginning to be exploited. Producing two or more crops a year is not an unmixed blessing. It sometimes creates deficiencies in minor soil nutrients or special problems of pest and disease control and water management. In some cases there is the problem of harvesting and drying grain while the monsoon is in full swing. Nevertheless, the potential benefits are arousing the interest of farmers and governments alike.

Multiple cropping in the equatorial latitudes makes a virtue of the very solar energy that has such a debilitating effect on human beings in these regions. Fortunately, its potential is greatest where hunger and malnutrition are most acute—in the tropical and subtropical regions, which are well endowed with solar energy and rainfall and have temperatures favorable to year-round crop growth. The Indian Agricultural Research Institute, which has field stations located throughout India, is experimenting with various multiple-cropping combinations. One four-crop rotation includes rice during the wet season, a short-season vegetable crop, wheat during the winter season, and an oilseed crop in the spring. In both India and Pakistan, the combination of tubewells (cylindrical shafts driven into the ground to tap the underground water supply) and new fast-maturing crop varieties has generated considerable opportunity for the expansion of multiple cropping.

Farmers in temperate southern Brazil are beginning to double-crop winter wheat and soybeans. Double cropping also helped Mexico to achieve a fivefold increase in sorghum production over five years. The potential of multiple cropping is suggested by the experience of the diligent Taiwanese farmers, who expanded the multiple-cropped area from 18 per cent of total cropland in 1946 to the point where now they are harvesting an average of two crops on *all* their land. Estimates are that nearly half the farmland in China is doublecropped, but only about 18 per cent of India's fields are currently being exploited in this fashion.

Some multiple cropping is practiced in the United States, mainly in the South, but the climate so far has prevented multiple cropping on a sizable scale. When U.S. agriculture was faced with chronic overproduction, relatively little attention was paid to the potential for multiple cropping in regions such as the corn belt, but in the future research efforts on multiple-cropping potential may bring valuable results. The consecutive planting of winter wheat and soybeans, for example, is already being tried to a limited degree on the southern fringe of the corn belt.

As more nations press against limited arable-land endowments, interest in multiple cropping in both tropical and temperate zones is certain to intensify. The availability of water will be an important factor in the spread of the practice; another will be the development of earlier-maturing varieties of various crops, enabling additional harvests to be squeezed into growing seasons.

In contrast to multiple cropping, fallowing—the withholding of farmland from production on a rotating basis—results in less than one crop per acre per year. In modern agricultural systems, fallowing is used primarily to conserve moisture and soil. Holding land idle allows a buildup of its moisture content, thereby permitting cultivation in some areas that have only marginal rainfall. Without fallowing, soil moisture in these regions would be reduced to the point where crop yields would be very low, crop failures would become frequent, and soil losses to wind and water would rise, often forcing abandonment of the land. Fallowing thus permits the extension of agriculture to areas that would not otherwise be cultivable.

Nearly all the world's fallowed farmlands at present are in the drier, wheat-growing regions of Canada, the United States, Australia, and the Soviet Union. In the future the practice is likely to become commonplace in many developing nations as efforts increase to halt the spread of deserts, reduce soil erosion, and bring new lands into production in areas with low rainfall.

In the United States, the wheat-growing area held fallow (almost all of it in low-rainfall regions west of the Mississippi) has consistently exceeded one third of the total wheat-producing area since World War II. Should the fallowed acreage fall below the estimated 28 million acres of 1974—a total considerably lower than during the previous two decades—there would be a serious risk of a return to dustbowl conditions in some regions.

In many less developed tropical regions of sub-Saharan Africa, Southeast Asia, and parts of Latin America, an age-old variation of fallowing is practiced to preserve soil fertility. Under what is known as shifting cultivation, or "slash and burn" agriculture, families, clans, or small tribal groups clear a forested area, often by burning the forest cover in order to take advantage of the nutrient in the resulting ashes. The cleared land is farmed for two or three years until its fertility is dissipated. It is then abandoned,

TABLE 6-3. AREA OF SUMMER FALLOW AND AREA OF WHEAT SOWN, UNITED STATES, 1911–74.

Years	Cultivated Summer Fallow (million acres)	Area of Wheat Sown (million acres)	Fallow per 100 Acres of Wheat Sown (acres)
1911–20	5	56.4	8.9
1921–30	8	64.9	12.2
1931–40	17	69.4	24.4
1941–50	20	69.1	29.6
1951–60	29	63.5	46.6
1961–70	36	55.7	65.4
1971	34	53.8	63.2
1972	38	54.9	69.2
1973[a]	31	59.0	52.5
1974[b]	28	70.7	39.6

[a] Preliminary.
[b] Estimate.
SOURCE: U.S. Department of Agriculture.

often for decades, until the natural forest cover has had a chance to return. The system is ecologically sound but depends upon a high ratio of uninhabited land to human numbers, as well as on the willingness to preserve a traditional way of life. As populations expand in many tropical regions, farmers are forced to abandon the practice, for the rapid clearing of land upsets the ecological balance and results in reduced soil fertility and progressive deforestation.

7.

WATER AND BREAD

In the final quarter of this century, the lack of fresh water rather than of land may be the principal constraint on efforts to expand world food output. Indeed, in the Green Revolution countries, it is already the dominant constraint on increasing the area planted to the high-yielding seeds. In the Soviet Union, it is frustrating attempts to expand feedgrain production to keep pace with the growth in demand for livestock products.

Competition for water among countries with common river systems has become increasingly intense in the past two decades. Protracted negotiations were required to allocate the waters of the Indus River between India and Pakistan. Without the mediating role of the World Bank, the irrigation potential of this river system might never have been realized. Competition is also keen between Israel and the Arab countries for the waters of the Jordan. Difficult negotiations were required to allocate the Nile River waters between Sudan and the United Arab Republic. The distribution and pollution of the Colorado River waters are a continuing irritant to U.S.–Mexican relations. As the supply of fresh water for irrigation becomes scarcer, the link between bread and water becomes increasingly obvious.

DEVELOPMENT OF IRRIGATION

Irrigation has played a major role in expanding the earth's food-producing capacities. Nature distributes rainfall very unevenly over the earth's land masses, but man's intervention in the hydrological cycle has enabled him to bring into profitable cultivation vast areas of the world that would otherwise be unusable or only marginally productive. Early efforts were very primitive and small in scale, but in time man learned to build rather ambitious structures for this purpose and also to utilize water-lifting devices powered by men, animals, wind, or fossil fuels and to tap underground water from wells.

It was irrigated—not rain-fed—agriculture that provided the surplus food and spurred the social organization necessary for the earliest civilizations in Mesopotamia and Egypt. In these lands of little or no rainfall, great rivers carried rich silt from mountain sources and, over the millennia, deposited a fertile alluvium that could be worked easily with light implements. In the river valleys, man did not have to shift cultivation every few years to renew depleted soil, as was the practice in the uplands; silt deposits during periodic floods renewed the soil naturally. Man's problem was to make the rivers work for him.

Controlling the Tigris and Euphrates rivers was no easy task, for they are turbulent and often dangerous. Their floods are unpredictable and can be violent. By contrast, the flood of the Nile is comparatively gentle, punctual, and ideally synchronized with the actual growing season. The unique behavior of this river is indeed why Herodotus called Egypt the "gift of the Nile."

Irrigation expanded in the Tigris-Euphrates Valley and along the Nile, developing into complex systems capable of supporting growing populations and successive civilizations. In the past, many areas of the Middle East, such as the Tigris-Euphrates Valley, contained populations substantially larger than those that inhabit them today. The American conservationist Walter Lowdermilk estimates that at its zenith the Tigris-Euphrates Valley supported between 17 million and 25 million inhabitants; in contrast, the total population of Iraq today is only 10 million. Because of man's neglect and ignorance, desert sands and extremely arid conditions have made much of the region uninhabitable.

Irrigation also developed early along the major rivers of southern Asia, particularly along the Indus and the Hwang Ho (or Yellow) River of China. Both of these regions gave rise to great ancient civilizations. Thus some irrigated areas have been under continuous cultivation for several millennia. Irrigation apparently evolved independently in the New World before the arrival of Europeans, in the coastal valleys of Peru, in the Andes, in central Mexico, and in the North American Southwest.

Although man practiced irrigated agriculture as much as 6,000 years ago, it was not until the twentieth century that irrigation covered a significant share of the earth's land surface. In 1800 an estimated 20 million acres of the world's cropland was irrigated. By 1900 this had expanded to 100 million acres, and by 1950 to 260 million acres. But the greatest expansion in the world's irrigated area has occurred since 1950, with the irrigated area nearly doubling in twenty years to reach about 460 million acres in 1970. Irrigated land in China alone, long the world's most populous country, has increased by 60 million acres since 1950 to reach about 100 million acres; this has been achieved largely through the massive mobilization of China's abundant manpower.

The explosive growth in the demand for food during this century, particularly since World War II, has given impetus to the growth in irrigated acreage, but other factors have also spurred this expansion. The increased availability of chemical fertilizers in recent decades has raised the return on investment in water resources. Irrigation also has been an important target for investment by the World Bank and by bilateral aid programs, such as American assistance for irrigation expansion in India, Pakistan, and elsewhere, and Soviet aid for Egypt's Aswan Dam Project. A further incentive to invest in irrigation works was provided when large-scale irrigation structures became geared to provide hydroelectric power as well as water for crops.

IRRIGATION TODAY

Irrigation is today much more widely used in some regions than in others. Western Europe, which is favored with an abundance of rainfall well distributed throughout the year, has relatively little irrigated land; Asia, in contrast, is heavily dependent on irrigation. Rice, which accounts for 40 per cent of the region's total food-energy supply, is grown almost entirely on either irrigated land or rain-fed paddy fields. China and India together have nearly half the world's irrigated land.

Most of the irrigated land in Africa is in the Sudan or in Egypt, one of the few countries in the world with virtually all of its cropland under irrigation. Egypt's crop yields are therefore far above those of most other developing countries. Spain, with its semiarid Mediterranean climate, has more irrigated land than all other West European countries combined. The Soviet Union contains the major share of the irrigated land in Eastern Europe. In the Western Hemisphere, the United States, with extensive cultivated areas in the Southwest almost entirely dependent on irrigation, leads in irrigation agriculture, with Mexico ranking a distant second, followed by Argentina, Chile, and Peru. Among the continents, Australia is unique with respect to irrigation, for, unlike most land bodies of continental scale, it has no large rivers and therefore has limited potential for irrigation.

One crop—rice—occupies more irrigated land than all other crops combined and is the only cereal produced largely under irrigation. The possibilities for expanding the area planted to wetland rice are therefore limited by the potential for expanding the area under irrigation.

In the earth's more arid areas, the difference between irrigated and unirrigated land is the difference between land that is cultivated and that which is not. Irrigation not only contributes directly to higher yields but also expands the possibility for profitable use of other yield-raising inputs, particularly fertilizer. Irrigation is also essential to an increase in multiple cropping in many parts of the world, especially those with a monsoon climate and a long dry season.

Like many of man's other interventions in natural cycles, his reshaping of the hydrological cycle has had unwanted side effects. In some regions, it has raised the underground water table by diverting river water onto the land. Over a period of time, the downward percolation of irrigation water and the accumulation of this water underground may gradually raise the water table to within a few feet or even a few inches of the soil's surface. This not only inhibits the growth of plant roots by waterlogging but also results in saltiness in the surface soil as water evaporates through it, leaving a concentrated deposit of salts in the upper few inches.

Such a situation developed in Pakistan after its fertile plain had been irrigated with water from the Indus for several decades. By 1960 Pakistan was losing 60,000 acres of fertile cropland per year because of waterlogging and salinity. Meanwhile its population was expanding 2.5 per cent yearly. Pakistan's very existence as a nation was threatened by the progressive abandonment of its irrigated cropland. At the request of President Ayub to President Kennedy, an interdisciplinary study team of U.S. scientists led by Roger Revelle, then Science Adviser to the Secretary of the Interior, was dispatched to Pakistan in 1961. The team gathered data on river flows, irrigation rates, plant utilization, percolation, and evaporation and simulated a model of the Indus River system on a computer. After studying numerous possible approaches, it recommended, among other things, a system of tubewells that would lower the water table by tapping the underground water for intensive irrigated agriculture. By discharging large amounts of water on the surface, the wells would also wash the soil's salt downward.

The stratagem worked, and the salty, waterlogged land of Pakistan was gradually reclaimed. By 1966 the amount of abandoned land being brought back into production began to exceed that being lost. The continuing progress made since then, bringing the problem under control, constitutes one of the most exciting successes in the short history of international technical assistance.

This sequence of the diversion of river water onto land for irrigation, followed eventually by waterlogging, salinity, and abandonment of the land, has been repeated many times throughout history. The result has invariably been the decline and sometimes the disappearance of the civilizations based on such interventions in the hydrological cycle. The remains of civilizations buried in the deserts of the Middle East attest to early experiences similar to those of contemporary Pakistan.

Archaeologists have uncovered evidence that the salting of soil and the consequent undermining of irrigation systems, or of irrigated agriculture, preceded by as much as a century the decline of some civilizations in Mesopotamia, which historians have long believed was caused primarily by the invasion of nomadic hordes or by intercity warfare.

Irrigation and the Green Revolution

The new high-yielding seeds of the Green Revolution are generating an enormous thirst for irrigation water among millions of farmers in the poor countries where they are being introduced. Water has suddenly become the key to a better life. With an adequate supply of water, farmers can use the new wheats or rices and raise their living standards; without it, they may remain tied to traditional agriculture, merely scratching out a subsistence living.

The new seeds and associated technologies are abruptly altering the economics of both water use and water-resource development. They produce more grain with a given amount of water than traditional varieties, since their superiority in yields usually surpasses the increase in water use. The four-month maturation cycle of the dwarf rices (rather than the five or six months required for traditional varieties) reduces the irrigation period. Now that water has become the pivotal factor in determining whether the new seeds can be used, its value is climbing sharply.

The new seeds, combined with price supports for farm products, are influencing irrigation strategies. Tubewells and electrically powered pumps have suddenly become popular with farmers, and governments are putting more emphasis on small-scale irrigation that farmers can install in a matter of days or weeks than on huge irrigation systems that take many years and millions of dollars to construct.

Farmers in poor countries such as India and Pakistan have also turned to tubewells because large irrigation works, often the byproducts of multipurpose hydroelectric dams, have sometimes proved inefficient. The multipurpose dam so fascinating to engineers has potential in the poor countries, but it has yet to live up to the dreams of its promoters. Such projects tie up large blocks of capital for long periods of time. Seventy-two major irrigation projects undertaken in India between 1951 and 1965, having a total command area of 13.4 million hectares, had managed to deliver water to only one fourth of this area by 1966—and the story is much the same in other countries.

Further, the delivery of irrigation waters from a large centralized system to vast numbers of peasant farmers requires a degree of coordination that is beyond the managerial skills of most poor countries. When a farmer realizes that he can recover his own investment in a tubewell in as little as two years and at the same time get irrigation waters subject to his immediate control, he will act. The new seeds have brought this opportunity to hundreds of thousands of farmers throughout Asia, as witness the fact that "peasant farmers" in Pakistan installed more than 60,000 private tubewells from 1965 to 1971. During that six-year period, the total number of private and public tubewells in Pakistan increased from 33,000 to more than 100,000. The installation of each 5,000 tubewells in that country has added an estimated 1 million acre-feet to the yearly supply of irrigation water. Most important, this new source is under the farmer's personal management, enabling him to control very precisely the amount and timing of water delivered to his crops.

In India, the number of private tubewells rose from 113,000 to 550,000 between 1965 and 1971. In the same six years, the number of pump sets (diesel and electric)—many of which replaced traditional bullocks or hand-powered lifting devices—increased from 979,000 to 2.7 million units.

The dramatic turn to tubewells in the Indian subcontinent was spurred in 1965 and 1966 by two successive monsoon failures that underlined the risks of overdependence on the monsoon and surface-water supplies. Even in good years, rainfall is concentrated in a few months of the year. To make water available in the dry season—when the yield potential of the new seeds, particularly rice, is higher because of the greater availability of solar energy, and when many of the resources of traditional farms are underutilized—it is necessary either to impound and conserve monsoon rains or to augment the water supply by other means. Tapping underground water resources, which are independent of seasonal variations in the monsoon, is one obvious way to increase the water supply and minimize the risks of monsoon failure.

The electrification of rural communities is facilitating the rapid spread of small-scale irrigation. The cost of irrigation water for farmers who are able to use electric pumps is usually about a third less than for those in similar circumstances who have to rely on diesel engines. Throughout most of Asia today farmers are being encouraged to invest in small-scale irrigation and thereby reduce pressures on government budgets.

Farmers in the delta areas of Southeast Asia and Bangladesh are investing heavily in pumps to lift water from low-flowing streams and canals to field levels during the dry season. The combination of high-yielding rices and favorable prices makes such investments highly profitable; it means that fields once idled during the dry season are now green with a second crop of rice. In Bangladesh, it is proving less costly to expand production of the new rice varieties by using wells and pumps during the dry season than by massive investment in flood control to create conditions suitable for these varieties during the wet season. Of 22 million cultivated acres in Bangladesh, an estimated 5 million can be irrigated for dry-season cultivation. Yet the latest available data indicate that barely one fifth of that area is actually being irrigated in this manner—illustrating the country's untapped productive potential.

MORE AMBITIOUS INTERVENTIONS

As the demand for food has soared, national governments are being forced to consider far more ambitious interventions in the hydrological cycle. During the late 'fifties, the Soviet Union, under the leadership of Khrushchev, launched the virgin-lands project, which brought an estimated 100 million acres of new land under cultivation and inspired Soviet political leaders to predict that the U.S.S.R. would overtake the United States in per capita production of meat, milk, and eggs by 1965. When it was belatedly discovered that much of the new land lacked sufficient moisture to sustain continuous cultivation, Soviet plans were thwarted. Instead of attempting to extend the cultivated area into marginal areas, the planners decided to concentrate on intensifying production on existing cultivated areas. But this required more water, and river waters in agricultural areas were already being rather fully utilized. Planners therefore seized upon the idea of reversing the flow of four rivers that flow northward into the Arctic Ocean by blocking their northward passage and constructing new southward channels, thus greatly augmenting the supply of irrigation water in the southern part of the Soviet Union. Once these plans became public, however, the international meteorological community was quick to respond, arguing that interrupting the flow of warm water into the Arctic would alter the climate in the Arctic and trigger compensatory adjustments throughout the global climatic system. One study estimated that rainfall in central North America would be measurably reduced if the Soviets were to proceed with these plans.

In late 1973, it was reported that construction had begun on a 175-mile canal to divert a portion of the waters of two Siberian rivers into arid Central Asia. If the Soviets proceed with the project, it may be decades before the full water-diversion plan is implemented. In the meantime, the U.S.S.R.'s perceptions of the dependability of its grain import supplies—most of which must come from the United States—may help shape its decision whether or not to carry through this expensive, meteorologically risky program.

As the technology of climate modification advances, new possibilities for expanding fresh-water supplies are beginning to emerge. The technology is now available to cause it to rain in some situations where it otherwise would not. In the United States, there are now rainmaking firms that will contract their services to national governments, local governments, farmers' associations, or any other concerns willing to pay for their services.

A few years ago, the state of Florida contracted with a rainmaking firm to interrupt an extended drought that was damaging agricultural crops and threatening wildlife in the Everglades. In this case, the rainfall gained through atmospheric intervention was at the expense of the surrounding ocean. But the interesting question is: What if Texas were to sign such a rainmaking contract? How would this affect relations between the United States and Mexico? That this type of international conflict has become a pressing possibility was underscored in December, 1973, when Rhodesia initiated a nationwide cloud-seeding operation, which authorities hoped would increase the country's rainfall by at least 10 per cent. The plan—if it is successful—is likely to be at least partly at the expense of neighboring African nations, whose share of the region's rainfall may be reduced. The government of Niger, in the Sahelian zone of Africa, which has been plagued by years of drought, hired an American company to seed clouds in 1973 and 1974. The program has apparently had some success, but the effects on neighboring nations and the region's meteorological patterns are unknown.

The FAO projects that global demand for fresh water will increase by 240 per cent by the end of the century. Needless to say, this will generate great pressures on countries to use whatever technologies are available or can be developed to expand their fresh-water supplies. Since efforts to expand fresh-water supplies often have transnational if not global consequences, the international community must seriously consider the regulation of national interventions in the climatic system. The combination of growing demand pressures and advancing technologies is shifting the prospect of meteorological aggression from the pages of science fiction to the daily headlines.

WATER FROM THE SEAS?

Man has long dreamed of utilizing the waters of the oceans, which cover 72 per cent of the earth's surface, for food production. In some measure, desalination already has made an impact. Worldwide desalting operations today produce more than 110 million gallons of fresh water daily, compared to 8 million gallons in 1960. More than 800 plants are currently operating throughout the world, primarily in the United States and around the Mediterranean, the Persian Gulf, and the Caribbean.

But the prospects of significantly increasing agricultural production through desalination are limited. Although it may aid the relatively small-scale production of garden crops in arid regions, when the investment and operating costs of desalination—principally the cost of needed energy supplies—are considered, desalted water becomes an unlikely factor in opening large regions to the production of staple crops. A partial solution to the cost problem may lie in a breakthrough in utilizing fusion power, but such a development is not at all certain and, in any event, is at least a generation away.

Desalination processes using combustible fuels and electricity were expensive even before global energy prices soared in 1973 and would be still more costly to farmers now. Most proposed plants—except perhaps those located near the natural-gas deposits of the Middle East—will consequently rely on nuclear energy. Yet nuclear operations also carry a heavy price, and the inherently high costs of construction, plus long break-in periods, are prohibitive for many countries. Drawing seawater and disposing of wastes also require great expenditure, as do transporting and storing the desalted water, particularly in regions where evaporation presents a serious problem.

Many of these problems may be overcome eventually, but it remains doubtful whether even the most elaborate desalting systems now conceivable could satisfy a significant portion of future agricultural needs. The largest nuclear desalination plants yet designed would produce only enough grain to meet a small fraction of the yearly growth in world demand. In any case, with construction and production costs for such plants steadily rising, the overall expense of desalted water will remain higher than most of the world's farmers and consumers can afford in the foreseeable future.

FUTURE PROSPECTS

The prospect of expanding the area under irrigation from large-scale river irrigation systems is much less favorable for the last quarter of this century than for the quarter now ending. The easiest large-scale irrigation projects, whether in China, India, the Soviet Union, the Middle East, Africa, or North America have already been completed. The irrigation potential of most of the world's major rivers—including the Nile, Yellow, Indus, Ganges, and Colorado—has largely been realized. Among those yet to be exploited are the Mekong and the Amazon. But the latter is an exceedingly difficult river to harness because of its vast width and broad flood plains.

The great burst of investment in large-scale irrigation projects throughout the world during the third quarter of this century will not be repeated during the last quarter. Thus, while the world irrigated area expanded by nearly 3 per cent annually between 1950 and 1970, it will probably grow at barely 1 per cent a year in the remaining years of the century (Table 7–1).

There is considerable potential for further development of underground water supplies in many areas of the world. However, the

TABLE 7-1. Estimated World Irrigated Area, 1900-2000.

Year	Estimated Irrigated Area (million acres)	Annual Rate of Increase (per cent)
1900	100	
		1.9
1950	260	
		2.9
1970	460	
		1.1
2000	640	

Sources: FAO, *Production Yearbook* (various issues) and authors' estimates.

potential is by no means unlimited. Over the long term, the volume of water used cannot exceed the recharge rate of the water table. For this reason, the rate of drilling and installation of irrigation wells in India and Pakistan in the past several years cannot continue indefinitely.

In some regions, wells are being used to tap underground water supplies that are not renewable. Once these so-called fossil water reserves are exhausted, the land will have to be abandoned. Such is the case with nearly a million acres now under cultivation in the high plains of West Texas. Water tables in other parts of the United States are being drawn down as irrigation and other claims on underground water supplies begin to exceed the recharge rate. In considering future prospects for increasing food output, it must be recognized that, whereas most yield-raising inputs, such as fertilizer, improved seeds, pesticides, and possibly energy, can be increased severalfold, the worldwide potential for expanding irrigated areas is comparatively limited.

The possibilities of vastly expanding the irrigated area depend on continued technological progress in other areas. Breakthroughs in the cost of desalting seawater and in atomic fusion processes, which would lower the cost of energy used to desalt and transport water, would undoubtedly permit extensive irrigation expansion, but a source of power much more economic than any now existing will be needed to make vast desalting and desert-irrigation projects possible.

With water becoming increasingly scarce, man will have to pay more attention to the efficiency with which crops, particularly cereals, *use* water. Rice, the staple food of half of mankind, is an extravagant user of water. Wheat usually yields far more calories and proteins for a given amount of water than does rice. Under some circumstances, an equivalent amount of wheat can be produced with one third the water needed for rice, and in some areas where both can be grown, including parts of Asia, rice eventually may have to be phased out in favor of wheat production as water becomes scarce. Fortunately, the new high-yielding varieties of both wheat and rice are more efficient in using water than are traditional varieties.

Among the cereals, the most efficient user of water is sorghum, which responds well to intensive irrigation and also tolerates drought far better than all other cereals. In the event of severe stress, sorghum simply becomes dormant, resuming growth when moisture supplies are replenished. These characteristics, plus sorghum's high protein content, are making it increasingly popular in tropical and subtropical countries as a dry-season crop to be grown in seasonal rotation with rice. With enough water and fertilizer, certain varieties of sorghum generate new stems and leaves (or "tiller") after harvest to produce second and third crops of grain from the original planting.

Agricultural water requirements, like per capita grain requirements, escalate as populations improve the quality of their diets. Professor Charles C. Bradley has calculated the total water requirements for producing various food products. A person subsisting on a vegetarian diet of 2.5 pounds of bread a day is indirectly utilizing 300 gallons of water daily. Production of food for an affluent diet of two pounds of vegetable matter and one pound of beef and animal fat a day, by contrast, requires a total of about 2,500 gallons of water daily. The "water cost" of a pound of beef—which includes that used to produce feed as well as that drunk by the animal—is about twenty-five times that of a pound of bread!

Water has played a crucial role in the rise and fall of civilizations throughout history. The efficiency with which it is used will increasingly determine the adequacy of food supplies in the future.

8.

ENERGY AND AGRICULTURE

The evolution of modern agriculture can be described as the harnessing of more and more energy inputs to increase the productivity of land and labor. The three distinct forms of agriculture in existence today are best characterized by the principal form of energy employed to till the land—the power of human muscle, draft animals, and the internal-combustion engine—all plus the sun, without which there would be no photosynthesis. In some areas of the world, all three types of energy can be found within a single country. In Colombia, for example, Andean Indians living in mountainous regions practice hand cultivation, family-size farms in the lowlands employ draft animals, and the large commercial farms use tractors.

The limited availability of energy in traditional agriculture, which depends almost entirely on human muscle and animal power tied at least four fifths of the population to the land in most regions. The efficient use of modern energy sources has multiplied the productivity of agricultural labor dozens of times. Today mechanical power (driven by fossil fuels) and chemical fertilizers and pesticides (often produced from and applied with the aid of fossil fuels) have made it feasible in the United States, for example, to feed the entire population and to export considerable quantities of food as well with less than 5 per cent of the population directly employed in agriculture.

Given the strong dependence of modern agricultural systems on energy inputs, it is apparent that the global energy crisis of the mid-'seventies will affect future food-production prospects. It seems inevitable that food will be more costly and less abundant as energy supplies tighten and petroleum reserves are depleted. It is becoming increasingly important therefore, to economize on agricultural energy uses where possible and to ensure that scarce fossil fuels are allocated according to rational priorities.

In the past, little research attention has been given to global uses of energy in agriculture. The useful studies that are now beginning to appear are primarily the work of ecologists, who are introducing energy accounting into agriculture. The most detailed data available are for the U.S. food-producing system, and for that reason the United States will receive special attention in this chapter.

ENERGY INTENSITY OF FOOD SYSTEMS

If energy accounting rather than financial accounting is used to evaluate the efficiency of food-production systems, a surprising fact emerges: The books are not balancing for the more advanced agricultural systems, which are running up an energy deficit. As the geographic distance from producer to consumer lengthens, as the degree of processing increases, and as energy is substituted for labor and land, the deficit increases accordingly.

In some of the simplest agricultural systems, the return on energy applications is very high. For example, in the shifting cultivation (slash and burn) practiced in many tropical regions, the estimated return for every calorie of human labor invested is 20 calories of food energy. The figure is similar for wet rice cultivation, where the principal input is human labor at planting and harvesting times. The intensive cultivation of corn and soybeans, range-fed beef, and grass-fed dairy cows also yields an energy surplus. Intensive egg production and feedlot beef, however, may easily consume three to fifteen times as much energy as the products contain.

With the modernization of agriculture and society, the amount of energy used to produce food relative to the energy it contains rises steadily. According to Carol and John Steinhart, the energy content of the food produced by U.S. farmers in 1910 was slightly greater than the energy used to grow, process, and transport the food. Shortly thereafter, however, the amount of energy used in the American agricultural system began to exceed that which it produced. By 1920 the system was using half again as much energy as its products contained. By 1970 nearly nine calories were being consumed by the system for every calorie contained in the food produced.

David Pimentel and his colleagues at Cornell University have estimated that in 1945 the production of an acre of corn in the United States required 925,500 kilo-calories. Of this total, well over half was in the form of gasoline used to operate farm equipment. By 1970 the total energy used to produce an acre of corn had increased to 2,896,800 kilo-calories, of which 941,000 kilo-calories were accounted for by the use of chemical nitrogen fertilizer, which is produced from fossil fuels. In other words, the energy required to provide the nitrogen applied to an acre of corn in 1970 exceeded the total energy inputs required to produce the acre of corn twenty-five years earlier.

Pimentel's computations take into account all the important inputs used in corn production, from human labor to the production of machinery to the production and use of gasoline, chemical fertilizers, seed used for planting, irrigation, pesticides, energy for drying, electricity, and transportation. The only one of these inputs that has declined in importance in terms of kilo-calories consumed is farm labor, which declined by three fifths. The ratio of calories contained in the corn to those used to produce it was 3.7 in 1945 but only 2.8 in 1970.

If the food-producing system ended with on-farm corn production, it would remain on the plus side of the energy accounting ledger. Even at this level of the food producing system, however, the equivalent of 80 gallons of gasoline currently is used to produce an acre of corn. Much of the corn produced is fed to livestock, and the animal products in turn are then processed, packaged, and transported. By the time the consumer has the final product on his plate at home, the total calories expended are many times those contained in the food he is eating.

However energy-intensive the on-farm production of food may be in the United States, it is the processing, transportation, and distribution of food that absorb most of the energy. Only 24 per cent of the energy consumed by the U.S. food system in 1970 was used before the food products left the farm. As processing techniques have evolved to ever more sophisticated levels, the amount of energy used has increased considerably. The preservation of food by drying—an ancient practice—uses very little energy, particularly when the sun is the source of the energy used for drying. Even today rice farmers in Southeast Asia dry their rice by spreading it in the sun. In the U.S. corn belt, however, farmers use dryers powered by electricity or natural gas to remove moisture from the corn before storage. Canning of footstuffs uses more energy than drying but is not excessively energy-intensive. Freezing, which is effective in preserving food quality and freshness, is not only energy-intensive in the freezing process but requires a continuous use of energy for storage of the frozen food. And as populations become urbanized, the distance between farm and consumer also increases, requiring the use of more energy in the transportation of food.

ENERGY AND LAND PRODUCTIVITY

As we have noted, in some of the most "primitive" agricultural systems, such as shifting cultivation, the energy inputs are quite minimal. At the same time, however, land farmed in this way has limited capability to support humans—perhaps only one person per square mile.

As countries traditionally dependent on draft animals to power farming operations have switched to tractors, large amounts of land previously used to produce forage crops have been freed for other purposes. Within the United States, for example, the massive transition from horse to tractor power between 1930 and 1950 not only provided farmers with several times more energy but freed 70 million acres that had previously been used to produce feed for horses.

In response to the increasing pressure of population on land, various methods have been devised for intensifying cultivation on existing crop areas—in effect, substituting energy for new land, which is no longer available. The application of fertilizer (particularly nitrogen fertilizer), irrigation, and the use of higher yielding seeds such as those of the Green Revolution are ways of increasing food production where there is no more new land.

There are, however, limits to the amount of energy that can be used to raise land productivity. In the United States this point of diminishing returns is now being approached as the additional food output per unit of energy used drops sharply. Unless techniques can be found to improve the efficiency of photosynthesis itself, it will be difficult to overcome the effects of these diminishing returns.

The Steinharts point out that at present levels of energy and technology, U.S. corn producers arc already achieving food-energy yields equal to almost half the photosynthetic limit of production. "Further applications of energy," they observe, "are likely to yield little or no increase in this level of productivity. In any case, no amount of research is likely to improve the efficiency of the photosynthetic process itself."*

ENERGY AND LABOR PRODUCTIVITY

In early agricultural systems, as we have noted, the level of food output per person was quite low, and many people were therefore obliged to live on the land. It was not until man learned to harness draft animals that labor productivity in agriculture increased enough to release a few people from food production for other activities. On the eve of the Industrial Revolution, only a small percentage of the population of Europe lived in cities. Even today, more than four fifths of some societies are still engaged in agriculture.

Man has devised innumerable ways of substituting energy for his own labor. Almost all major farming operations have been mechanized, including tillage, planting, cultivating, and harvesting. Not only have field operations been mechanized, but farmers today also use electrical power to milk cows, to incubate eggs, and to brood chicks. A farmer who must milk cows by hand cannot easily manage more than fifteen cows, but a farmer who uses electric milking machines can milk, feed, and care for perhaps sixty animals.

Over the past generation or so there has been a dramatic and

* Carol E. and John S. Steinhart, "Energy Use in the U.S. Food System." *Science,* No. 184, April 19, 1974, p. 312.

rapid decline in the size of the U.S. farm-labor force. It is often pointed out that one farm worker feeds fifty people off the farm. This figure is useful but somewhat illusory, for it fails to measure the off-farm labor required to support the farm-labor force, such as equipment manufacturers, agricultural-chemical salesmen, and the many employees of the U.S. Department of Agriculture. It is likely that at least two such nonfarm workers are required to support each farm worker.

The massive substitution of energy for human labor in the past half-century in the United States is now tapering off. This suggests that we may be reaching the point at which the profitability of the substitution of energy for human labor is rapidly diminishing and that the labor input on U.S. farms is not likely to decline much further.

CONSERVING ENERGY IN FOOD SYSTEMS

As energy becomes more scarce and more costly, it becomes more worthwhile to identify areas in which we can conserve energy in the food system. Within the low-income countries, where minimal energy is used to produce food, there are few opportunities for conserving energy in food production, but within the more agriculturally advanced countries, the opportunities are abundant.

As noted earlier, in more affluent societies most of the energy used in the food system is not used in production but is consumed after the food leaves the farm gate. The greatest single inefficiency along this route, particularly in the United States, is in the transportation of the food from the market to the home. As has been pointed out, the use of a two-ton vehicle—the family car—to transport 30 pounds of food several miles once a week is grossly inefficient in engineering terms.

In most highly industrialized countries, a great deal of energy is also consumed unnecessarily in the processing and distribution of food. In some instances more energy is embodied in the container than in the food itself. One way of reducing this inefficiency would be to eliminate throwaway containers, using only those that are returnable.

In the United States, a growing share of agricultural commodities and processed foodstuffs is transported by truck. In part this is because the railroad system has been neglected and permitted to deteriorate. This is unfortunate, because far more energy is required to transport food by truck than by rail.

For the production of many crops, chemical fertilizer now embodies more energy than any other input used, including the fuel to operate farm equipment. Now that energy—and therefore nitrogen fertilizer—is becoming increasingly costly and nitrogen runoff is causing growing environmental problems, it is time to reconsider the use of organic fertilizers and the rotation of legumes in order to reduce the need for nitrogen fertilizer. This would mean reversing the trend of the past twenty-five years of substituting nitrogen fertilizer for nitrogen fixed by leguminous crops.

As the feeding of beef cattle in the United States has become more intensive in recent years, large amounts of animal waste have been concentrated in relatively few areas, with no easy means of getting the waste back to the land, where it is needed. Not only is an important source of plant nutrients being lost, but a steadily worsening waste-disposal problem has been created. It may well be desirable from the ecological—if not the economic—point of view to decentralize feedlots and return the feeding of beef cattle to family-size farms, permitting greater use of manure on fields. Spreading several tons of manure on a field requires a significant amount of energy, but far less than that required to produce a similar quantity of chemical nutrient.

Another area of potential saving in modern agriculture is in the reduction of the use of pesticides. Both the manufacture and the application of pesticides require significant amounts of energy. To the extent that effective biological pest controls, including insect- and disease-resistant crop varieties, can be used, this demand for energy can be substantially lessened. In addition, if pesticides were used only when needed rather than applied automatically, as is often now the case, substantial energy savings could be realized.

As population growth and rising affluence generate ever more demand for food, pressures will grow for using more and more energy in food-producing systems. There will be a far greater need to substitute energy for land that is no longer available and, in many nations, to substitute energy for labor. Particularly as global society becomes increasingly urban, there will be pressures to use more energy in food processing and distribution.

One of the obvious questions raised by the growing global scarcity of energy supplies is the extent to which the developing countries should follow the path of the more developed nations in increasing energy inputs in their food-producing systems. Certainly it would be unwise to advocate indiscriminate emulation of a system that is so costly in energy as that of the United States. In the developing countries, much of the energy used in food processing, packaging, and transportation could be minimized and greater use of human labor could hold down some direct on-farm uses of fossil fuels.

Having said this, however, we must add that major increases in energy inputs per acre, especially in the form of chemical fertilizers and irrigation, will be necessary in the developing countries if their future food needs are to be met. With known technologies, there is no real alternative to increasing the use of energy in agriculture in these countries. Coaxing high yields from the soil generally requires substantial inputs of energy—in some combination of human, animal, and mechanical power. At least some mechanical power is often necessary for proper tillage, planting, weeding, pesticide and fertilizer application, and harvesting. If multiple cropping is the goal, very often mechanical power is needed for quick harvesting and rapid seedbed preparation and planting.

ESTABLISHING GLOBAL ENERGY PRIORITIES

Fossil-fuel scarcity now makes it necessary to re-examine the ways in which available energy is now being used in the world. Priorities must be more clearly established, and governments must ensure that available supplies are used where they are most needed. In particular, it is necessary to distinguish between essential energy uses in agriculture and unnecessary uses, such as in oversized private automobiles. In establishing global energy priorities, we must also take into account that in the developing countries the returns for additional inputs of energy in the form of greater food output are far greater than in the agriculturally advanced nations.

A key question, then, is whether sufficient energy supplies for such basic needs will be available in the future at a price that the poorest quarter of mankind can afford to pay. With all mankind drawing on common reserves of petroleum concentrated in a few countries, it is apparent that the consumption of great amounts of energy for nonessential purposes by some people will deprive others of access to energy for essential purposes, such as the production of food.

In addition to wasteful energy-consumption patterns in the more affluent countries, another major form of energy waste is the flaring of the natural gas that is a by-product of petroleum pumping in many oil-producing countries. It is sometimes more attractive economically to get rid of the gas by burning it than to convert it into usable forms such as nitrogen fertilizer. In 1972, more than three fifths of the natural gas produced in the principal oil-exporting countries was flared—enough to produce twice as much nitrogen fertilizer as the world now uses. Given the acute global scarcity of nitrogen fertilizer and the dangerous implications of that shortage for world food supplies, those who control nitrogen-fertilizer technology and those who control flared gas must soon find a means to combine their expertise and materials.

David Pimentel and his colleagues emphasize the need for some fundamental rethinking of priorities. These experts maintain that, if all the world were to adopt the protein-rich U.S. diet and food-producing system, and if petroleum were the sole source of energy for agriculture, *all known world reserves of petroleum would be exhausted within a mere twenty-nine years.* These calculations, of course, do not include the demands of nonagricultural uses of petroleum or of food processing and transportation. They spotlight the need for increased attention to energy conservation within food systems, for a more rational global allocation of available energy supplies, and for holding future growth in the demand for food to manageable levels.

9.

THE ROLE OF FERTILIZER

While the world area of cultivated land has expanded only modestly since 1950, the use of chemical fertilizers has expanded fivefold. At least one fourth of the world's food output is directly attributable to the use of chemical fertilizers. The food supply of at least a billion people is directly dependent on the output of the fertilizer industry.

Since 1973, critical world shortages of fertilizer have emerged, and consequently the prices of many key fertilizers doubled or tripled between 1973 and 1974. Many populous developing countries that are highly dependent on fertilizer imports—including China, India, Indonesia, and the Philippines—were unable to buy needed amounts of fertilizer at any price. Price increases and scarcity of fertilizer are certain to cut food production at a time when world food reserves are at a modern low and food prices are at a historic high. The current fertilizer shortage is due primarily to a lag in the construction of new production facilities. But even if construction catches up with demand—perhaps by the late 'seventies—fertilizer prices will remain high because of the high cost of essential energy inputs.

FERTILIZER AND WORLD FOOD OUTPUT

Agricultural man has long known that manure, bones, and ashes somehow help to make soil more fertile and productive. However, it was not until von Liebig's major discoveries in soil chemistry in the early nineteenth century that man learned to apply the same nutrients—nitrogen, phosphorus, and potassium—in *inorganic* forms. Von Liebig identified the importance of these nutrients for plant growth and demonstrated that the natural fertility of the soil could be enhanced or restored by adding these nutrients in proper proportions.

In von Liebig's day, available land resources in much of the world provided ample opportunity for expanding the area under cultivation. The application of chemical fertilizers did not become widespread until this century, when the pressure of population and the disappearance of frontiers compelled man to substitute fertilizer for expansion of cropland to meet mounting food needs.

World use of chemical fertilizers has soared particularly since World War II. While the combined use of nitrogen, phosphate, and potash was less than 10 million metric tons in 1938, by 1973 the total was more than 78 million tons—including 36 million tons of nitrogen, 23 million of phosphate, and 19 million of potash. In 1974 the total used will surpass 80 million metric tons. (Other nutrients are also added to the soil, but not in commercially significant quantities.) In the mid-'seventies, an average of nearly 50 pounds of chemical nutrient is being applied for every acre of arable land in the world. Roughly half of all fertilizer used is applied to cereals.

But chemical-fertilizer use varies widely among geographic regions (see Table 9–1). In some poor countries, chemical fertilizers are scarcely used at all. In other countries, particularly the densely populated industrial countries located in the temperate regions with high rainfall, use is intensive. The application of chemical fertilizers in combination with other inputs and practices can double, triple, or quadruple the soil's productivity. In countries practicing intensive agriculture, such as Japan and the Netherlands, more than 300 pounds of chemical fertilizer are applied per acre yearly. If the use of chemical fertilizers were discontinued in these countries, soil fertility would decline rapidly, and food production could easily drop by at least half.

The data in Table 9–1 deserve some further explanation, for varying cropping and environmental patterns in different nations directly affect the opportunities for efficient fertilizer use. The U.S.

TABLE 9-1. FERTILIZER CONSUMPTION PER ACRE OF ARABLE LAND, FIFTEEN MOST POPULOUS COUNTRIES, 1972.

Country	Pounds/Acre
West Germany	363
Japan	347
United Kingdom	239
France	231
Italy	104
United States	72
U.S.S.R.	40
China	35
Brazil	32
Mexico	26
India	14
Pakistan	12
Indonesia	11
Bangladesh	7
Nigeria	1

SOURCE: FAO, *Annual Fertilizer Review, 1972.*

figure is distorted by the large acreage held idle at that time under government programs, as well as land held fallow for conservation purposes; in fact the average nutrient application per *harvested* acre in 1972 was about 100 pounds, in contrast to the 72 pounds indicated. Further, the figure given for the United States is an average, masking the fact that large fertilizer applications are not feasible on much of the acreage planted to wheat, which tends to be grown in drier regions. Much well-watered U.S. cornland receives more than 250 pounds of nutrients each year. Similarly, some of China's rice fields that have good water supplies and drainage facilities may be receiving nutrients at rates approaching Japanese levels— or close to the useful maximum—while such intensive use of fertilizers is not practical in China's drier areas.

Very little chemical fertilizer—less than one fifth of the world total—is currently being applied in the developing countries of Asia (including China), Africa, and Latin America. However, commercial-fertilizer demand in these regions is increasing at more than 10 per cent annually—nearly twice as fast as in the more developed countries. The use of the new high-yielding wheat and rice varieties has spurred fertilizer demand in Asia, since these varieties are far more efficient users of chemical nutrients than the traditional ones they are replacing.

Despite their shortcomings, the figures on the intensity of current fertilizer use in various nations provide a rough indication of where the comparative advantage lies for future growth in world food production. When fertilizer is initially applied, assuming adequate soil moisture, yields increase very rapidly, but as greater and greater amounts of fertilizer are added, the gain in yield diminishes rapidly, as is illustrated in Figure 9–1.

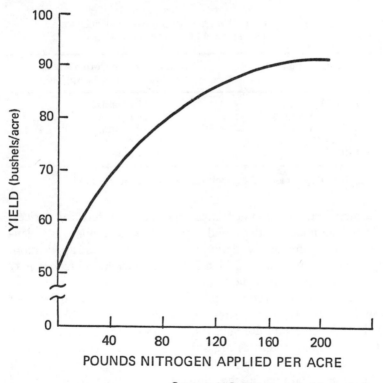

Source: U.S. Department of Agriculture.

Figure 9-1. Typical Fertilizer Response Curve
(Corn Yield in Iowa, 1964)

The data in Table 9–2 demonstrate even more vividly that production returns from fertilizer use decline sharply as successive increments are applied. At application rates of 40 pounds of nitrogen fertilizer per acre, each pound of nitrogen applied in this region in 1964 increased the production of corn by about 27 pounds. As nitrogen applications approached 200 pounds, however, the weight of additional corn produced scarcely equaled the weight of the additional fertilizer added. Since the cost per pound of nitrogen fertilizer is several times that of corn, financial losses began to be incurred at application rates between 120 and 160 pounds per acre.

TABLE 9–2. Corn-Yield Gains from Successive Fertilizer Applications.

Nitrogen Applied	Average Gain in Corn Yield per Pound of Nitrogen Applied
First 40 pounds	27 pounds
Second 40 pounds	14 pounds
Third 40 pounds	9 pounds
Fourth 40 pounds	4 pounds
Fifth 40 pounds	1 pound

Source: U.S. Department of Agriculture. Data from Iowa, 1964.

Farmers, of course, must take into account fertilizer prices, projected commodity prices, and expected yield response in calculating their economically optimal level of fertilizer application. Improvements in seeds and in many other farming practices may raise average yields and move the position of the response curve upward, but for any crop in a given region at a given level of technology, the shape of the response curve resembles Figure 9–1.

Since they currently use very little or no fertilizer, most farmers in the developing countries are still near the low end of the fertilizer response curve, with the largest and cheapest yield gains still in the future. Farmers in the agriculturally advanced nations of Western Europe, Japan, and the United States, in contrast, are far up on the curve, with crop yields relatively unresponsive to additional chemical fertilizer. As a general rule, the use of an additional ton of fertilizer in the agriculturally advanced nations will not yield more than 5 additional tons of grain, and in some cases much less than that. In the developing countries, an extra ton of nutrient will often produce 10 extra tons of grain, and in some situations 15 or more. Professor Raymond Ewell, a leading fertilizer expert, has calculated that in the more developed nations raising grain production by 100 million tons would require an additional 24 million tons of chemical nutrients. In the less developed countries, the same production increase would require only 10 million additional tons of fertilizer.

Boom and Bust Cycles

The world fertilizer industry has a history of boom and bust cycles, with periods of overexpansion and depressed prices followed by periods of short supplies and high prices. When supplies of nitrogen and phosphates became tight in the mid-'sixties, production facilities were rapidly expanded in both the developed and the less developed countries. Several multinational oil companies entered the fertilizer industry in a big way for the first time. Inevitably, massive overconstruction in the industry resulted in plummeting prices, a virtual cessation of new investments, and failure to replace older plants when they wore out.

Nitrogen and phosphate prices reached a low in the 1969–71 period and then began an upward trend as demand started overtaking existing production capacity. Remembering the experience of the previous decade, however, the industry was slow to respond with new investments and construction. By 1973, serious shortages of nitrogen and phosphates had developed. The prices of potash fertilizers also rose, largely as a result of transportation bottlenecks.

The high prices and short supplies of food since 1972 have encouraged a sharp rise in total world acreage planted to crops and in farmers' demands for fertilizer, placing great additional strain on already tight fertilizer supplies. In 1973 and 1974, shortages and high prices of natural gas and naphtha—critical raw materials in nitrogen-fertilizer synthesis—developed in many nations. The over-all results have been record prices for many key fertilizer products, a critical shortage of supplies in relation to world food-production needs, and a tendency for major exporting nations—

TABLE 9-3. WORLD FERTILIZER PRICES, 1967-74.

	Urea (Europe)	Potash (Canada)	Triple Super Phosphate (U.S.)	Phosphate Rock (Morocco)
	(dollars per ton)			
1967	79	26	47	12
1968	66	24	38	12
1969	56	22	39	11
1970	48	32	43	11
1971	46	33	43	11
1972	59	34	68	12
1973	125	43	100	14
1974[a]	300	45	200	63

[a] Estimate.

SOURCES: International Monetary Fund and authors' estimates.

Europe, the U.S.S.R., Japan, and the United States—to reduce their fertilizer exports.

The exceptionally high 1974 prices are encouraging a considerable expansion in fertilizer production facilities worldwide, but the long lead time required to bring new plants into operation—two to four years or more—will keep production from expanding rapidly. Many experts are hopeful that phosphate production will catch up to world demand within a few years and that the worrisome gap between nitrogen production and demand will be closed by the end of this decade (although some doubt that the massive investments required will materialize rapidly enough to catch up with spiraling world needs in the foreseeable future). Present world potash capacity is adequate to meet world needs, but shortages will emerge in a few years if capacity is not expanded.

FERTILIZER PRODUCTION AND RAW MATERIALS

Although nitrogen, a critical building block of plant and animal growth, is in ample supply—it constitutes 79 per cent of the earth's atmosphere—plants and animals are incapable of utilizing this abundant resource unless it is converted into certain chemical compounds (fixed).

Nature supplies the earth's plants with large quantities of usable nitrogen. Lightning and ultraviolet radiation create vast amounts of nitrogen compounds in the atmosphere, and an estimated 10 million tons of usable nitrogen is washed into the earth's soils annually by rainfall. Most significantly, perhaps 170 million tons annually are extracted from the air and converted into readily usable ammonia by nitrogen-fixing bacteria (including some that live in a symbiotic relationship with leguminous plants and others that survive on their own in soils). By comparison, man is currently applying to the land only about 40 million tons in the form of inorganic chemical fertilizers.

Historically, farmers often designed crop rotations to include nitrogen-fixing leguminous plants (such as clover, alfalfa, soybeans, or peanuts) to restore periodically the soil's natural fertility. But man has discovered various chemical processes by which nitrogen can be synthesized into usable compounds. The result is relatively inexpensive chemical fertilizer that can be applied rapidly and with dramatic effects on crop yields.

Modern factories combine nitrogen with hydrogen to produce anhydrous ammonia, which is 82 per cent nitrogen and can be either applied directly as fertilizer or further processed into other fertilizer products. Urea, with a nitrogen content of 46 per cent, is rapidly becoming the world's most widely used nitrogen product. Solid products like urea are often more convenient to transport, store, and apply than ammonia.

Nearly all the manufacturing processes for the synthesis of ammonia require a hydrocarbon feedstock to supply the needed hydrogen, and this feedstock represents an important part of the production costs. The cheapest processes use natural gas as the basic raw material, but in Europe and Asia petroleum derivatives —particularly naphtha and fuel oil—are being used. Coal can serve as the hydrogen source, but its use considerably raises production costs. Where extremely cheap electric power is available, as in Egypt, ammonia is produced by first obtaining hydrogen through the electrolysis of water.

In the early 'sixties, American companies developed efficient new technologies for the synthesis of ammonia that have altered the nature of the industry. Extremely large plants—often producing a thousand tons of ammonia a day and using natural gas as the feedstock—have a significant economic advantage over smaller plants. This means that those countries with abundant supplies of natural gas, such as the oil-producing nations, the U.S.S.R., and China, have the greatest economic potential for significantly expanding low-cost nitrogen fertilizer production in the future.

Currently, about four fifths of the world's nitrogen fertilizer is produced in the economically developed regions of North America, the U.S.S.R., Japan, and Europe. Many developing countries are rapidly increasing nitrogen production within their borders, but the demand for fertilizer in those countries is escalating so rapidly that it has been difficult for new construction to keep up. Since the early 'sixties, China and India have been, respectively, the world's number one and number two importers of nitrogen fertilizer. In a move that reflected the importance it attaches to expanding indigenous supplies of nitrogen fertilizer, China in 1973 hired a leading U.S. firm to construct 10 large new nitrogen plants in China—a highly complex multiyear project that will eventualy reduce China's import needs.

Whenever the current global lag in the construction of new nitrogen fertilizer production facilities is corrected, prices can be expected to fall somewhat from their present scarcity-induced levels. But there is virtually no likelihood that prices will again return to the low levels of the late 'sixties and early 'seventies, for the costs of plant machinery, construction, and labor have risen considerably in the last two years, and energy prices as well have reached new levels.

Although phosphate fertilizers are used in several chemical forms, nearly all fertilizers in this category are produced from phosphate rock. Sulfur is also essential for the production of the most popular phosphate products, since sulfuric acid is used to break down phosphate rock and to produce phosphoric acid.

World reserves of phosphate rock are widespread, but the largest sources are concentrated in just a few locations—principally North and West Africa, the United States, and the Soviet Union. As Table 9-4 indicates, Morocco and the United States together account for 64 per cent of known world phosphorus reserves. Exports of phosphate rock are similarly concentrated. The implication of this concentration in market power became evident in late 1973, when Morocco unilaterally tripled its export price from $14 to $42 per ton. Other exporters quickly followed suit. In mid-1974, Morocco again raised the price, this time to $63 per ton, and other exporters are expected to raise prices again as well.

TABLE 9–4. WORLD PHOSPHATE RESERVES.

Country	Phosphorus[a] (million short tons)	Share of World Total (per cent)
Morocco	3,764	41
United States	2,142	23
U.S.S.R.	628	7
Australia	182	2
Spanish Sahara	155	2
People's Republic of China	148	2
Tunisia	116	1
Algeria	92	1
Other Africa	551	6
Other	1,462	15
World total	9,240	100

[a] Economically accessible at $144 (1972) per ton of contained phosphorus.

SOURCE: U.S. Bureau of Mines.

Much of the phosphate rock from Morocco is processed into fertilizer in Europe. The United States, Belgium, Canada, and the Netherlands together account for over 60 per cent of world phosphate-fertilizer exports. Although the developing countries—with Tunisia and Morocco in the lead—are gradually increasing their share of world exports as processing facilities are constructed within their boundaries, as a whole they remain net importers of phosphate fertilizer.

Sulfur for phosphate fertilizer production is in tight supply in 1974, but this situation is expected to be temporary. Large quantities of sulfur are available in ground deposits, but even more important in the future will be the production of sulfur and sulfuric acid as by-products of pollution-control efforts. As reliance on high-sulfur coal increases and as techniques for removing sulfur from smokestacks and nonferrous-metal smelter stacks improve, these will become important sources.

The expansion of phosphate rock production is having serious ecological side effects. The rock is customarily strip-mined, and its subsequent treatment involves major problems of water pollution. In the United States, concern over the environmental impact of this process has limited expansion of the phosphate industry.

Chemical nitrogen that is unused by plants tends to wash out from the soil and thus must be replenished in full each year. Phosphates and potash, by contrast, tend to accumulate in the soil. Thus a temporary shortage of these fertilizers has less impact on food production than a shortage of nitrogen.

Potash ranks third in use among the three primary nutrients, mainly because many of the earth's soils are inherently high in potash. Over 90 per cent of the 19-million-ton global total in 1973 was used in the developed countries. Although potash is abundant, its reserves are geographically much more concentrated than those of phosphate. Canada, the U.S.S.R., and the two Germanys hold a total of 94 per cent of recoverable reserves (Table 9–5). Canada alone could easily meet world potash needs for well over a century.

For several years the world potash market has been characterized by an excess of production capacity. After world demand for

TABLE 9–5. WORLD POTASH RESERVES.

Country	Potassium[a] (million short tons)	Share of World Total (per cent)
Canada	21,300	42
U.S.S.R.	13,200	26
East Germany	6,640	13
West Germany	6,320	13
Jordan and Israel	1,290	3
United States	295	1
Other	1,155	2
World total	50,200	100

[a] Economically accessible at $60 (1972) per ton.

SOURCE: U.S. Bureau of Mines.

potash rose sharply in 1974, prices increased somewhat, and temporary shortages developed, particularly in the United States. But these shortages have been a result more of transportation bottlenecks than of limited supplies.

The (perhaps temporary) scarcity of fertilizer and growing awareness of the adverse ecological consequences of expanding applications of chemical fertilizers and of the probable limits on supplies of fossil-fuel feedstocks have heightened interest in alternate means of providing nutrients to crops. The possibility of making greater use of organic fertilizers—animal, human, and plant wastes—is receiving growing attention. Sludge from human-sewage treatment plants is already being used for agricultural purposes in some developed countries, and the Chinese have long assiduously returned organic wastes to their fields with beneficial results. Successful recycling of organic wastes as fertilizers has the added benefit of reducing the pollution problems of waste disposal. We have noted that the huge and growing amount of manure produced by large commercial feedlots in the United States, for example, is posing an environmental challenge. Disposal of human sewage presents both environmental and health problems in many nations.

Unfortunately, there are serious economic obstacles to the widespread use of organic fertilizers. The nutrient content of manures and vegetable matter for composting is quite low, and massive volumes must be transported and often treated to provide the needed amounts of nutrient for crops. Health hazards may arise if the wastes are not properly handled. Nevertheless, the potential usefulness of organic fertilizers deserves greater exploration, especially in the developing countries, where labor is abundant and cheap. In South Asia, the greatest obstacle to the use of animal manures for fertilizers is the critical need to use dried dung for cooking fuel.

Efficient use of available organic fertilizers cannot substitute for chemical nutrients, as China's soaring need for chemical fertilizers indicates. Recycling wastes can, however, fulfill some limited portion of needs and also have beneficial ecological side effects. Composts and manures help improve soil structure, reduce soil erosion, and reduce chemical-fertilizer runoff.

The wider and more systematic use of legumes in crop rotations is also receiving more attention now that fertilizer prices are high. In addition, some scientists are trying to develop symbiotic relationships between nitrogen-fixing bacteria and grain crops, paralleling those already existing for legumes. Whether such a union is possible and whether the yield of the resulting grain plants can be boosted to competitive levels at present remain speculative points.

THE DISTRIBUTION QUESTION

Shortages of fertilizer, as of food or any other resource, raise questions of an economic and moral nature regarding not only production but also distribution. As nitrogenous fertilizers became critically scarce in late 1973, the immediate reaction of Japan, the United States, and exporting nations in Europe was to reduce exports and maximize the domestic supply, even though farmers in these nations already get diminishing yield returns from additional applications of fertilizer. The developing countries are still dependent on imports from the developed regions for about half of their fertilizer needs and are therefore exceedingly vulnerable in times of shortage.

Thus, as a result of shortages and the distribution patterns we have noted, food production is being constrained—and hence future food-import (and food-aid) needs are being raised—in the developing nations. For every dollar's worth of urea India is unable to import, it may later have to import five dollars' worth of grain. Further, total world food production is being reduced below what it would have been given a more efficient distribution of available fertilizers.

Until world production capacity catches up with world demand, particularly in the case of nitrogen fertilizers, special attention to fertilizer distribution patterns will be required. When food is in short supply, the international community simply cannot afford to leave unexploited the food-production potential of densely populated developing countries through a failure of rational fertilizer allocation. Assistance to help raise the efficiency of existing fertilizer plants in developing countries is one obvious immediate need.

But for several years at least it will also be necessary for fertilizer-exporting nations to restore exports at least to 1973 levels instead of reducing them, as they did in early 1974. In the immediate situation of acute global shortages, it may also be necessary to reduce the nonessential, nonfarm uses of fertilizer. In the United States, for example, more than three million tons of nutrient are applied to lawns, gardens, and golf courses—equal to the *total* amount of fertilizer used in India.

At a time when scarcity has induced extremely high food prices, it may be profitable for individual farmers in the agriculturally advanced nations to apply virtually all the fertilizer they can buy, even if the extra yield return is extremely low. But if the extra 10 pounds of nitrogen such a farmer uses would have produced double or triple the amount of extra food in another region, his financial gain is dwarfed by society's loss.

FUTURE PROSPECTS

Although for many years trade in nitrogen fertilizers has flowed from the developed to the developing countries, this situation is not likely to last indefinitely; indeed, it is likely to be reversed within a decade. The comparative advantage in nitrogen-fertilizer production has increasingly shifted to countries with abundant supplies of the energy raw materials required as feedstock. The natural gas that is still being wastefully flared at oil-wellheads in the Middle East and elsewhere could be utilized to produce vast quantities of comparatively low-cost nitrogen. Saudi Arabia, Kuwait, Nigeria, Venezuela, Indonesia, Iran, and Libya—as well as Canada and the Soviet Union—could become important world suppliers of nitrogen fertilizer in the future.

Nitrogen synthesis is highly complex, and production in these nations will not rise rapidly without the technical cooperation of experienced U.S., European, and Japanese firms. Such cooperation, whether through joint ventures, management-assistance contracts, or official bilateral and multilateral aid channels, is an urgent global necessity. Unless ample supplies of low-cost nitrogen can be produced very quickly, there is little hope of raising world food production to safer levels, and even less hope that farmers and consumers in the poorest countries will be able to pay for needed fertilizer and the food it produces.

Unfortunately, the large fertilizer-manufacturing companies of the industrial nations have been reluctant to commit themselves to rapid building of new production capacity in the Middle East —apparently because of the fear that political and economic instability in these regions might threaten their investments. The energy-surplus countries, for their part, have not shown an urgent interest in putting their excess capital and energy into nitrogen production to supply the future needs of the developing world. Both parties must recognize the very pressing need to begin constructing the next generation of world nitrogen-fertilizer plants in areas where nitrogen can be produced most cheaply.

Although new investments to build world fertilizer-production capacity must be encouraged in order to ensure adequate food supplies, this will have little impact on the current world shortage of fertilizers. New plants take from two to four years to enter into production once the decision to invest has been reached. To alleviate the current crisis, a crash effort is needed to increase the efficiency of existing nitrogen plants in developing countries, many of which, in India, are producing at two thirds or less of their theoretical capacity. This unfortunate situation has many causes, including unreliable supplies of power and raw-material feedstocks, difficulties in obtaining spare parts and rapid repairs, and many other technical and managerial problems. Increased international efforts to provide technical assistance for plant management and repair, extra supplies of natural gas or naphtha, or spare parts where needed for fertilizer production could do much to mitigate the current shortage.

With fertilizer prices at historic highs, major investments in fertilizer industries are virtually certain. Some industry representatives are in fact already apprehensive about the danger of once again expanding capacity too rapidly and thus knocking the bottom out of the market, as happened in the late 'sixties. While this prospect does not appear to be likely for several years, if ever, it is clear that more rational planning is necessary if the fertilizer industry is to produce and distribute adequate supplies of fertilizer at reasonably stable prices.

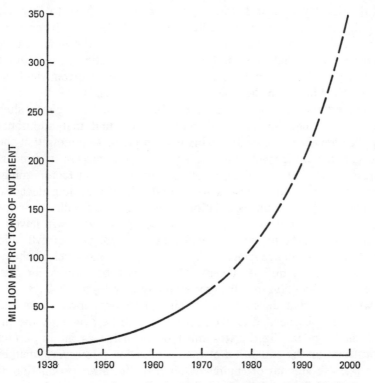

Sources: Food and Agriculture Organization and author's estimates.

Figure 9-2. World Chemical Fertilizer Use, Projected to 2000

An international agency, such as the World Bank or the Commission on Fertilizer recently organized by the FAO, could systematically monitor and publish up-to-date information on investment, production, demand, and distributional trends. A more rational and comprehensive international flow of basic information and analysis would perhaps encourage a steadier long-range expansion of fertilizer production capacity in keeping with world needs.

It is impossible to predict precisely the level of chemical-fertilizer use that will be required to meet the world's growing demand for food. Little is known about the fertilizer responsiveness of crops in the scientifically uncharted growing conditions of much of the developing world, where fertilizer use will have to increase rapidly. But in most cases the best farmland is already in production, and it seems certain that production on the increasingly marginal lands that must be brought into production in the future will require higher applications of fertilizer for a given yield increase than has been the case with more fertile lands.

The growth in world fertilizer use will eventually begin to slow down as farmers in more and more regions find that additional applications bring negligible gains in crop yield. Assuming that the world demand for food continues its exponential growth, it remains unclear just what agricultural input or combination of factors might begin taking up this slack in food production in coming decades.

If the U.N. medium population projection of 6.5 billion for the year 2000 materializes, current global food production will have to double (at least) to meet the demands of population growth and modest dietary improvements. As a result, the total level of chemical fertilizers required at century's end may be more than four times the 80 million tons being used today (see Figure 9–2).*

Assuming that the massive capital and energy supplies required to produce the needed levels of fertilizer will be available, the inevitably high fertilizer prices must be regarded as an important constraint on the expansion of food production. However, whether the massive amount of capital required for fertilizer production at these projected levels will be forthcoming remains in doubt. A large number of resource industries, including those producing energy and many minerals, also will require huge increases in capital investment. Environmental-control efforts in heavy industries are pushing up global capital needs still further. World-wide, the capital needs of the fertilizer industry in the next twenty-five years will be more than four times the investments in chemical fertilizer made thus far in this century. The difficulty of meeting future needs for fertilizer—as for land, water, and energy—suggests that existing demand trends must be altered by slowing population growth everywhere and simplifying diets among the more affluent.

* Fertilizer projection based on forecasting technique developed by Raymond Ewell.

PART THREE

Areas of Concern and Hope

10.

THE GREEN REVOLUTION: OPPORTUNITY LOST?

In the early 'sixties, food production was falling behind population growth in country after country in the developing world. The adverse trend in the relation of food production to population was brought into sharp focus in the mid-'sixties when monsoons in the Indo-Pakistan subcontinent failed for two consecutive years, bringing a vast portion of mankind to the brink of famine. Efforts to fill the food-supply gap reduced world food reserves to a dangerously low level.

This was the global setting in which the newly developed high-yielding dwarf varieties of wheat and rice, together with enlightened economic policies providing incentives and inputs to producers, gave rise in several countries to what later became known as the "Green Revolution."

THE NEW SEEDS

Many of the efforts to raise crop yields in the poor countries in the 'fifties and early 'sixties did not succeed. When farmers in these countries attempted to use varieties of corn developed in Iowa, for example, they often failed to produce any corn at all. When Japanese rice varieties were introduced into India, they proved to be unsuitable either to local cultivation practices or to consumer tastes. The yield response of local cereal varieties to intensive fertilizer applications was limited and occasionally even negative. It was in this climate of frustration that the Rockefeller Foundation's team in Mexico first developed the high-yielding dwarf wheats. Three unique characteristics of these wheats appealed to farmers in many countries: high fertilizer responsiveness, lack of sensitivity to day length, and early maturation.

The traditional wheat varieties, characterized by tall, thin straw, often fell over ("lodged") when farmers applied more than 40 pounds of nitrogen fertilizer per acre, causing severe crop losses. In contrast, crop yields of the short, stiff-straw, dwarf varieties of Mexican wheat continued to increase with applications of up to 120 pounds of nitrogen per acre. Given the necessary fertilizer and water and appropriate management, farmers could easily double the yields of previously used indigenous varieties.

Further, the reduced sensitivity of these dwarf varieties to day length permitted them to be used within a wide latitudinal range stretching from Mexico, which lies partly in the tropics, to Turkey, in the temperate zone. Because the "biological clocks" of the new wheats were much less sensitive than those of traditional strains, planting dates were much more flexible.

Perhaps the most important characteristic distinguishing the newer seeds was the fact that they permitted far more efficient use of various agricultural resources. Under appropriate conditions, the new wheats and rices could easily yield twice as much grain as other varieties per acre of land, per pound of fertilizer, and per cubic foot of water.

The high-yielding dwarf wheats owe their existence to a dwarfing gene first incorporated into Japanese wheat varieties. The dwarfing gene was brought to the United States in 1947, but the Japanese variety did not adapt well to U.S. growing conditions. It was only when Dr. Orville Vogel of the U.S. Department of Agriculture incorporated the Japanese dwarf gene into local breeding materials that a successful dwarf variety was developed in the United States. The so-called Gaines wheat produced world record yields in the irrigated regions of the Pacific Northwest.

Meanwhile Dr. Norman Borlaug, director of the Rockefeller Foundation's wheat-breeding program in Mexico, obtained some of Dr. Vogel's breeding materials containing the dwarfing gene and refined Gaines wheat to make it more suitable for use in Mexico. In the process he achieved the second major breakthrough in wheat plant breeding. Dr. Borlaug wanted to develop a dwarf wheat that would perform well under the varied growing conditions of Mexico. He amassed germ plasm from Japan, the United States, Australia, and Colombia and then, to speed up the breeding program, began growing two crops each year, using two different sites. He planted a summer crop just south of the U.S. border and a winter crop near Mexico City, some 800 miles away. The two sites differed in day length, or photo period, as well as in many other environmental factors.

The high-yielding dwarf wheats Borlaug developed proved to be remarkably adaptable to a wide range of growing conditions. Today, Mexican dwarf wheats are grown successfully in latitudes near the equator, where days are of uniform length, and also at higher latitudes, where day lengths vary greatly from season to season. This adaptability was something new; hitherto, wheat varieties had performed well only under conditions comparable to those under which they were first bred.

Buoyed by the success of the Mexican wheats and keenly aware that most of the world's poor eat rice, the Rockefeller Foundation and the Ford Foundation joined forces in 1960 to establish the International Rice Research Institute in the Philippines. A top-level team of scientists drawn from several countries was assembled under the direction of Dr. Robert Chandler to produce a cosmopolitan dwarf-rice strain comparable to the Mexican wheats. The team assembled some 10,000 strains of rice from every corner of the world and patiently began the process of crossbreeding. Success came early when a tall, vigorous variety from Indonesia was combined with a dwarf rice from Taiwan to produce IR-8, the first of the "miracle rices." Properly managed, IR-8 was easily capable of doubling the yields of most local rices under the appropriate growing conditions in Asia.

These plant-breeding breakthroughs were remarkable feats of biological engineering, with important implications for the welfare of much of mankind. For his role in developing the new wheat strains, Norman Borlaug was awarded the 1970 Nobel Peace Prize.

ACROSS NATIONAL BOUNDARIES

Once the adaptability of the new seeds became evident, an international effort was launched to introduce them into the principal wheat- and rice-producing countries. India, Pakistan, and Turkey were among the first countries to import samples of Mexican wheats for testing. Once the seeds' adaptability to local conditions was established, these countries imported them from Mexico by the shipload, at prices only marginally higher than world market prices for wheat imported for consumption. Since these countries were already importing wheat, the real additional cost was only the modest difference between the cost of the Mexican wheat seed and the world market price.

Not only was the new technology essentially free, but, because the seeds could be imported in bulk, the time required for seed multiplication was greatly reduced. (Normally the development of a new variety begins with a handful of seeds which is multiplied to a half-bushel and then to a quarter-ton, to 10 tons, to 400 tons, eventually leading to the production of enough to release the seed commercially.) Pakistan imported 42,000 tons of new seed wheats, enough to plant more than a million acres, in 1967–68. When this crop was harvested, it provided enough seed to cover all of Pakistan's wheat land, thus telescoping into two years a process normally requiring several years.

Imports of seed rice from the Philippines similarly accelerated the diffusion of the high-yield dwarf rices. Perhaps more important than the actual tonnage of dwarf wheats and rices imported is the fact that they are a prototype which local plant breeders can refine and modify specifically for local growing conditions. The development of the new seeds ushered in a renaissance of agricultural research, challenging agricultural scientists in the developing countries to make the prototype locally suitable. Local improvements on the dwarf wheat prototypes are already in widespread use in India and Pakistan. Norman Borlaug has called India's wheat-breeding program perhaps the best in the world today. As plant-breeding efforts continue, the first generation of high-yielding varieties is being replaced by a second generation, and in some cases by a third.

There is no precedent for the speed with which the new seeds have spread in several Asian countries. The area planted to high-yielding cereals in Asia in the 1964–65 crop year was estimated at 200 acres—and that largely for experimental purposes. Thereafter, according to Dana G. Dalrymple of the U.S. Department of Agriculture, who has become official keeper of the numbers, the acreage in Asia and North Africa spread swiftly as follows:

Year	Acres
1965	200
1966	41,000
1967	4,047,000
1968	16,660,000
1969	31,319,000
1970	43,914,000
1971	50,549,000
1972	68,000,000
1973 (prel.)	80,200,000

IMPACT OF THE NEW SEEDS

The rapid spread of the high-yielding wheats and rices has had a significant impact on India, Pakistan, Turkey, the Philippines, Indonesia, Malaysia, and Sri Lanka. During the late 'sixties, the Philippines was able to achieve self-sufficiency in rice, ending a half century of dependence on imports. (Unfortunately, this situation was not sustained because of a variety of factors, including civil unrest, the susceptibility of the new rices to disease, and the failure of the government to continue its support of the rice program.) Rice farmers in Taiwan have been using improved seeds and practices for several decades and, as Figure 10–1 illustrates, achieve yields considerably higher than those of other Asian developing countries.

Pakistan greatly increased its wheat production, emerging as a net exporter of grain in recent years. In India, where advances in the new varieties have been concentrated largely in wheat, the results also have been encouraging. Over a period of only seven years, 1965 to 1972, India expanded its wheat production from 11 million to 26 million tons—an increase in production of a food staple unmatched by any other country in history. Unfortunately, the pro-

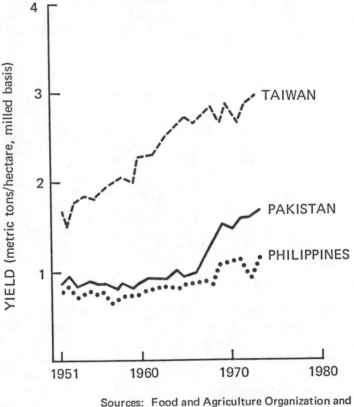

Sources: Food and Agriculture Organization and
U.S. Department of Agriculture.

Figure 10-1. Rice Yields in Selected Countries, 1951-73

duction of rice, India's principal food staple, has not risen so dramatically, partly because rice breeders have been less successful in developing high-yielding varieties well adapted to Indian conditions, and partly because the necessary control of water supply and drainage often has not been available in rice-growing regions.

One result of the dramatic advance in wheat production in India was the accumulation of unprecedented cereal reserves and the attainment of economic self-sufficiency in cereals in 1972. This at

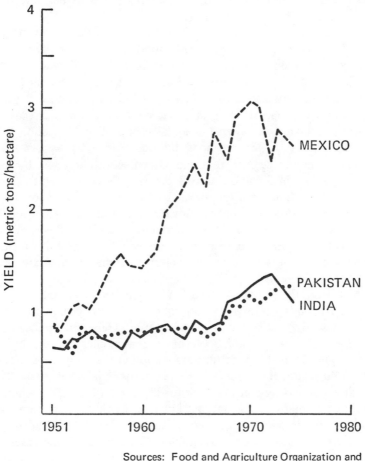

Sources: Food and Agriculture Organization and
U.S. Department of Agriculture.

Figure 10-2. Wheat Yields in Selected Countries, 1951-74

least temporarily eliminated the need for imports into a country
that only a few years before had been the principal recipient of
U.S. food aid. However, economic self-sufficiency in cereals—
which merely means the ability to produce as much as consumers
can afford to buy at prevailing prices—is not to be confused with

nutritional self-sufficiency, which requires much higher levels of productivity and purchasing power.

In late 1971 and throughout 1972, India was able to draw nearly 2 million tons of grain from its own food reserves, initially to feed nearly 10 million Bengali refugees during the civil war in East Pakistan and later to provide food aid to newly independent Bangladesh. A poor monsoon in 1972 forced India back into the world market as an importer of grain, but on a much smaller scale—about 4 million tons—than the massive import of 10 million tons that followed the 1965 monsoon failure.

This is not to suggest that the Green Revolution has by any stretch of the imagination solved the world's food problems, on either a short-term or a long-term basis. Gains will be short-lived if the population tide is not stemmed soon. And the 1972 drought clearly demonstrated that Indian agriculture is still at the mercy of the weather. A second monsoon failure would seriously disrupt the pattern of progress that has characterized Indian agriculture over the past eight years.

Moreover, the global shortage of nitrogen fertilizers that emerged in 1973 is having disastrous consequences in many regions where the new seed varieties are now widely used. Generous applications of chemical nutrients are necessary for attainment of the higher yields, and the inability of farmers to obtain these amounts means that food production is far below previously anticipated levels. The result is not only a severe setback for the agricultural and economic progress of many Asian nations but also the immediate threat of food shortages and famine, particularly in India. Until adequate fertilizer supplies become available—through rapid increases in internal production, increased imports, or both—food import needs may remain high, and any progress in upgrading diets in most of Asia will be in abeyance.

The intensive agriculture of the Green Revolution also requires ample energy supplies, particularly to operate tubewells and irrigation pumps. This critical need for fossil fuels was vividly dramatized when the global energy crisis hit India in late 1973 and early 1974. Farmers in some communities reportedly waited in line for days to obtain diesel fuel for their pumps—providing a stark counterpoint to the hour-long waits in their automobiles that some

Americans suffered as they lined up to purchase gasoline in early 1974. According to the U.S. Department of Agriculture, the combined shortages of energy and fertilizer played a principal role in reducing India's 1974 wheat crop from the original projections of 30 million metric tons to the estimated 23 million tons finally harvested. Each million tons lost could have sustained five million people for a year.

TABLE 10-1. PER CAPITA PRODUCTION IN COUNTRIES USING HIGH-YIELDING VARIETIES (KILOGRAMS PER YEAR), 1960–73.

	Philippines: Rice	India: Wheat	India: All Cereals	Mexico: All Cereals	Pakistan: All Cereals
1960	88	25	164	136	202
1961	90	26	162	135	205
1962	88	27	161	137	197
1963	82	24	159	138	232
1964	83	21	160	140	251
1965	82	26	136	142	265
1966	80	21	134	127	267
1967	78	23	154	139	280
1968	81	32	162	178	274
1969	92	36	165	184	258
1970	91	37	173	190	286
1971	84	43	166	171	262
1972	78	47	149	174	226
1973 (prel.)	89	43	168	182	272

SOURCE: U.S. Department of Agriculture.

In several Asian nations over the past decade, there has been a disconcerting decline in the per capita availability of protein-rich pulses (beans and peas). Some observers feel that improvements in the quantity of food available have been accompanied by a worsening in the nutritional quality of food supplies in many areas, and that the availability of high-yielding grain varieties may have accelerated that trend by making grains more attractive for farmers to grow than pulses. The evidence on this matter is not clear, however. The trend toward declining pulse acreage appears to have begun many years prior to the Green Revolution. Where the increase in per capita supplies of grain has been large enough, consumers may still have ended up with more protein in their diets than they had previously. In any case, there is clearly an urgent need for research to make pulses more productive and hence more attractive for farmers in developing nations. The protein content of pulses is double that of wheat, triple that of milled rice, and twenty-five times that of cassava, and pulses have even greater advantages in terms of protein quality. Any advancements in the production and consumption of pulses would be highly beneficial in poorly nourished regions.

New Potentials for Multiple Cropping

The shorter maturation periods required by the new high-yielding seed varieties in some cases can reduce the growing season by a third, making various new cropping combinations possible. Farming around the calendar with two and occasionally even three or four crops per year is becoming feasible in some tropical and subtropical regions. As multiple cropping spreads, it is profoundly altering the way of life in the countryside, divorcing it from the traditional seasonal crop cycle, which dictated not only planting and harvesting times but the timing of religious festivals, weddings, and a host of other social events as well.

The new agricultural technologies are helping farmers in the tropics discover the potential for expanding food production during the dry, sunny season; the genetic potential of the new seeds can be fully realized only with an abundance of sunlight. Data from both Indonesia and the Philippines show higher yields in the dry season than in the wet season for several high-yielding rice varieties grown at different sites. In central and northern India and in parts of Pakistan where rice is normally grown during the rainy season, it is now possible to harvest the early-maturing dwarf rice in time to plant a crop of high-yielding wheat in the dry season. Scientists in the Philippines are harvesting 8 tons of grain a year from a single acre planted successively with rice and sorghum. Farmers in much of Asia harvest scarcely half a ton per year.

The economic advantages of farming during the dry season are obvious. Increased utilization of farm labor, draft animals, and farm equipment formerly left idle in the dry season—together with the higher yields attainable in dry-season conditions—makes dry-season cropping exceedingly profitable. The likelihood of substantially higher profits justifies investments in dry-season irrigation facilities such as tubewells or water-impounding structures that may not have been financially attractive with the older varieties.

In countries where holdings are small and the possibilities for enlarging them nonexistent, more intensive use of land through multiple cropping may be the only avenue to a better life. Intensive cropping is in many ways ideal for small family farms, where labor is abundant and relatively inexpensive. Replacing a single crop of the traditional variety with two high-yielding crops broadens a farmer's economic base, enabling him both to expand his food supply and to create a store of feed grains for a small livestock operation.

DISTRIBUTING THE BENEFITS

One of the questions frequently raised about the Green Revolution is: "Who benefits from the adoption of these new technologies?" Many critics argue that only large farmers benefit. In answering this question, however, one must be specific not only about the country, or even the region within the country, but also about the crop.

The new seeds can be used with uniform success regardless of farm size, assuming that farmers have access to the requisite inputs and supporting services. In countries and locales where farmers with large holdings have better access to credit and to technical advisory services, rich farmers often get richer and poor farmers often get poorer.

But many different factors determine which farmers can use the new seeds. One is the crop they grow; widely adapted high-yielding varieties exist only for wheat and rice. Thus in Mexico most farmers growing wheat have benefited considerably from technological progress, while those growing corn, mostly small, subsistence farmers, have gained little. Likewise, the principal beneficiaries of the Green Revolution in India are the wheat farmers, since success in adoption of the high-yielding rices has been modest by comparison.

Perhaps the most important single factor determining whether or not a given farmer can use the new seeds is access to an adequate supply and control of water. Thus wheat farmers on the high-rainfall coastal plain of Turkey have benefited enormously from the new seeds, while those of the arid Anatolian Plateau have scarcely been affected. In the Philippines, farmers with irrigated rice land have successfully exploited the genetic potential of the new seeds, whereas rice farmers in Bangladesh, who rely on natural flooding of the river plain during the monsoon for their water supply, have benefited very little, because the short-strawed rices cannot survive a deep flooding.

Available evidence suggests that use of the new seeds has usually generated substantial increases in labor requirements per acre, thus helping to alleviate underemployment of family labor and providing more jobs for landless laborers. However, this positive effect is tempered by a disturbing rise in the number of landless laborers in areas where landlords, recognizing the increased profitability of their land, have reacted by displacing their tenant farmers. Unwarranted government subsidies for large-scale agricultural mechanization have further mitigated the potential employment benefits of the high-yielding varieties. In the late 'sixties, farmers in Pakistan, for example, paid only half the actual cost for imported tractors and therefore often found it privately profitable to mechanize even when the true economic costs outweighed the benefits to society. Appropriate government policies in land reform, security of land-tenure contracts, and the cost of capital can do much to eliminate the negative phenomena that in some areas have accompanied the spread of the new seeds.

ASSESSMENTS AND PROSPECTS

It has been fashionable in many circles to criticize the Green Revolution and to emphasize the very real problems—ranging from displaced tenant farmers to overloaded marketing systems to the new dependence on chemical fertilizers—that it has helped to spawn in some regions. Critics are quick to point out that per capita food output has not improved very much in the countries where the new seeds are being used. This is certainly the case in the majority of countries, but to focus on this is to miss the essential point: Without the production boost made possible by the new seeds, there would have been a disastrous *decline* in per capita food production in Asia. And although relatively little progress has been made in raising per capita production of cereals in the poor countries as a whole, there have been spectacular localized successes.

Critics have also focused on the traumatic social consequences associated with introducing seeds that double yields within a few years. There is no doubt that a doubling of yields is a traumatic experience both for individual farmers and for rural communities. But in societies with little new land and populations that double every twenty or twenty-five years, what are the alternatives to introducing the new seeds? Surely widespread famine is a likely one.

In sum, the Green Revolution does not represent a solution to the food problem; rather, it has been a means of buying time—perhaps an additional fifteen years—during which to find some way to apply the brakes to population growth. For the governments of countries in which conditions permitted the achievement of a breakthrough in the late 'sixties, the Green Revolution presented an option of major importance: These governments could use the breathing space afforded by the new production gains to begin to bring population growth under control, or they could defer making the difficult policy changes until they were again confronted with crises. Unfortunately, all too many countries have followed the latter path. Almost a decade has now passed since the launching of the Green Revolution, but there are few success stories in family-planning programs in the poor nations. Among the population giants of Asia, China appears to be substantially reducing its birth rate, and India is slowly bringing its birth rate down, but there have been only minimal reductions in Indonesia, Pakistan, and Bangladesh. The futility of relying solely on the new agricultural technologies to "solve" the population problem is evident in Mexico, where the Green Revolution began. Fifteen years of dramatic advances in wheat production made Mexico a net exporter of cereals by the late 'sixties, but a population growth rate that ranks among the highest in the world has again converted that country into an importer of food.

The introduction of any important new technology into a society invariably tests that society's responsiveness to change as well as the effectiveness of its social and economic systems. That heightened social tensions and widened income disparities have sometimes accompanied the introduction of the new seeds is not surprising. It is important to keep in mind, however, that high-yielding crop varieties did not *create* the political, social, and economic institutions that produce such tensions and disparities. Rather, their productive potential has, in many cases, brought into sharp focus the critical importance of long-needed institutional reforms. The new seeds do not provide a technological panacea that can alone eliminate hunger and unemployment. They do represent a landmark technological advance that can, if properly used, measurably improve the basic welfare of a sizable segment of mankind.

There are few countries in the world that cannot effectively employ at least some of the new varieties of wheat or rice, given available technologies; supporting institutions to provide credit, seeds, fertilizers, and marketing facilities; and economic incentives to encourage use of the new varieties. Unfortunately, a large number of governments, principally in sub-Saharan Africa and in Latin America, have not yet made the major effort necessary to provide these critical links in the process of agricultural modernization.

11.

DEEP TROUBLE IN OCEANIC FISHERIES

The oceans have long been considered a major potential source of food. But the hope that man will be able to turn to the oceans to satisfy his food needs as pressures on land-based food resources mount is being shattered. Indeed, quite the opposite is now occurring, and as the world fish catch declines, pressures on agricultural resources for protein are growing. World fisheries are in serious trouble. Daily newspapers in Tokyo, London, and New York tell of increasing competition and growing conflict among countries over scarce supplies of fish.

FISH IN THE WORLD FOOD ECONOMY

The importance of fish in the human diet has steadily increased over the past generation as man's capacity to exploit oceanic fisheries has improved. Today the fish catch occupies a prominent position in the world food economy. At nearly 70 million metric tons in live weight, the world fish catch now accounts for a large share of world animal protein consumption. Globally, it averages nearly 40 pounds per person annually, well above world beef output.

The great bulk of the world fish catch comes from oceanic fisheries; the inland and fresh-water catch amounts to less than 15 per cent of the total. Mainland China leads the world in fresh-water catch, primarily as result of the extensive managed production of fish in ponds. Roughly two thirds of the world catch is used for direct human consumption. The remaining third is consumed indirectly in the form of fish meal, which is fed mainly to poultry and hogs in the more industrialized countries.

The importance of fish in the national diet varies widely by country. Among the most populous countries, consumption is highest in Japan and the Soviet Union. As population pressure built up during the late nineteenth and early twentieth centuries, the Japanese were forced to turn to the oceans for their animal protein, using their very limited land resources to produce rice to meet minimum food-energy needs. As a result, the Japanese evolved a fish and rice diet. Annual fish consumption per person in Japan now exceeds 70 pounds in edible weight, the highest of any major country.

The Soviet Union, experiencing difficulties in expanding its livestock industry at a satisfactory rate, has also turned to the oceans for animal protein in the past two decades. It has invested heavily not only in fishing fleets but also in floating fish-processing factories and sophisticated fishing technologies, which enable its fleets to travel the world's oceans, locating and taking fish wherever they find them. The direct consumption of fish by the average Soviet consumer now amounts to about 23 pounds a year, about double the American levels.

In the United States fish are important in the diet, but direct consumption is only about 13 pounds per capita, compared with about 230 pounds of meat, including poultry, in 1973. However, data on direct consumption understate the importance of fish in the diet, for some of the poultry and pork that is consumed is produced with fish meal. In many recent years, the amount of fish utilized for animal feed and industrial purposes in the United States has exceeded the total consumed directly.

TRENDS IN WORLD FISH CATCH

The quarter-century since the end of World War II has witnessed a great expansion in world fishing fleets. Investment has multiplied severalfold during this period as the industry has increasingly resorted to sophisticated technologies and techniques, such as the location of fish by sonar.

TABLE 11-1. ANNUAL PER CAPITA DIRECT CONSUMPTION OF FISH
AND SHELLFISH, FIFTEEN MOST POPULOUS NATIONS.

	Pounds, Edible Weight
China	8
India	2
U.S.S.R.	23
United States	13
Indonesia	9
Japan	71
Brazil	6
Pakistan	4
West Germany	9
Nigeria	11
United Kingdom	19
Italy	14
Mexico	4
France	18
Philippines	44

SOURCE: FAO and U.S. Department of Commerce. Latest available data.

Between 1950 and 1970 the world fish catch increased steadily and reached a new record virtually every year, rising from 21 million tons to 70 million tons. During this period it increased by an average of nearly 5 per cent yearly, thus greatly outstripping population growth and greatly boosting per capita supplies of marine protein. In 1970 the trend was abruptly and unexpectedly reversed. Since then it has fallen for three consecutive years, clouding the prospects for a continuing expansion of the catch. Many marine biologists feel that the global catch of table-grade species may be approaching the maximum sustainable limit.

There is no doubt that potential exists for further expansion of the total catch from the seas. Some regions, such as the Indian Ocean and the South Atlantic, are far from fully exploited, and in most areas certain species remain unexploited because of low commercial demand in the past. Probably the greatest hope of expanding marine protein supplies lies in the possibility of moving down the marine food chain, increasing the catch of the smaller fish and crustaceans that are now consumed by the larger commercially preferred species, such as tuna and salmon.

The Antarctic krill, an abundant small crustacean that in the past fed the now decimated Blue Whale population, probably presents the greatest potential in this direction, for its extraordinary concentration in one region makes it more economical to fish for than plankton of other kinds. The possibility of harvesting the krill, probably for fishmeal rather than for direct human consumption, has been explored intensively by the Soviet Union since the early 'sixties, but technical and economic obstacles still block commercial krill operations. With an estimated potential annual harvest of 25 million to 50 million tons, research on low-cost methods to catch and process the krill is sure to continue.

Although there is untapped potential for extracting food from the sea, it is unlikely that the dramatic growth in the world fish catch of the 1950–70 period ever will be repeated. As human populations continue their rapid growth, the per capita supply of table-grade fish, which has already fallen by more than one tenth, will likely continue to fall. Higher prices and growing international competition for available supplies seem to be inevitable.

Overfishing, generally discovered only when the catch begins to decline in a sustained fashion, has become a serious global problem. The catch of a large number of the thirty-odd leading species of table-grade fish exceeds the maximum sustainable level; that is, the species' regenerative capacity cannot maintain even the present level of catch over time. Francis T. Christy, a leading fisheries economist, observes that "the number of depleted fish stocks is large and growing rapidly."* The result is that the catches of many important species have been declining.

COMPETITION AMONG COUNTRIES

The net effect of these disturbing new trends in the catch of many commercial species of fish—at a time when the world demand for protein is soaring—has been increasingly intense international competition in world fisheries. In the North Atlantic, Great Britain and Iceland have experienced serious conflict over the fishery resources off the coast of Iceland. The Icelandic econ-

---

* Francis T. Christy, Jr., *Alternative Arrangements for Marine Fisheries* (Washington, D.C.: Resources for the Future, May, 1973), p. 11.

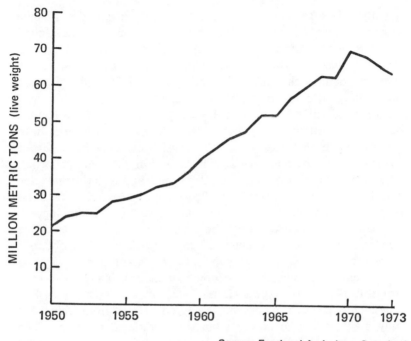

Source: Food and Agriculture Organization.

Figure 11-1. World Fish Catch, 1950-73

omy is closely tied to its fisheries, as is evidenced by devaluations of the krona following poor fishing years in 1967 and 1968. Iceland has therefore extended its offshore limits to 50 miles in order to prevent British ships from competing for its fishery resources; the result was the "Cod War" of 1973. Soviet fishing trawlers operating just beyond the 12-mile offshore limits on the eastern coast of the United States are exploiting fisheries that were once the exclusive domain of American fishermen. The State of Massachusetts is threatening to extend its offshore limits to 200 miles in order to prevent the demise of its once vigorous fishing industry.

In the north Pacific, the expanding Soviet and Japanese fishing fleets find themselves in direct competition. U.S. fishermen off the North American West Coast face stiff competition from Soviet, Japanese, and Korean trawlers, and the U.S. Coast Guard frequently seizes foreign vessels caught fishing inside the 12-mile territorial limit. Off the west coast of Latin America, the United States is in continuous conflict with Peru and Ecuador. During a recent twelve-month period, Ecuador seized fifty-six U.S. fishing trawlers found within its unilaterally imposed 200-mile offshore limit, fining them a total of $2.3 million.

The competition in oceanic fisheries has exacerbated the conflict between the rich and the poor countries. As the rich countries have exhausted the resources of northern fisheries, they have turned increasingly to the Southern Hemisphere. For the poor countries, whose protein and foreign-exchange needs are desperate, the invasion of modern fleets and floating fish-processing facilities poses a serious problem. Lacking the capital and technology to compete, they are extending their territorial limits beyond the traditional and widely accepted 12 miles in an effort to obtain a more satisfactory share of the world's marine-protein supply. At least twenty-one countries have now extended their claims to control of fishing rights beyond 12 miles, ten of them as much as 200 miles. Their position has recently received support from China, the only major power to depart from the traditional position. Then Foreign Minister Edgardo Mercado Jarrin of Peru spoke for many developing countries when he said:

> Unrestricted freedom of the seas has been claimed as being necessary for the profit of the international community as a whole. But the developing countries have learned that while absolute freedom indisputably is necessary for international communications, when applied to sea resources the result benefits only those maritime powers with the means of exploiting them—which they do for their own advantage and in disregard of the needs of the coastal states.*

In recent years a number of developing countries have emerged as major fishing nations. For nearly a decade before the collapse of the coastal anchovy fishery in 1972 (see pp. 155–57), Peru had led the world in total fish catch. Other developing countries that are becoming major participants in world fisheries include South

---

* Edgardo Mercado Jarrin, "Utilizing Sea Resources for Human and Social Welfare," *Pacific Community* 3, No. 2 (January 1972): 310.

Korea, India, and Pakistan. In per capita terms, however, the poor countries lag far behind the rich countries in the share of the world catch consumed.

As growth in the world catch of table-grade fish slows and, for some important species, begins to decline from overfishing, the Soviet and Japanese populations are especially vulnerable. If they find themselves increasingly unable to meet protein needs from oceanic resources, they will be forced to offset this decline by stepping up their imports of feed grains and soybeans to expand indigenous poultry and livestock production, exerting substantial additional pressures on exportable food supplies.

TABLE 11–2. COMMERCIAL CATCH, TEN LEADING FISHING NATIONS, 1972.

	Thousand Metric Tons Live Weight
Japan	10,248
U.S.S.R.	7,757
China	7,574
Peru	4,768
Norway	3,163
United States	2,650
Thailand	1,679
India	1,637
Spain	1,617
Chile	1,487
World total	65,600

SOURCE: FAO, *Yearbook of Fishery Statistics, 1972.*

THE NORTHWEST ATLANTIC FISHERY

The Northwest Atlantic Fishery consists of the offshore fishing area extending from Rhode Island northward to the southern coast of Greenland; today it accounts for 5 per cent of the total world fish catch. Its 350-year history makes it one of the world's oldest oceanic fisheries and, in effect, a microcosm of world fisheries. The countries fishing in this area in 1949 formed the International Commission for the Northwest Atlantic Fisheries (ICNAF) for the purpose of collectively overseeing and managing the fishery.

The catch of this biologically rich region totaled 1.8 million tons in 1954 and increased steadily until 1968, when it reached 3.9 million tons. It then dropped to 3.2 million tons in 1970, a decline of 18 per cent, and has remained at this lower level even though the level of fishing effort has continued to rise dramatically.

The catch of several individual species peaked in the 'sixties and then began to decline. Since there was no diminution of effort during this period, this decline was very likely the result of overfishing. The haddock catch, for example, reached a high of 249,000 tons in 1965 and then dropped steadily until in 1972 it was only one seventh what it had been six years earlier. The catches of cod,

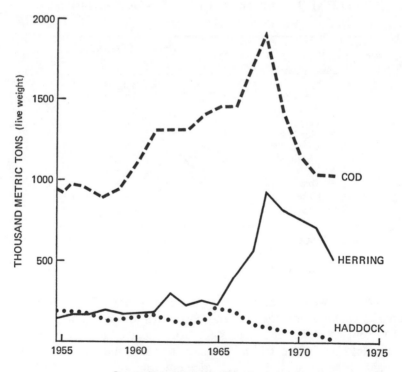

Source: International Commission for the Northwest Atlantic Fisheries.

Figure 11-2. Annual Catch of Selected Species
in the Northwest Atlantic, 1954-72

halibut, and herring peaked in 1968 but have all dropped sub-stantially since then, with declines ranging from over 40 per cent for herring to over 90 per cent for halibut.

The relative importance of various countries in the Northwest Atlantic fishery has changed greatly since 1954. At that time only eleven countries were involved—all members of the Atlantic com-munity. Since then, Japan, Romania, Poland, and, most important, the Soviet Union have entered the fishery. As of 1972 the Soviet Union was threatening to displace Canada, traditionally the fish-ery's leading country, as the nation with the largest catch. Poland had reached fifth place, close after the United States.

Efforts by the ICNAF to impose quotas within the past few years have had limited success. The most commonly used formula has sought to limit the total catch and to allocate it among ICNAF member countries, with 40 per cent of the allocation determined by the average national catch of the preceding ten years, 40 per cent determined by the average catch of the preceding three years, 10 per cent based on territorial proximity, and 10 per cent for newcomers and special factors. In 1973, the Commission went a step farther and, for some regions within its jurisdiction, placed national quotas on the total catch of *all* species that were lower than each nation's combined quotas for individual species.

Difficulties in obtaining agreement to the quotas by the many nations involved as well as in enforcement of those quotas that have been reached have caused considerable conflict among Com-mission members. The United States has been especially con-cerned both over the decline in its share of the region's fish yield in the face of massive efforts by relative newcomers to the north-west Atlantic and over the dwindling stocks of many important species.

THE PERUVIAN ANCHOVY FISHERY

Beginning in the late 'fifties, the fishing industry in Peru under-went spectacular expansion. By the early 'sixties, Peru had emerged as the world's leading fishing nation, with its vast anchovy fishery accounting for one fifth of the total world fish catch in several recent years. The increase in Peru's anchovy catch was matched by the growing demand for high-protein feed for livestock production in the increasingly affluent industrialized world. About 90 per cent of all fishmeal produced is mixed into poultry feeds, with hog rations accounting for nearly all the remainder. Europe, Japan, and the United States supplied a lucrative export market for Peruvian fishmeal, which replaced copper as Peru's number-one export product. In many recent years Peru supplied nearly two thirds of world fishmeal exports.

Peru is fortunate in having coastal and current conditions hospitable to an extraordinary concentration of marine life. Gerald Paulik described the anchovy fishery graphically in 1971:

> The true capacity of the Peruvian Fleet is staggering. On April 28, 1970, the total catch reached 9.5 million metric tons. The fishery continued for ten more days, taking 100,000 metric tons per day. This fantastic catching power could have taken the whole U.S. yellowfin-tuna catch in one day, or the entire U.S. catch of all Pacific salmon in two and a half days. Obviously, this type of destructive power must be handled most carefully, and precise management and regulation are essential.*

During 1972 and most of 1973, the anchovies seemingly disappeared from the traditional offshore fishing areas. At first this did not cause great alarm, for slight shifts and temperature changes in the Humbolt current (known as *El Niño*) had caused the anchovies to move away before, at least temporarily. There is considerable evidence, however, that the very heavy annual catches, ranging from 10 million to 12 million tons in the late 'sixties and early 'seventies, exceeded the regenerative capacity of the fishery. This overfishing may have seriously damaged the anchovy fishery, at least temporarily.

A careful biological study conducted in 1970 by an international team of experts led by the FAO estimated the maximum sustainable yield of the Peruvian anchovy fishery at 9.5 million metric tons per year. The catches of 1967, 1968, 1970, and 1971 all exceeded this level.

Following the 1972–73 debacle, the Peruvian government in 1973 nationalized the fishmeal-production industries as part of an

---

* Gerald J. Paulik. "Anchovies, Birds and Fishermen in the Peru Current," in W. W. Murdock, ed., *Environment: Resources, Pollution and Society* (Stamford, Conn.: Sinauer Associates, 1971), p. 157.

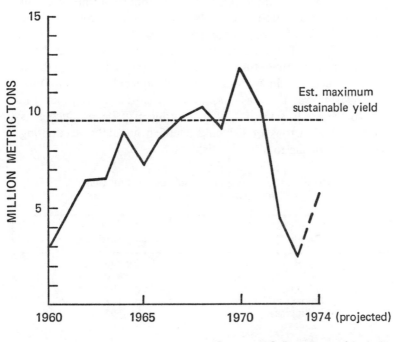

Figure 11-3. Peruvian Anchovy Catch, 1960-74

effort to reduce overcapacity and economic waste. Extremely careful management of fishing levels was also instituted when larger
numbers of anchovies finally began to reappear in early 1974.
Indications in mid-1974 were that a total catch of only 5 million
tons or so would be allowed in 1974 in order to encourage recovery
of the stock. Presumably, the Peruvian government will allow
marine biologists to exercise much closer control over fishing
efforts in the future so that fishmeal production can be restored to
sizable—and sustainable—levels within a few years.

Fish Farming: Status and Prospects

On land, man long ago learned to farm and thus has increased
the earth's food-producing capacity several hundredfold. But in the

oceans he is still a hunter. One of the important questions in assessing food-production prospects for the future concerns the possibilities for fish farming, or aquaculture.

The concept of fish farming is not new. In Asia it has been practiced for more than three thousand years. There have been many local successes in various forms of aquaculture, both fresh water and salt water, in a number of countries throughout the world. In the early 'seventies, fish farming may be producing as much as 5 million tons of fish and shellfish annually, accounting for 6 per cent of the total world fish catch.

TABLE 11–3. ESTIMATED PRODUCTION OF FISH
THROUGH AQUACULTURE.

Country	Production[a] (1,000 metric tons)
China	2,240
India	480
U.S.S.R.	190
Indonesia	141
Philippines	95
Thailand	88
Japan	85
Taiwan	56
United States	40
Pakistan and Bangladesh	38
Other	204
Total	3,657

[a] Excludes shrimps and mollusks. Latest available data.

SOURCE: T. V. R. Pillay, "The Role of Aquaculture in Fishery Development and Management," FAO, 1973.

Fish farming is a complex undertaking. In its simplest form, it means providing supplementary feed for various species of fish in water bodies where the fish can be harvested in a controlled and systematic way. Its more sophisticated forms involve not only the domestication of various fish species but also breeding them; controlling their environment, including nutrients, temperature, and light; and controlling disease and pests of various kinds.

Many proposals have been set forth for both fresh- and salt-water aquaculture, ranging from the use of circular atolls in the Pacific as pens or corrals for whale farming to the culture of oysters in marine estuaries. They also include the artificial creation of large upwelling areas that can carry nutrients from the ocean floor to the surface in order to sustain a larger population of plankton and the fish that feed on them. One of the most interesting possibilities of fish farming involves the use of human sewage as a source of nutrients in fresh-water bodies. Sewage is now used very effectively in some fresh-water fisheries, particularly in the carp ponds of Asia and southern Germany. The possibility of using thermal pollution to create a more productive habitat for certain species of fish in selected locations is also being given serious attention.

Aquaculture is practiced most extensively in China, where at least 2.2 million tons of carp and other species are harvested from ponds each year, accounting for about 40 per cent of the nation's fish harvest. Probably the next most prevalent fish cultured by man is the milkfish, an important protein source, particularly in Indonesia, the Philippines, and Taiwan. In a method used for many centuries, the young of this species are gathered in shallow shore-line waters and transferred to inland ponds, where they feed on algae, bacteria, larvae, and other organic matter until they reach the desired size.

Shrimp and oysters are the most commercially valuable marine species to be raised artificially. The culture of shrimp larvae first captured from the ocean has been practiced for centuries in Japan, the Philippines, and elsewhere in Asia. Japanese scientists in this century have learned to raise shrimp from egg to adulthood. However, the relatively high cost of shrimp produced in this manner means that shrimp culture of this type has been economically feasible only in Japan, where this food is especially valued and consumers have a high average income. Oysters also are being farmed widely, because of both their high market value and their biological characteristics, which are well suited for artificial culture. The practice dates back at least to ancient Rome. Today oyster culture is prevalent in Japan, the United States, and Europe.

In the United States, fish farming has so far become significant only in the cases of catfish and trout. The production of these two fresh-water species has grown very rapidly over the last several years and now amounts to over half a pound per capita. But this is still a negligible share of animal-protein intake.

The economic feasibility of some types of fish farming will depend in part on the costs of the protein-high feeds that may be necessary. The sharp rise in the prices of soy and fishmeals in early 1973 had a depressing influence on the emerging fish-farming industries in the United States. Aquatic pollution presents the greatest threat to the future of aquaculture; already pollution has made large aquaculture areas in the United States and Japan unfit for fish or shellfish culture.

Recent advances in man's understanding of the complex conditions under which fish live, reproduce, and grow have, if anything, diminished hopes of farming the oceans extensively. There is no doubt that there will be a substantial expansion of both fresh-water and salt-water fish farming in the coming decades, but it is not likely to expand fast enough to alleviate world protein shortages substantially. In the words of FAO expert C. P. Idyll, "instead, sea farms will probably prove to be profitable operations for some investors, and they will supplement the production of fish, shrimp, and other seafoods that are in high demand."*

There is growing interest in the potential for expanding the farming of food fish in the developing world, thus providing both economically viable industries and vital protein. The limited data gathered so far in Asia and Africa suggest that only a small portion of the areas with high potential for fish farming, such as lagoons, mangrove swamps, ponds, and reservoirs, are currently being exploited for fish production. The expansion of aquaculture in the developing countries will require a considerable increase in biological and economic research and technical manpower training. International development-assistance agencies could profitably provide greater support for research and development of aquaculture industries in the years ahead.

Although the prospects for progress in aquaculture are good, it is starting from a rather small base and faces numerous constraints.

---

* C. P. Idyll, *The Sea Against Hunger* (New York: Thomas Y. Crowell, 1970). p. 90.

The transition from fisherman to farmer of the ocean is not imminent. Man's primary hopes for increasing protein supplies in the immediate future lie not with the ocean but with the land.

POLLUTION OF OCEANIC FISHERIES

Besides being a source of food for man, the ocean serves as the ultimate waste receptacle for the planet. Deliberately and accidentally, man is adding to the oceans thousands of waste products —frequently highly toxic—including oil, chemical effluents, lethal chemical-warfare gases, radioactive wastes, junk metal, trace elements, organic wastes from humans and animals, automobile exhaust products, pesticides, and detergents.

The long-term biological effects of polluting the ocean with industrial, military, municipal, and agricultural wastes are not yet fully known. Both the quantity and the variety of oceanic pollutants are growing faster than man's ability to collect information about them and about their individual and synergistic consequences for the marine biosphere. It is certain, however, that oceanic pollution has reached alarming proportions, that it is global in scale, and that it poses an increasingly serious threat to oceanic food resources.

Pollution of inland and offshore waters has killed some fish outright, jeopardized the existence of others, and rendered still others unfit for human consumption. In the United States, thirty-three states have banned commercial fishing in at least some fresh-water bodies during the past few years because of dangerous levels of mercury content in fish. Early in 1971 quantities of tuna and swordfish were withdrawn from American markets after detection of excessive mercury content. Illness and death have been blamed on mercury-contaminated fish in Japan. In 1969, some 3,200 pounds of coho salmon caught in Lake Michigan were banned from interstate commerce by the Food and Drug Administration because of contamination by DDT.

Oil pollution also is among the most serious threats to life in the sea. Approximately a million tons of oil are spilled from freighters, tankers, and offshore oil rigs each year. Several million more tons of crude-oil products are added to the oceans in the form of gasoline solvents and waste motor oil. Oil floating on the surface interferes with the flow of light and oxygen in the sea, making areas at least temporarily uninhabitable.

Pesticides spread on the land find their way into estuaries and coastal waters, often carried far from the points of application by rivers, rain, and winds. Winds have borne pesticides thousands of miles. DDT is affecting shrimp, clams, and oysters, as well as trout, salmon, and other fish. Even small amounts of DDT in the water— no more than a few parts per billion—can prevent reproduction in some species or greatly reduce their numbers. A concentration of eight parts per million in the ovaries of sea trout in an estuary off the Texas coast prevented spawning. As little as one part in 10 billion of DDT in water can severely cut the growth rate of oysters.

Man is faced with some difficult trade-offs in deciding whether to use fresh-water bodies and the oceans for waste disposal or for food production. It now seems clear that the level of pollution in both fresh-water bodies and oceans is worsening and will continue to deteriorate even further before it gets better. Fish have virtually disappeared from some of the more polluted rivers in the industrial countries. Pollution levels are rising in both the Mediterranean and the Baltic at an alarming rate. In Japan's coastal waters, once-rich nearby fishing areas, such as Tokyo Bay, Osaka Bay, and Hiroshima Bay, are now "dead seas," and the Inland Sea may soon follow.

COOPERATIVE MANAGEMENT OF OCEANIC FISHERIES

Examination of overfishing and stock depletion in oceanic fisheries highlights the urgency of evolving a cooperative global approach to their management. Failure to do this will result in continuing depletion of stocks, reductions in catch, and soaring seafood prices. The prices of some preferred species of table-grade fish could double within a few years. Without global cooperation, fishery resources could dwindle in the same way that the world catch of whales has dwindled over the past decade. And a declining world fish catch will put severe added pressure on land-based food resources.

To reverse this trend, it will be necessary to impose limits on the annual intake of fish on a species-by-species, region-by-region basis. Once the over-all limit is agreed upon, a formula must be devised for allocating the catch among countries, based on their historical share, coastal proximity, investment in fishing facilities, size of population, nutritional needs, and other factors. If even a few of the countries involved in a particular fishery refuse to cooperate, it will not be possible to preserve stocks and maintain the catch at optimum levels.

Regional fishery arrangements already in existence need to be greatly strengthened, and many others must be devised. Countries must exercise patience and forbearance in negotiating quotas. This will be most difficult when the countries participating in negotiations represent widely varying levels of development. It is in this context that all nations have a direct interest in the successful negotiation and implementation of cooperative fishery agreements at the U.N. Law of the Seas Conference convened in Caracas, Venezuela, in mid-1974, and at subsequent UN conferences.

12.

NON-CONVENTIONAL FOOD SOURCES

In an age of great scientific achievement, it is not surprising that many new technologies have been developed for satisfying man's nutritional needs. Scientists are currently working on a wide range of possibilities, including the production of food from oil, the nutritional improvement of grains, the creation of protein foods from leaves, and the recycling of animal manures as livestock feed. Only some of the most significant experimental areas are surveyed in this chapter. One other major development—the production of imitation meat products from vegetable-protein sources—is discussed in Chapter 14.

Nutritious new foods and food additives, as well as various means of meeting human food needs without recourse to conventional agriculture, have long held allure as possible shortcuts to eliminate malnutrition. But experience has shown that no new technologies can substitute for reducing poverty, improving the distribution of available food, raising agricultural production, and putting the brakes on world population growth. Nevertheless, many potential non-conventional sources of food do hold the promise of contributing over time to the struggle to provide an adequate diet for all of the human race.

High-Protein Cereals

Since cereal grains account for some two thirds of the total caloric intake in many developing countries, any improvement in the protein content of cereals could directly improve nutrition. Cereal proteins lack one or more of the essential amino acids. Corn, for example, is deficient in lysine and, to a lesser extent, in tryptophan, both of which are essential for human metabolism. Corn-consuming populations therefore tend to be vulnerable to malnutrition due to the shortage of these amino acids in their diet.

Plant breeders at research centers in the United States and elsewhere around the world are working to develop cereal varieties with greater protein content and quality. However, the process is not a rapid one. Analyzing the protein content and quality of currently grown strains is itself an arduous task. Locating genetic lines with desirable qualities involves painstaking study of thousands of varieties, and breeding and cross-breeding take years. Incorporating high protein content while retaining high yield potential, desirable cooking and eating qualities, and high insect and disease resistance can be incredibly complicated.

The first important breakthrough came in 1963, with the discovery of a high-lysine corn gene, called opaque-2, by Edwin T. Mertz and his associates at Purdue University. A description of this discovery in the July, 1964, issue of *Science* attracted the attention of scientists throughout the world and sparked a flurry of efforts to upgrade the protein content of cereals through breeding.

The development of high-lysine corn is important to many nations of Latin America and sub-Saharan Africa, where corn accounts for a large portion of the food-energy supply—at least half in Guatemala, Kenya, Rhodesia, Zambia, and Malawi. Diets will improve markedly if the new high-lysine corn varieties can eventually replace traditional corn. If it is used as livestock feed, the need for costly protein supplements will be sharply reduced.

Despite the exciting potential, opaque-2 and related hybrids of high-lysine corn so far have been used commercially only in Colombia, Brazil, and the United States, and even there to a very modest extent, owing to the fact that high-lysine corn has lower yields per acre than traditional varieties, greater susceptibility to insects and disease, and kernel characteristics and cooking qualities that are unacceptable to many consumers.

There is nevertheless no reason for discouragement about the longer-term prospects of high-lysine corn. None of the problems that have limited the spread of the hybrid thus far appears to be insurmountable. Researchers in the United States, at the International Maize and Wheat Improvement Center (CIMMYT) in Mexico, and in several other countries are making steady progress toward developing newer varieties as high in protein quantity and quality as the early opaque-2 lines but without their disadvantages. Within a few years, more and more high-lysine corn seeds with increasingly competitive qualities should begin emerging from the experimental plots. Their use will spread gradually as governments, food processors, and livestock feeders become aware of their nutritional advantages.

After seven years of research sponsored by the U.S. Agency for International Development (AID), Purdue scientists John Axtell and Rameshwar Singh announced the discovery of two high-lysine sorghum varieties in late 1973. Any success in developing more nutritious sorghum for widespread use will benefit those who live in the more arid regions of Asia and Africa, where sorghum is often the primary source of food.

After examining more than 9,000 sorghum varieties from all over the world, the researchers found two obscure strains in Ethiopia—the ancestral home of sorghum—that contain nearly one third more protein and twice the lysine of more commonly grown varieties. Although these two strains produce lower yields than other varieties, Ethiopian farmers have nurtured them over the centuries because of their distinctive and pleasing flavor. Further research is clearly necessary to develop strains with higher yields and other needed qualities. It is hoped that by the early 'eighties at least, high-protein sorghum will be widely available to help meet nutritional needs and also reduce the feed costs of livestock production.

Rice, the staple food of more than half of mankind, is relatively low in protein content, but scientists at the International Rice Research Institute (IRRI) in the Philippines have made considerable progress in the last several years in breeding experimental rices with a higher protein content. After studying 7,600 rice varieties, the Institute selected six with the highest protein content and crossed them with IR-8, the well-known high-yielding dwarf variety. IRRI scientists are now confident of obtaining high-yielding varieties with a protein content one fourth greater and with no adverse effects on cooking and eating quality. An increase of this magnitude in the protein content of rice could help reduce protein deficiency among children in Asia, whose main source of protein is rice. The first test harvests showing both high protein content and high yields appeared in 1973. IRRI reports that "if these lines maintain yields equal to IR-8 and high protein content through several more seasons, some might be suitable for commercial release."*

Wheat is less deficient in total protein and key amino acids than rice, corn, and sorghum; yet it, too, is incapable of supplying all the requirements of an adequate diet, primarily because of its lysine deficiency. Researchers in more than thirty countries are cooperating in a project led by the University of Nebraska and supported by AID to develop wheats combining high yields and improved protein quality and quantity. More than 16,000 wheats have been analyzed, and wide differences in protein content and patterns have been discovered. Strains with high lysine content and others with high total protein have been identified and are being crossed in breeding programs. Researchers are hopeful that an increase in protein content of 25 per cent or more will eventually prove possible in commercially viable varieties.

Breeding New Crops

Triticale, a cross between wheat and rye, is on the verge of becoming the first commercially successful man-made grain. Its particular appeal to plant breeders and nutritionists is that it is considerably higher in both protein quantity and protein quality than existing cereals. Some triticale varieties may also be more resistant to cold and drought than wheats. This could greatly benefit farmers in some regions where the use of high-yielding wheat varieties has not been possible.

Triticale was first bred in Germany in the late nineteenth century, but early versions, like those of many other crossed species, suffered from sterility, tall, weak straw, and shriveled grain. Since

* *The IRRI Reporter*, No. 3, 1973, p. 2.

1965, however, breeders at the CIMMYT in Mexico have been working to overcome these difficulties, with the financial and technical cooperation of the Rockefeller Foundation, the Canadian government, and the University of Manitoba. An important breakthrough occurred in 1968, when an accidental crossing of triticale with a Mexican wheat variety solved the fertility problem. Since then progress occurred in other areas as well. Dwarf varieties have been developed that can utilize more than 100 pounds of nitrogen fertilizer per acre without lodging and can attain yields approaching those of the more productive wheat varieties. Improvement of the grain quality is coming more gradually and remains a constraint on the spread of the new crop.

Triticale is already in limited commercial use. In 1972, nearly 500,000 acres were planted to triticale in Texas, Oklahoma, and Kansas for use as fall and winter forage for livestock. Five thousand acres were grown in Canada to supply a whisky distillery, and a small amount has been produced in Eastern Europe for human consumption. Interest in triticale is strong in a broad geographic range of countries, including Ethiopia, Algeria, Spain, India, the U.S.S.R., and China. As further research brings about improvements in the yields and grain quality of triticale, its commercial use is certain to spread. Triticale will probably be produced for both animal and human consumption. Its flour mixes well with wheat flour to produce tasty, nutritious bread, and food technologists are hopeful that it will also be used for making more nutritious tortillas, chapatis, pasta, and pancakes.

Triticale is the first potentially useful man-made grain, but it is not likely to be the last. CIMMYT reports that the "imminent success of triticale is stimulating many other proposals" for the crossing of grains to find products of greater use to man.* However, the progress of these efforts is not likely to be rapid.

Designing New Foods

Paradoxically, in many poor countries widespread protein hunger coexists with the availability of vast quantities of unused pro-

* CIMMYT, *Report to Trustees: Program Review, 1972–73,* p. 26.

tein meal, most of it the product of local vegetable-oil extraction industries. In India, Nigeria, and other smaller countries, millions of tons of peanuts are used in the production of peanut oil for cooking purposes. Other countries use coconuts or soybeans for cooking-oil production. The meal remaining after the seeds are crushed and the oil is extracted has a high protein content. Unfortunately, little of this protein finds its way directly into the food stream; most of the oil meal is fed to livestock or poultry, used for organic fertilizer, or exported to earn foreign exchange.

If some of the more than 20 million tons of peanut, cottonseed, coconut, and soybean meals available each year in the poor countries could be converted into attractive, commercially successful protein foods, the result would be a major contribution toward the reduction of protein malnutrition. There are, however, some serious technical problems: The foods have to be made palatable, and toxic compounds have to be eliminated. But these obstacles are slowly being overcome, and some new products have been marketed successfully in various parts of the world. Prominent among these are popular beverages using oilseed meals as a base, which have been developed by several private firms and are being marketed in Asia. The pioneer in this field is Vitasoy, which has been manufactured in Hong Kong for three decades and today, with sales of 150 million bottles annually, has captured more than one fourth of the Hong Kong soft-drink market, outselling popular conventional soft drinks. Other high-protein milky beverages are being manufactured and sold in Singapore, Thailand, India, and Malaysia. The success of these drinks in Asia is due to their resemblance to traditional beverages, low cost, and long shelf-life, and the fact that they have been skillfully advertised. Given the mounting popularity of soft drinks in many poor nations, even among the lowest-income groups, the manufacture and marketing of high-protein soft drinks could have a meaningful impact on nutrition patterns.

Perhaps of even greater potential importance are the various prepared foods, powders, and flours in which soy or other high-protein sources are blended with cereals. Corn-Soy-Milk mix (CSM), Wheat-Soy Blend (WSB), and similar products have assumed a growing role in the U.S. food-aid program. In 1972, nearly 300,000 tons of CSM and WSB were donated by the United States, primarily for use by the international voluntary agencies and the FAO World Food Programme in their efforts to fight malnutrition. More recently, as dried milk has become scarce, shipments of CSM have been reduced and replaced by a corn-soy blend used in baked goods. A new product designed by the U.S. Department of Agriculture and being tested in Latin America is a soy-whey blend that serves as a milk substitute for babies and young children. Another new product designed in the United States is soy-fortified grits, developed specifically to battle malnutrition in the Sahel, since it resembles a traditional dish in the region.

While these products have greatest potential as weaning foods— the most critical category of need—they provide a valuable protein supplement for people of all ages. Their growing use in aid programs and in institutional cooking is, one hopes, paving the way for the more widespread commercial production and sale of high-protein blends by firms or governments within the developing countries.

To a limited extent, developing-country production of premixed foods is already occurring. By far the largest-selling such product is manufactured in India for child-feeding programs. The production of Bal Ahar (Hindi for "child's food"), which combines lysine-fortified bulgur with peanut meal and soy flour, may have reached 100 million pounds in 1973. Another interesting new product is the Nutribun, a combination of milk solids and wheat flour designed for elementary school children in the Philippines. Each bun supplies 38 per cent of the daily protein requirement in addition to important vitamins and minerals.

Probably the most widely known low-cost protein product is Incaparina, developed in the 'fifties at the Institute of Nutrition for Central America and Panama (INCAP) in Guatemala. Early versions of this mixture, which is generally prepared as a thin gruel, especially for infants, combined corn and cottonseed flour; more recent versions have used other protein sources, including soy flour and synthetic amino acids. The mixed history of Incaparina epitomizes many of the obstacles to commercial production of inexpensive high-protein foods.

Although the product has been successful in Guatemala, attempts to market it in several other Latin American countries, including Brazil and El Salvador, have failed, largely because of consumer resistance to paying a price considerably higher than that of simple corn flour (despite the relative nutritional advantages) and the unacceptability of the texture and taste. After producing and selling Incaparina in Colombia for several years, the Quaker Oats Company closed down its operations there when its losses began to mount in late 1973.

Panaceas of the Past

Over the past two decades, many other new high-protein foods have been proposed, but few have materialized. The use of algae on a massive scale as a source of nutritious food has frequently been suggested. To date, however, serious cost and palatability problems remain to be overcome. Probably the most widely discussed idea in the 'sixties was fish-protein concentrate (FPC). A powder with extremely high protein content and value, FPC is produced by processing low-grade species of fish that would not otherwise be considered edible.

Small amounts of FPC have been used in a variety of infant foods in special programs in the developing countries. However, major technological and economic problems block the use of FPC on a broad scale. Apart from palatability problems, the complex technology and high capital costs involved in producing acceptable FPC have pushed its price beyond commercially feasible levels. In contrast to the unwarranted international enthusiasm it attracted in the late 'sixties, FPC is now receiving relatively little attention from either the scientific community or food processors.

Particularly since 1967, when AID offered financial incentives for corporations to investigate possibilities of producing new high-protein foods, private industry has been deeply involved in this area. Despite early optimism about such ventures, the experience of private industry so far has not been encouraging. Apart from the difficulty of satisfying consumers' esthetic needs—as well as the occasional political problems raised when new products compete with locally manufactured traditional foods—the major problem limiting the profitability of private production and sale of high-nutrition products is cost. Suitable products generally are developed only after a lengthy, expensive period of research and testing, and industrial processing and packaging often push prices far out of the reach of those who most need the nutritional supplement. Alan Berg notes that "for all the technical ingenuity that has gone into the development of new products, corporate technologists have not yet been able to come up with a food that can be sold commercially for a profit and still be priced low enough to reach and help the masses of people who most need it."[*]

Nevertheless, Aaron M. Altschul's recent cautiously optimistic assessment of the experience with new protein foods puts their evolution into a useful perspective:

> What has been achieved thus far is minuscule compared to the size and gravity of the problem. If what has been achieved represents the limits of what can be reached by technology, then we would be forced to conclude that technology in this area has little to offer of social consequence. And even the few achievements are still in the test-market stage; their success is not assured. . . . What is visible is the first generation of products, faltering and still expensive. But enough is visible to offer promise that these efforts are in the right direction, make good technological sense, are basically cheaper than conventional protein sources, and can attain economic and social viability.[†]

FOOD FORTIFICATION

The fortification of existing foods with needed vitamins, minerals, and amino acids is often an inexpensive way to improve nutrition. In the United States, most flour and bread sold since World War II has been enriched with vitamins and minerals. This has helped to eliminate many of the vitamin-deficiency diseases that had been prevalent. The enrichment of Japanese rice with vitamin B-1 since World War II has virtually wiped out beri-beri, formerly a common cause of death.

---

[*] Alan Berg "Industry's Struggle with World Malnutrition, *Harvard Business Review*, January–February 1972, p. 134.

[†] Aaron M. Altschul, ed. *New Protein Foods;* Vol. 1A: *Technology* (New York and London: Academic Press, 1974), p. 26.

Scientists have invented ways of synthesizing amino acids economically, just as they earlier synthesized vitamins. This in turn has made it possible to upgrade the quality of protein in cereals, for example, simply by adding the necessary amino acids. Adding four pounds of lysine to a ton of wheat costs only four dollars but results in one third more usable protein. Additions of essential amino acids to plant protein can make it equal in quality to animal protein. Fortification with synthetic amino acids has far-reaching commercial potential for both food processing and feed mixing. In the United States, lysine is now used in livestock feed, particularly for hogs; it has already successfully reduced protein meal requirements and food costs. Japan is forging ahead in the use of lysine and other synthetic amino acids in both human food and livestock feed.

All three of the major cereals—rice, wheat, and corn—are deficient in the amino-acid lysine. Corn is also deficient in tryptophane, and rice in threonine. Thus the effective protein fortification of corn and rice is somewhat more expensive than that of wheat because of the need to add another amino acid along with lysine.

In the late 'sixties government bakeries in India began producing "Modern Bread," which was fortified with synthetic lysine as well as with critically needed vitamins and minerals. As the supply of donated lysine was terminated, soya and peanut flours have been substituted to provide the protein supplementation. The Indian government hopes to produce 100 million loaves annually of this bread—which may well be the most nutritious marketed anywhere. Perhaps more important, private-sector bakeries also have been stimulated to begin fortifying their products. With bread consumption surging upward at over 10 per cent a year in India and many other developing countries, any measure that can improve the nutritional quality of bread holds great promise.

A principal appeal of the fortification of products like bread, salt, or tea is that no changes are required in the eating habits of those benefiting from the enriched foods. As Alan Berg observes, "The principle of fortification challenges the long-standing belief that the consumer must consciously desire and be involved in nutritional change."* A significant disadvantage of both fortifica-

---

* Alan Berg, *The Nutrition Factor* (Washington, D.C.: The Brookings Institution, 1973), p. 108.

tion and the introduction of new high-protein foods is that they can reach and help only those who purchase a high portion of their food—mainly urban residents. But since the urban poor represent a large portion of the malnourished in many poor nations, both approaches deserve consideration. Many relatively simple and inexpensive opportunities to improve the welfare of sizable numbers remain to be exploited.

SINGLE-CELL PROTEIN

Currently, the most widely discussed possibility for augmenting food supplies involves the use of single-cell micro-organisms, principally certain strains of yeast, to convert petroleum derivatives or organic wastes into edible forms of protein, known as single-cell protein (SCP). Although the process has been actively researched by dozens of international oil companies, it is not yet in use on a significant scale in any country. Problems of economy, safety, and consumer resistance have limited the production of SCP.

Most SCP production so far has taken place in Europe, but owing to safety concerns production has been cleared only for consumption by livestock. British Petroleum, the leader in this field, has been operating pilot plants in France and Scotland and is now constructing a plant in Italy that will produce 100,000 tons of protein for animal feed annually. A few firms in Italy and the United Kingdom are entering the business with large plants, and some experts predict that by the late 'seventies SCP may be meeting as much as 3.5 per cent of the animal-feed protein requirements in Western Europe—a significant amount, but hardly an alternative to agricultural production.

The Soviet Union, with a serious deficiency in protein feeds that is hampering the desired expansion of meat production, is apparently opening at least one large SCP plant. In Romania, a government agency is joining with a Japanese firm to produce 60,000 tons of SCP for animal feed annually. In Japan, however, the plans of three companies to produce 300,000 tons of protein annually were recently scrapped—primarily as a result of extreme resistance on the part of consumers, who felt that even the indirect consumption of protein produced from petroleum by-products might not be medically safe.

Recent shifts in the world marketplace require new assessments of the economics of SCP production. High energy prices have pushed up the cost of SCP production by raising the cost of raw-material inputs. At the same time, however, higher prices for conventionally produced protein sources are helping to make SCP more competitive with soybeans and fishmeal in feed rations. Since world prices of high-quality protein are likely to remain high in the future, the production of SCP for animal feeds can be expected to grow.

Producing SCP for human consumption presents vastly more difficult problems. Not only is consumer resistance likely to remain strong, but continuing experimentation on humans with many kinds of single-cell micro-organisms has revealed adverse gastro-intestinal and other physical effects. This has not been true of all forms of SCP in all experiments, but the need has been well established for very careful testing of industrially produced protein products on both animals and humans. Safe and economically feasible SCP is being developed for human consumption, but its introduction into diets will not be rapid. The Protein Advisory Group of the United Nations, under the leadership of Dr. Max Milner, has sponsored several world conferences on the problems and potential of SCP and has established detailed guidelines for the testing and evaluation of SCP that should help prevent the possibility of hazardous side effects and gradually build consumer confidence in the product.

That the discovery of industrially produced micro-organisms acceptable for human consumption should be a slow process is hardly surprising. Dr. Nevin Scrimshaw of the Massachusetts Institute of Technology reminds us that "difficulties arise because in searching for SCP for food use man is trying to compress into a few decades the selection and evaluation that have extended over millennia for higher plants."*

FEEDING FERTILIZER TO CATTLE

Some American cattlemen have adopted a novel compromise between conventional and unconventional technologies in the

* Nevin S. Scrimshaw, "Single Cell Protein for Human Consumption: An Overview," in *Single Cell Protein II* (Cambridge, Mass.: MIT Press, 1974).

production of beef—the most popular source of animal protein in the American diet. They are feeding cattle urea, which is commonly used as a nitrogen fertilizer. Farmers can thus reduce to some extent the protein content of other rations and can rely more heavily on roughage, such as cornstalks, corncobs, straw, and even sawdust, made more palatable by the addition of molasses. Microorganisms in the rumen combine the nitrogen and carbohydrates to form protein, which the cattle can then absorb. Where roughage supplies are adequate, as in the U.S. corn belt, feeding urea to cattle can measurably reduce the cost of producing beef. But this method should result in even greater economies in the tropics, where low-cost roughage can be produced easily all year round.

By 1972, some 800,000 tons of urea—far more than is used as fertilizer in many nations—were fed to cattle in the United States. The use of urea in U.S. cattle feeds has grown 14 per cent annually over the last decade. European cattle growers are also showing interest in this technique.

The successful use of urea in feed rations requires exceedingly careful management and feed mixing lest the animals' health be impaired, a requisite that has thus far impeded its use. Until the price of urea subsides from the record levels of the mid-'seventies, its use in feeding is not likely to expand so rapidly as in the past.

The possibility for the expanded feeding of manufactured fertilizer to cattle is nevertheless promising, because it permits, within constraints, the substitution of atmospheric nitrogen for increasingly scarce agriculturally produced high-quality proteins. The use of urea as cattle feed makes it possible to convert roughage that might otherwise be wasted into beef—a high-quality protein product that is in great worldwide demand.

PART FOUR

Responses

13.

PUTTING ON
THE DEMOGRAPHIC BRAKES

Throughout most of the estimated 2 million years of man's existence as a distinct species, his numbers were comparatively low. At the time agriculture was developed, some 10,000 years ago, world population probably did not exceed 10 million. World population at the beginning of the Christian era nearly two millennia ago has been estimated at 250 million, almost exactly the size of the population of the Soviet Union in 1974. From the beginning of the Christian era until the beginning of the Industrial Revolution, global population increased to 1 billion. By the beginning of the present century it had reached 1.55 billion, by 1950 it had climbed to 2.5 billion, and by the time the U.N. Population Conference was convened in Bucharest in August of 1974 it had reached nearly 4 billion.

The global population increase of nearly 700 million during the 'sixties roughly equaled that of the entire nineteenth century. This increase of more than 20 per cent brought a corresponding decline in per capita natural resources, since these are in fixed supply. For each person, there was nearly one fifth less fresh water, arable land, marine protein, fossil-fuel reserves, mineral reserves, living space, waste-absorptive capacity, and natural recreation areas in 1970 than in 1960.

The significance of this dramatic decline in natural amenities,

The analysis and recommendations in this chapter are presented in much greater detail in Lester R. Brown, *In the Human Interest: A Strategy to Stabilize World Population* (New York: W. W. Norton, 1974).

which is continuing at an unabated rate, goes far beyond the mere arithmetic of the decline itself and the resulting pressures on food resources and ecological systems. The changing relationship between man and the finite natural system within which he exists has profound economic, political, and social consequences that we are only beginning to perceive.

UNDERSTANDING THE PROBLEM

While most of us understand the short-term consequences of a 3 per cent annual rate of population growth in terms of the need for food, water, housing, education, and other services, the fact that such a seemingly small rate of growth results in a *nineteenfold increase within a century* is not widely recognized, even by many national political figures whose leadership in this critical area is essential.

In a country of 15 million people—say, Algeria—a growth rate of 3 per cent would result in a population of 285 million a century hence. If Indonesia's current population growth rate of 2.7 per cent were to continue for a century, it would result in a population of 1.78 billion, or nearly half of today's entire global population. The need to put the brakes on population growth is imperative. The objective of completing the demographic transition—i.e., moving from a rapid population growth rate to a moderate rate— as rapidly as possible no longer suffices. The goal must now be population stabilization—an end to population growth—in every nation of the world.

If family-planning services were made available to every man and woman throughout the world, population growth rates would be measurably reduced. But this is only one part of the problem. The historical record indicates that human fertility does not usually decline much unless certain basic social needs are satisfied. That is, birth rates do not normally drop voluntarily in the absence of an assured food supply, reduced infant-mortality rates, literacy, and at least rudimentary health services. In the future, far more attention must be devoted to designing economic and social policies to distribute these fundamental improvements in well-being more evenly among national populations, even in nations where per capita income is still at a low level. Social progress for the poor in most developing nations will necessarily require agricultural progress that directly involves and benefits the broad masses—progress that will simultaneously mean higher food production.

The changes required to cope successfully with the population threat are not marginal or trivial. They strike at the very structure, functioning, and behavior of society and challenge many of the fundamental tenets on which our social and economic systems are based, including the pursuit of superaffluence among the rich and the desire for large families among the poor. Mankind as a whole can no longer afford to limit the role of women to childbearing and childrearing, a practice that still characterizes many traditional societies. The population threat demands an alteration of many aspects of our life-styles.

FAMILY-PLANNING SERVICES

A distressingly large share of the world's fertile population does not have ready access to family-planning services, either because the services are not locally available or because they are too costly for many who need and want them. In the more developed countries, the problem is not the lack of sufficient resources to provide family-planning services to all who require them but, rather, the fact that internal priorities have been focused elsewhere. For example, only since 1970, with passage of the Family Planning Services and Population Research Act, has the United States acted systematically to ensure the availability of family-planning services to all Americans regardless of geographic location or economic status.

A recent worldwide survey by the International Planned Parenthood Federation (IPPF) estimated that 31 per cent of all couples of fertile age were practicing birth control in some form as of 1971. The percentage varied widely from country to country, ranging from below 20 per cent to above 80 per cent. Of the 31 per cent average figure, roughly half relied on traditional techniques, such as withdrawal, the condom, and the rhythm method; the other half used more modern techniques, such as the pill, the IUD, and sterilization. Worldwide, the condom was probably the most widely used contraceptive.

One of the most revealing findings of the IPPF survey was the extent to which abortion was used as a means of limiting births; an estimated 40 million unwanted pregnancies are terminated by abortion each year. At the global level, expenditures for abortion apparently exceeded those of all other forms of contraception combined. In economic terms, it is far more costly to terminate a pregnancy through abortion than to avoid it through the use of contraceptive practices. Abortion is, however, used effectively in many countries as a back-up to contraceptive practices when they fail, as most do from time to time.

Among most of the less developed countries, family-planning services still do not reach the majority. The U.N. Fund for Population Activities (UNFPA) estimates that the cost of providing such services ranges between 50 cents and one dollar per year per capita for an entire population. (The actual cost per capita to those who need advice and contraceptives is several times higher, since the group at risk is only a small fraction of the total population.)

The only populous developing country that appears largely to have overcome the logistical and economic obstacles to providing universal family-planning services is China. If China is excluded from our calculations for this reason, the remaining developing countries contain roughly 2 billion people. Using the UNFPA estimate of one dollar per person as the cost of providing family-planning services, it would require an expenditure of $2 billion to provide universal family-planning services. If half of this amount were to come from internal resources, roughly $1 billion would be required annually from the international community, to be used for training personnel, for educational materials, for clinics, for transportation equipment (including jeeps and bicycles), and for contraceptives.

Probably no other expenditure of funds can approach the effectiveness of family-planning services in breaking the self-reinforcing cycle of poverty and high fertility. On the basis of surveys of desired and actual family sizes in the developing world, the Population Council reports that *if* the responses were genuine, and *if* family-planning programs could satisfy this demand, birth rates in the developing world would fall by nine to twelve points. In global economic terms, this expenditure would be quite small; in terms of its impact on human well-being, it could be of profound importance. The present flow of funds into the less developed countries for family-planning purposes from both public and private sources approximates $250 million, scarcely a quarter of what is needed.

But the mere availability of $2 billion cannot solve the problem of making family-planning programs available throughout the world. Obviously, major organizational and political problems would still plague this effort. Given the appropriate international political will, however, the *financial* resources required for such a family-planning effort would be almost insignificant in global economic terms. They would surely be trivial compared with the current military expenditures of national governments; yet uncontrolled human fertility poses a threat to our future well-being that may be greater than that posed by international aggression.

Because family-planning initiatives and programs usually originate with governments in the developing nations, there is a tendency to overlook the potential role of the commercial sector in the distribution of contraceptives. One reason for harnessing the distribution potential of the commercial sector is that it already supplies an estimated 40 per cent of all contraceptives used in the less developed world and an even larger proportion in the developed countries; therefore, personnel costs, which often absorb 90 per cent of the funds of family-planning programs, as well as organizational difficulties would be greatly reduced by capitalizing on these existing services and channels of distribution. Commercial services can satisfy the needs of a sizable segment of the population, thereby making it possible to concentrate official resources and programs on people who are not otherwise reached. Even economically advanced countries such as the United States need official programs to reach those whose need for advice and contraceptives is not satisfied by commercial services.

MEETING SOCIAL NEEDS

Filling the demand for family-planning services as rapidly as possible is essential, but it is not enough. Although the increased availability of such services will contribute to a significant decline in fertility in virtually every society, it is not likely to reduce markedly the fertility of the preponderant share of humanity that suffers from severe social deprivation unless a way can be found to satisfy their basic social needs and thus decrease the urgency they assign to ensuring their security by having large families.

In the absence of family-planning programs, the experience of Europe and North America during the past century—a general reduction in birth rates after incomes became relatively high—was long thought to be the norm for poor countries as well. However, in an increasing number of poor countries, including societies as different as China, Barbados, Sri Lanka, Uruguay, Taiwan, Cuba, and South Korea, as well as in some regions within countries, such as the Indian Punjab, birth rates have dropped sharply despite relatively low per capita income and despite the absence or relative newness of family-planning programs. In all these countries, a large portion of the population has gained access to modern social and economic benefits—such as education, health, employment, and farm credit systems—to a far greater degree than the citizens of most poor countries or most Western countries during comparable periods of development. Not only have birth rates dropped noticeably in these countries even before the introduction of family-planning programs, but such programs seem to be much more successful in countries that have assigned high priority to a more equitable distribution of income and social services.

The relationship between socio-economic change and fertility is admittedly complex. In every country there are special cultural or religious factors that have implications for population growth, as do variations in the means available for reducing the birth rate. Yet there is increasing evidence that the very strategies that cause the greatest improvements in the welfare of the entire population also have the greatest effect on reducing population growth.

William Rich has summed up the evidence:

> In a number of poor countries, birth rates have dropped sharply despite relatively low per capita income and despite the relative newness of family planning programs. The common factor in these countries is that the *majority* of the population has shared in the

economic and social benefits of significant national progress to a far greater degree than in most poor countries—or in most Western countries during their comparable periods of development. Appropriate policies for making health, education, and jobs more broadly available to lower income groups in poor countries contribute significantly toward the motivation for smaller families that is the prerequisite of a major reduction in birth rates. Combining policies that give special attention to improving the well-being of the poor majority of the population with large-scale, well-executed family planning programs should make it possible to stabilize population in developing countries much faster than reliance on either approach alone.*

An examination of several societies, both more and less developed, shows a very strong relationship between female educational levels and fertility levels. As educational levels rise, fertility levels fall. In a number of societies, the attainment of literacy brings with it a sharp fertility decline. Several studies show that as women acquire literacy the number of children they have falls by about one third. Studies in Chile and elsewhere show a correlation between a sharp drop in fertility and completion of elementary school. Evidence from Ghana shows the biggest drop in fertility occurring with the completion of secondary school. Women with university degrees had only 0.5 children each, a fertility level well below the average in any more developed country.

Several explanations have been offered for these findings. Education can affect people's values so that they begin to question traditional practices of their parents and other authority figures. People who attend school or who become literate tend to be more receptive to innovations and have greater opportunity to come into contact with "change agents," such as health planners and family-planning counselors. Extended education is likely to delay marriage and to suggest vocational alternatives to childbearing. Higher educational levels also may be associated with increased economic security, which in turn often means smaller families.

* William Rich, *Smaller Families Through Social and Economic Progress,* Overseas Development Council Monograph No. 7, Washington, D.C. January, 1973, p. 76.

Literacy is one of the easiest social needs to satisfy if governments are fully committed to this goal. In part, this is because most resources required to achieve universal literacy are available within the developing countries themselves, and also because imparting literacy is a one-time effort (unlike health services, for example, which must be provided on a continuous basis). In those countries in which successful literacy efforts have been launched, teachers, civil servants, in some cases the army, and volunteers from among recent university graduates have been mobilized for the campaign. A number of countries have progressed steadily and rapidly from being largely illiterate to becoming largely literate, including China since 1949 and Cuba in the early 'sixties. More recently, Brazil and Somalia have launched vigorous programs.

In the 'sixties, UNESCO estimated the cost of enabling a person to become literate in a developing country at about $8, slightly less for an adult, slightly more for a school-age child. Given the nearly 1 billion illiterates in the less developed countries, the elimination of illiteracy would require an outlay of $8 billion. If a global literacy program were spread over five years, the cost would come to $1.6 billion a year. And if the cost were allocated among the principal industrial countries, no one country would have to contribute more than a few hundred million dollars a year. The benefits to those who become literate and to mankind as a whole would be enormous, especially if one takes into account the effect of literacy on receptivity to family planning. As with family-planning services, the financial costs of an effort to eliminate illiteracy are by no means prohibitive. What is lacking is the necessary national and international commitment to this objective.

Two important indicators of the state of health in any given society are the rates of infant mortality and life expectancy. The two factors of course are not unrelated, and both correlate quite closely with fertility levels. As infant-mortality rates decline, so do birth rates, shortly thereafter. As life expectancy increases, birth rates decline. The provision of basic health services to a population is a prerequisite of a rapid drop in population growth. This relationship may appear somewhat paradoxical, since if the birth rate were to remain the same, a reduction in a society's death rate would, of necessity, result in a more rapid population increase.

Indeed, the postwar population explosion in most developing nations can be attributed to the initial lowering of death rates following the introduction of Western medicine, without a simultaneous reduction in traditionally high birth rates.

However, in those developing nations where birth rates have declined substantially, infant mortality is considerably lower, and life expectancy longer, than in the less developed world as a whole. The evidence suggests that the improvement of health conditions beyond a certain minimum level is closely associated with a falling birth rate.

Parents generally wish to ensure the survival of at least one son to care for them in old age and to continue the family name. Often a woman must bear six or more children in order to be certain that one son will survive to adulthood. Where mortality rates are very high, couples tend to have as many children as possible. Where death rates are relatively low and life expectancy is fifty years or more, however, additional reductions in the death rate lead to far greater reductions in the birth rate, thus resulting in slower over-all population growth.

In the mid-'seventies, following a quarter-century of dramatic medical advances, an estimated one third to one half of mankind still lives without access to health services of any kind. At least rudimentary health services, of the kind now being made available by "barefoot doctors" in China, must now be considered one of man's basic social rights. At a minimum, such services should include protection against infectious diseases through vaccinations, provision of safe water supplies in each country, and the practice of basic public-health measures in the area of preventive medicine.

An assured food supply also plays an important role in reducing birth rates. When malnutrition is widespread, even common childhood diseases are often fatal. It is no coincidence that virtually all well-fed societies have low fertility, and all poorly fed societies have high fertility—although the effect of nutrition on fertility is in large measure indirect, through its effect on the infant-mortality rate and on over-all life expectancy. Where malnutrition is widespread, it is virtually impossible to achieve low infant-mortality rates.

Given the close relationship between the incidence of malnutrition and high birth rates, any effort that effectively reduces malnutrition will contribute toward the stabilization of population growth. The mounting evidence that assured food supplies bring birth rates down by increasing the likelihood that existing children will survive lends new urgency to efforts to expand food output in the developing countries. Nothing less than an all-out effort will suffice. The pressing need is to accelerate rural development in the developing countries, for these are where half of mankind lives. In this light, the recent shift in emphasis by the U.S. Agency for International Development and the World Bank to increase aid for rural development is encouraging. The potential for extending multiple cropping and other innovations of the Green Revolution also needs to be exploited as rapidly as possible.

Intensified efforts to expand agricultural production can have a multiple payoff if their strategy is properly designed. When small farms in the developing nations are properly supported with credit, marketing, and technical advisory services and inputs, they not only become more efficient producers of food but also provide more jobs per acre than large estates cultivated with heavy equipment. The increased availability of meaningful employment opportunities associated with broad-based rural development will help to put purchasing power in the hands of those who need it to improve their diets as well as increase total food supplies.

ECONOMIC AND SOCIAL POLICIES

Given the need to reduce fertility and birth rates, it is now imperative for every society to create sufficient attractive employment opportunities for women to induce many of them to opt for these rather than for childbearing alone. Laws, customs, and regulations restricting women's rights to employment, to own property, to vote, to hold political office, and to pursue certain traditionally "male" professions must be stricken from the books. The demands by women for a more equitable role in society are not limited to the economically advanced countries. There are stirrings of the women's liberation movement in virtually every country in the world, including some of the most traditional societies, in which the role of women long has been highly circumscribed. In the future, more and more women can be expected to strive for a role in society virtually indistinguishable from that of men. They should be encouraged and assisted in every way, for it is in both their interest and that of society that they do so.

Making family-planning services universally available, meeting basic social needs, and encouraging new roles for women in society are the most important broad areas for action if birth rates are to be reduced rapidly. In addition, attention must be given to the national structure of economic and social incentives that affect attitudes on family size. In many nations, a variety of policies serve to provide indirect incentives for larger families, often even as the nation adopts the goal of reducing the rate of population growth.

Income-tax deductions for an unlimited number of children (currently offered in the United States), child-care allowances (offered in France), and unlimited subsidized maternity leaves and benefits all may create a situation in which couples feel no incentive to hold down family size and may even feel encouraged to have more children. Limiting such benefits to, say, the first two children can, on the other hand, make couples plan more carefully before having more children. Measures with a similar effect would include limitations on government-subsidized housing or scholarships after the second child.

Governments can even go one step farther and provide positive inducements for smaller families, perhaps by giving special tax bonuses or cash payments to those who remain single instead of penalizing them with extra taxes, as is now often the case, or offering special pension payments as an alternative source of old-age security to those who opt to remain childless or to limit the number of children to one or two.

A lengthening list of governments are beginning to use social and economic pressures to reduce births. Predominantly Muslim Tunisia limits child allowances to the first four children, has legalized the sale of contraceptives, and has passed legislation establishing equal rights for women. Bangladesh has raised the legal minimum age for marriage. The Philippines recently limited tax deductions to four children and accorded working wives the right to deduct 10 per cent of their gross income from their tax base. Singapore has introduced perhaps more disincentives to childbearing than any other country: income-tax deductions for the first three children only, paid maternity leave for the first two confinements only, a progressive rise in the delivery fee for each child after the first, and priority in subsidized housing for couples with no more than two children.

The natural desire of parents to ensure the survival of children to help care for them in old age points up the crucial role that social-security measures can play in reducing family size. Compulsory social-security programs in most economically advanced nations have greatly reduced the economic dependence of parents on their children and thus indirectly have contributed to a climate in which birth rates have fallen. Many poorer nations lack the administrative and fiscal capacity to undertake an identical approach. However, opportunities often exist to provide old-age security through farm cooperative or factory savings/retirement schemes.

Perhaps the best example of how an array of economic and social policies and programs can be used to slow population growth is the comprehensive effort now under way in Mainland China. To begin with, the Chinese government has worked hard to satisfy what it determined were the basic social needs of the Chinese people. For a country with limited economic and natural resources, China has been remarkably successful in achieving ambitious goals in mass literacy, nutrition, and public health. Most people are also provided with social security for their old age. At the same time, a nationwide network of family-planning clinics has been established, offering a full range of free contraceptive services—not only condoms but also the pill, the IUD, and sterilization. The nationwide availability of birth-control services is reinforced by an intensive educational program designed to instill an awareness of the relationship between China's future population growth and both individual and national well-being. Free abortion services are readily available in rural as well as urban areas. A recommended minimum age at marriage of twenty-eight years for men and twenty-five for women is another aspect of the Chinese effort to reduce births. Ration cards are reportedly issued for only three children per family, and in some localities possibly for only two children. Government-supported efforts to secure equal rights for women in all spheres of economic and political activity are designed to provide means of self-fulfillment other than childbearing.

A Proposed Stabilization Timetable

U.N. projections show three alternative levels of population for the year 2000—6 billion, 6.5 billion, and 7.1 billion. The middle-level projection, viewed by U.N. demographers as the most likely, assumes a world population growth rate of 2 per cent until 1985, followed by a gradual decline to 1.7 per cent by the end of the century. The low and high projections reflect corresponding variations in assumed growth rates.

The United Nations has very usefully projected world population growth beyond the end of the century, extrapolating the three alternative trends until world population eventually stabilizes. The essential assumptions common to the three projections are that fertility in all regions will eventually decline to replacement levels and will hold at those levels for several decades until population stabilizes. Replacement-level fertility is that level which enables couples to replace themselves—in effect, two children per couple. (In reality, it must be slightly more than two to allow for the small number of infants who do not reach reproductive age.)

It is highly disturbing to realize how long these assumptions suggest it need take for the world to reach population stability. Even under the "low" variant, population is not expected to stabilize until near the end of the twenty-first century at just under 10 billion. Under the "medium" variant, the one referred to by U.N. demographers as "relatively optimistic," stability is expected by 2125, with population at 12.3 billion. The "high" variant projects population stability at 16 billion in 2135.

The explicit assumptions underlying these alternative projections are almost exclusively demographic. They deal with such matters as fertility behavior and life expectancy but do not examine the effect of these various population levels, supported at acceptable levels of consumption, on the amount of waste and thermal pollution generated, the extent of pressure on oceanic fisheries, the amount of energy required, the stress on food-producing ecosystems, or the level of unemployment. If the ecological, economic, social, and political stresses associated with the enormous projected increases in population are taken into account, even the "low" projection of just under 10 billion people becomes unrealistic.

Many of those who work in the population field have tended to accept totals of this magnitude as inevitable regardless of the consequences, of which they are often aware, since it appears next to impossible to alter the trend. This tendency makes it all the more urgent for those who believe that the combined effect of huge population growth and continuously rising affluence will put more pressure on the earth's resources, food-producing capacity, and ecosystem than these can withstand to examine more radical alternatives. It is now imperative to explore the possibility of achieving a different demographic future—one that holds future population to a sustainable size.

In that spirit a world population stabilization timetable is proposed in this chapter (Table 13–3). Keeping our future numbers down to the total suggested as possible—just under 6 billion in the early twenty-first century—would involve for many nations a much more abrupt shift from past trends than many have considered possible. Weighed against the consequences of failure to bring about such a change in habits, however, such a program begins to appear more necessary and more feasible.

Because of the current sharp contrast in fertility levels between the developed and the less-developed countries, it is useful to think of these two groups of countries separately when considering appropriate strategies. In the more developed countries, where populations are growing slowly, it should be possible to achieve stability much sooner than in less developed countries, where population growth rates generally remain rather high and the proportion of the population of childbearing age is also high. Nearly a score of developed countries are approaching or have already dropped below replacement-level fertility.

Three European countries—West Germany, East Germany, and Luxembourg—have achieved population stability within the past few years (see Table 13–1). Births and deaths in these three countries, which have a total population of 79 million, are essentially in balance. Another group of more developed countries containing 310 million people have birth rates that are low and declining.

These countries—including Austria, Belgium, the United Kingdom, Sweden, Finland, Hungary, the United States, and Switzerland— could attain population stability by 1980 if the recent decline in birth rates continues. Given the low birth rates now existing in most industrial countries, a relatively modest further reduction in the crude birth rate would result in population stability. It is not unreasonable, then, to suggest that all the *more developed* countries should strive for *population stability no later than 1985.*

TABLE 13-1. COUNTRIES ACHIEVING OR APPROACHING
POPULATION STABILITY, 1973.

	Population (million)	Crude Birth Rate	Crude Death Rate	Annual Rate of Natural Increase (per cent)
East Germany	17	10.6	13.7	−0.31
West Germany	62	10.2	11.8	−0.16
Luxembourg	0.3	10.9	12.0	−0.11
Austria	7	12.9	12.3	+0.06
Belgium	10	13.3	12.1	+0.12
United Kingdom	56	13.9	12.0	+0.19
Finland	5	12.2	9.3	+0.29
Sweden	8	13.5	10.5	+0.30
Hungary	10	15.0	11.8	+0.32
United States	208	14.9	9.4	+0.55
Switzerland	6	13.6	9.8	+0.58

SOURCE: United Nations.

Once the genuine urgency of slowing population growth is recognized, given the record already established by several less developed countries, it should be possible for all *less developed* countries that make the appropriate effort to *reduce birth rates to 25 births per thousand population in 1985.* If the less developed countries can accomplish this in the next eleven years, a much smaller group of youngsters will enter the prime reproductive ages in the years between 2005 and 2015; at that stage, it should be possible to take the final step of bringing the birth rate into balance with the death rate. Until 2005, birth rates in most less developed nations would remain at about where the U.S., West German, and

Soviet birth rates were in the early 'sixties (20–25 per thousand). From then until 2015, they would essentially be repeating what we have suggested above for the developed countries between 1975 and 1985—bringing moderate growth down to zero.

The ambitious goal of reducing crude birth rates in the less developed countries to 25 per thousand by 1985 will require far more rapid changes in fertility than most observers have considered possible. But if we examine the performance of those less developed countries which have been most successful in reducing population growth rates, the goal begins to appear much more attainable. It is useful to remind ourselves that seven developing countries, with a total population of 33 million, had already reduced their crude birth rates to 25 per thousand or less by 1973 (Table 13–2). Two other countries, Argentina and Uruguay, both with relatively high average incomes, had also achieved crude birth rates of less than 25. Another group of countries—Sri Lanka, South Korea, Cuba, and quite possibly China—had achieved crude birth rates of 30 or less by 1973.

TABLE 13–2. CRUDE BIRTH RATE DECLINE IN SELECTED
DEVELOPING COUNTRIES.

Country	Time Span	Average Annual Decline in Crude Birth Rate	Crude Birth Rate, 1972
		(births per thousand per year)	
Barbados	1960–69	1.5	22
Taiwan	1955–71	1.2	24
Tunisia	1966–71	1.8	35
Mauritius	1961–71	1.5	25
Hong Kong	1960–72	1.4	19
Singapore	1055–72	1.2	23
Costa Rica	1963–72	1.5	32
South Korea	1960–70	1.2	29
Egypt	1966–70	1.7	37
Chile	1963–70	1.2	25

SOURCE: United Nations and U.S. Agency for International Development.

Some knowledgeable observers may declare the proposed target for the less developed nations to be unattainable. However, consideration of the population size with which many nations will be burdened *even if they meet these stringent goals* indicates that we have little choice but to radically revise our family-planning goals and the scale of our efforts to meet them.

Even under our proposed timetable, China, already becoming dependent on grain imports to preserve adequate nutrition for its 800 million people, would reach a total of 1.33 billion just four decades from now. India, already struggling to feed and maintain political and economic order among a population of almost 600 million, would have to cope with the food needs of nearly 1 billion in 2015. Bangladesh, whose estimated population of 77 million is badly overcrowded and existing on a threadbare margin of survival today, would have to find means of supporting 50 million additional people. Mexico, already dependent for alleviation of its unemployment crisis on the emigration of an estimated quarter of a million workers annually to the United States, would grow from 55 to 103 million people. Nigeria also would face an increase in numbers from 55 million to nearly 100 million. Egypt, now with a population of about 35 million, would have to squeeze 26 million more people into the Nile Valley.

TABLE 13-3. A PROPOSED POPULATION-STABILIZATION TIMETABLE.

	1970	1975	1985	2000	2005	2015
World population (billions)	3.6	3.9	4.5	5.3	5.5	5.8
Annual growth rate (per cent)	1.9	1.7	1.1	1.0	.9	0
Annual increase (millions)	69	65	50	52	49	0

Under the proposed timetable, substantial declines in birth rates between 1975 and 1985 in both the developed and the less developed countries (as the former group moved to population stability and the latter lowered their crude birth rates to 25) would reduce the annual world-population growth rate from 1.9 per cent in 1970 to 1.1 per cent in 1985. This period would be one of steadily declining fertility throughout the world.

Despite continuing stringent efforts to limit births, there would be little further decline in the growth rate from 1985 to the end of the century, as populations in the more developed countries would already have stabilized while large groups in the less developed countries would be in the prime reproductive years as a result of the large number of births during the 1960–75 period. The second phase of the push toward stabilization would come during the decade from 2005 to 2015, when the sharply reduced group born after 1985 would be entering the prime reproductive years. This would yield a stabilized world population of just under 6 billion by 2015. Even with these extraordinary efforts, the 1970 world population by then would have increased by nearly two thirds.

Most demographers have viewed replacement-level fertility (an average family slightly above two children) as the lower limit on national fertility reductions, primarily because there is little historical precedent for a sustained fertility level much below that. The U.N. projections cited previously assume the attainment and maintenance of replacement levels in all nations by the mid-twenty-first century. But meeting the timetable proposed here will require the reduction of fertility levels to below replacement in many societies for at least a period of years. In some countries, it will mean that for short periods the average family may be closer to one child than to two. This is obviously not an easily attainable target. It implies changes in human fertility behavior more comprehensive than any in history, and it can be accomplished only through extraordinary global efforts to change attitudes, to ensure the universal availability of family-planning services, to create new social roles for women, and to reorient national and international economic policies to meet the basic social needs of all people.

The population prospect is critical if it is permitted to continue unchecked. But it is not hopeless, even at this late hour, if the complexity of the problem is recognized and accepted, and if the right combination of measures is launched. A rational and humane solution to the population problem is well within the capability of mankind provided that the appropriate decisions are taken both nationally and internationally. However, if the recent trends that have resulted in a worsened nutritional outlook for hundreds of millions are allowed to continue, there will be little chance of bringing birth rates down rapidly enough to avert disaster.

14.

SIMPLIFYING DIETS

Efforts to ensure an adequate diet for all mankind can no longer concentrate almost wholly on expanding the supply of food. A reduction in the projected future demand for food must be considered at the same time. In Chapter 13 we outlined a strategy for putting on the demographic brakes. Almost equally important is the need to curb the growth in per capita consumption among the more affluent people in the world, those who are already overeating.

ECONOMY, ECOLOGY, AND HEALTH

Today, several important factors are encouraging simplification of diets among the affluent: the need to economize on food expenditures in order to counter the effects of inflation at the household level; the need to reduce various ecological stresses associated with efforts to expand food production continuously; and the need to reduce intake of livestock products for health reasons. In addition to these self-interest reasons, there is of course a moral reason for simplifying diets. In a world of scarcity, if some of us consume more, others must of necessity consume less. The moral issue is raised by the fact that those who are consuming less are not so much the overweight affluent but the already undernourished poor.

The economic advantages of simplifying diets derive from some basic variations in the cost of different foods. Protein is much more costly than carbohydrates. Animal protein is more costly than vegetable protein, and some forms of animal protein are much more costly than others (Table 14–1). Many of us consume far more protein than we need. These are the factual bases from which we can derive a strategy to reduce food expenditures substantially while improving our health.

The pressures to economize on food expenditures derive in part from rising prices as more and more people in the world compete for inadequate food supplies. Reducing protein intake or substituting vegetable protein for animal protein helps to cut down on individual food expenditures. It also helps to cope with inflation in general. The simplification of diets among the affluent will also help lessen global inflationary pressures.

TABLE 14–1. COST OF ONE THIRD OF DAILY PROTEIN NEEDS, FROM SELECTED SOURCES.[a]

Food	Cost of 20 Grams of Protein (cents)
Peanut Butter	13
Dry beans	19
Eggs	20
Chicken	21
Milk	23
Hamburger	25
Canned tuna	25
Ham	31
Frankfurters	43
Chuck roast of beef	44
Lamb chops	65
Bacon	66
Porterhouse beefsteak	69
Veal cutlets	73

[a] April, 1974, prices, United States.

SOURCE: U.S. Department of Agriculture.

The ecological reasons for simplifying diets are quite persuasive. We need to remind ourselves that per capita claims on the world's food-producing resources vary among countries not by a modest percentage but by as much as a factor of five to one. The ecological costs of continuous efforts to expand food supplies have become increasingly evident. They manifest themselves in the form of eutrophication of fresh water lakes and streams as chemical fertilizer use multiplies and as feedlots, with their tremendous waste disposal problems, grow in size and number. Ecological stresses also result from the sharply accelerating world use of pesticides, as well as from the clearing of more and more land for agriculture. Even a modest decline in the consumption of livestock products among the more affluent could help relieve pressures on the earth's agricultural ecosystem.

The health reasons for simplifying diets may be the most persuasive of all. The American Heart Association has become quite convinced of the relationship between the rise in consumption of livestock products, particularly the fattier meats, and the incidence of coronary heart disease among Americans. It is now recommending that Americans reduce per capita meat consumption by about one third. Beyond this it recommends that the meat consumption patterns be shifted to de-emphasize beef and pork and emphasize poultry, which is lower in saturated fats.

Purchasing power in the more affluent countries has climbed steadily since World War II, reducing economic constraints on the amount of livestock products consumed. Most people have continued to increase the amount of meat in their diets without pausing to consider what the optimum level might be. Today doctors, particularly those specializing in heart disease, are forcing that question upon us. They are saying, in effect, that we are eating more meat than is good for us. If per capita meat consumption in the United States does decline, it may be possible again to resume the upward trend in life expectancy for American males, which has been arrested over the past decade. Harvard nutritionist Jean Mayer dramatizes the urgency with which the medical community is viewing the problem:

Coronary atherosclerosis is the number-one health problem in the United States, with one million Americans killed or permanently disabled every year. In many ways it must be considered a "disease of civilization" brought about in part by our mode of life: a diet overabundant in calories derived from saturated fat (and sucrose) and too high in cholesterol, an almost total lack of physical activity.

and heavy cigarette smoking. These have created conditions new to the human race. The United States is particularly hard hit by this new pandemic. The quintupling of our health expenditures in the past 20 years, the results of the most fertile period in medical research ever, have been nullified by the ever mounting tide of heart disease.*

The various arguments cited here in behalf of a significant decline in per capita consumption of livestock products in the United States, and therefore in per capita claims of Americans on the earth's agricultural resources, will appeal to different individuals in varying degrees. There are few Americans who will not be influenced in some measure by at least one of these factors. The 1973 decline in per capita beef consumption in the United States from 116 to 109 pounds was largely, though not entirely, economic in origin. But ecological and health considerations also are beginning to influence the dietary habits of growing numbers of people. Many young people in the United States and other developed countries have become semivegetarians or vegetarians for a variety of health and spiritual reasons.

Adjustment in the consumption of livestock products among the more affluent for health reasons is probably only beginning. But it is worth noting that the warnings of doctors probably did help reduce U.S. per capita consumption of eggs from 334 in 1960 to 293 in 1973. There is now a near-consensus among doctors on the contributive role of animal fats to heart disease. Any doctor treating a heart attack victim in the United States who did not prescribe a restricted intake of animal fats would probably be suspected of malpractice. As the possible adverse effects of excessive beef consumption become more widely recognized, reduction similar to that of eggs may follow. Meanwhile, nutrition-education programs should take into account the growing case against overconsumption of livestock products.

As Table 14–2 shows, only a few other industrialized nations (Australia, Canada, West Germany, France, and the United King-

* Jean Mayer, "Heart Disease: Plans for Action," in J. Mayer, ed., *U.S. Nutritional Policies in the Seventies* (San Francisco: W. H. Freeman, 1973), p. 44.

dom) have yet approached U.S. levels of meat consumption. The converging economic, ecological, health, and moral considerations may discourage these and other nations from trying to follow in American dietary footsteps. Most European nations, for example, might well think in terms of stabilizing, if not actually reducing, per capita consumption of livestock products. The consumption of beef in particular might be discouraged in favor of poultry, which takes fewer resources to produce.

TABLE 14–2. GROWTH IN PER CAPITA MEAT CONSUMPTION IN SELECTED INDUSTRIAL COUNTRIES, 1960 TO 1972.

Country	1960 Meat Consumption[a]	1972 Meat Consumption[a]	Increase (per cent)
	(pounds per year)		
United States	208	254	22
Australia	234	235	0
France	168	212	26
Canada	167	211	26
United Kingdom	158	171	8
West Germany	144	192	33
Sweden	109	112	3
U.S.S.R.	80	104	30
Italy	70	136	94
Yugoslavia	62	75	21
Spain	51	96	88
Japan	14	51	364

[a] Includes beef, veal, pork, mutton, lamb, goat, horse, poultry, edible offals, other.

SOURCES: OECD, *Meat Balances in OECD Member Countries, 1959–1972* (Paris, January, 1974). U.S.S.R. data from U.S. Dept. of Agriculture.

VEGETABLE OILS FOR ANIMAL FATS

In examining the prospects for the substitution of vegetable protein for animal protein, it is instructive to review the substitution of vegetable oils for animal fats over the past generation in the United States. In 1940, on the eve of World War II, Americans were consuming large quantities of animal fats; butter and lard were staples of the diet and were widely used for cooking in virtually every American home. At that time Americans were consuming 17 pounds of butter a year and only 2 pounds of margarine. Since 1940, however, butter consumption has declined steadily while margarine consumption has increased, until today the average American consumes 12 pounds of margarine annually and less than 5 pounds of butter. This has occurred despite intensive resistance by the dairy industry—particularly during the 'forties—to the encroachment of margarine on the market for butter.

The gradual shift from butter to margarine has been the most conspicuous example within a more general substitution of vege-

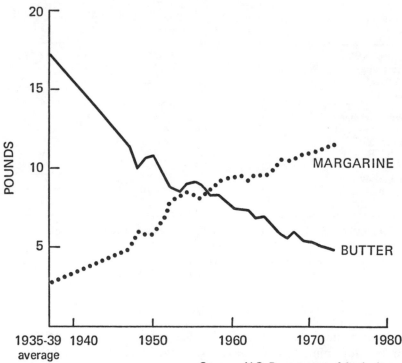

Source: U.S. Department of Agriculture.

Figure 14-1. U.S. Per Capita Consumption of Butter and Margarine, 1935-73

table oils for animal fats. The shift has been most impressive in the United States since 1950. In that year, consumption of animal fats and that of vegetable oils were almost exactly the same, just under 24 pounds each. As of the mid-'seventies, consumption of vegetable oils had climbed to nearly 40 pounds, while that of animal fats had dropped below 15 pounds. The ratio is now almost three to one in favor of vegetable oils.

This experience demonstrates that major transformations of dietary habits are possible. Just as the technological advance represented by hydrogenation (the conversion of a liquid vegetable oil into a solid at room temperature) greatly facilitated this process, so the process for producing textured soya protein is helping to set the stage for the potentially extensive substitution of vegetable protein for animal protein. How rapidly this will take place remains to be seen. We do know that a number of major food-processing firms are now mobilizing their research and marketing capacities with this in mind.

VEGETABLE PROTEIN FOR ANIMAL PROTEIN

The nutritional attractiveness of animal proteins derives from the excellent balance of the amino acids they contain. As already noted, amino acids are the building blocks from which protein is made. High-quality protein has a good balance of amino acids while low-quality protein is deficient in one or more of the essential amino acids. But animal protein is not the only available source of an appropriate balance of amino acids. The same balance can be achieved by consuming vegetable products in the right combination. For example, a proper combination of cereals and pulses (beans, peas, soybeans) usually provides an adequate and appropriate balance. Furthermore, synthetic amino acids can easily be added to manufactured vegetable food products in order to establish the proper protein balance, much as foods are enriched with vitamins.

Among the more prominent ways of substituting vegetable protein for animal protein are the use of vegetable-derived meat extenders for chopped meats, substitutes or imitation livestock products of vegetable origin, and alternatives to the consumption of livestock products in the form of high-quality protein vegetable products. In the United States, the production and marketing of soya-based extenders for chopped meat has accelerated dramatically since late 1973. Regulations have been altered to permit up to 30 per cent of chopped meats in school lunch programs, and any proportion (when properly identified) in commercial sales, to consist of soya protein. Increasing quantities of soya protein are being incorporated into various prepared meats and foods such as sausages and chili. Soya protein extenders already have been widely introduced in institutional cooking facilities throughout the United States, and as of mid-1974 direct commercial sales to the public also have become significant. The addition of textured vegetable protein to chopped and processed meat products not only reduces their cost but frequently also improves their flavor, cooking qualities, and nutritional value.

Another way of substituting vegetable protein for animal protein is through imitation livestock products that are actually of vegetable origin. The development of a technique for spinning soya protein into fibers, much as synthetic textile fibers are spun, makes it possible to simulate the fibrous texture of meat. Food technologists can now compress soya fibers into meat form and, with appropriate flavoring and coloring, came up with acceptable substitutes for beef, pork, and poultry. With livestock protein becoming more costly, this technique is likely to gain a strong commercial foothold in the near future.

The first important meat product for which substitution has succeeded commercially is bacon. The substitute looks and tastes like bacon, and while the extent of substitution is still small, it is growing. The substitute product has the advantages of being high in protein and low in fat, and it is storable without refrigeration. A large plant in Cedar Rapids, Iowa, processes soybeans from the surrounding countryside into "Bacos"—in direct competition with farmers in the community who still convert soybeans, along with corn, into bacon in the more traditional way, by feeding them to hogs.

Still another way to encourage substitution of vegetable products for animal products in the diet is to introduce alternative foods from the cuisine of other nations. In the Far East, for example, bean curd, made from soybeans, is an important source of high quality protein in the daily diet. Beans, peas, or lentils—all of which can be prepared in a variety of ways—are nutritious meat substitutes. A number of cookbooks have been published recently in the United States that offer nutritious and tasty recipes utilizing these and other non-livestock products. In 1974 the prestigious and scientifically cautious National Academy of Sciences gave its stamp of approval to vegetarian diets, concluding that "a vegetarian can be well nourished *if* he eats a variety of plant foods and gives attention to . . . critical nutrients."* However, one need not become a vegetarian to enjoy occasional creative meals that use little or no meat.

In the United States, at least some progress is being made in all these potential substitution areas. Indeed, it now seems doubtful that per capita beef consumption in the United States will reach the 140 pounds projected by the U.S. Department of Agriculture for 1985. The combination of factors at work suggests that we will probably not come close to that and in fact raises the prospect that per capita beef consumption could even decline from the level of the early 'seventies.

Nevertheless, beef plays a unique role in the world food economy. Grass-fed beef permits the conversion of vast quantities of roughage produced on land that is not suitable for the raising of crops into a high-quality, much sought-after protein product. Thus a substantial share of the world beef supply is produced with resources that could not be used to produce other foodstuffs.

However, when cattle are transferred from the range to the high-intensity feedlot, as they often are in North America, Europe, the Soviet Union, and Japan, they become extremely inefficient converters of grain into protein. Cattle fed on grass in grazing areas require no grain, but those on feedlots consume about *10 pounds* of grain for every pound of meat added. The total amount of grain used to produce a given amount of beef, then, depends upon how much time is spent on the feedlot. In the United States in recent years, the combination of range and feedlot production

* Committee on Nutritional Misinformation, National Academy of Sciences, "Vegetarian Diets," Washington, D.C.: May, 1974.

has resulted in an over-all average use of more than 4 pounds of grain for every pound of beef produced.

The crucial point is that, once grazing areas are more or less fully utilized, it becomes very costly in resource terms to satisfy additional growth in consumer demand, requiring the use of croplands and grains that could otherwise be used to meet human needs directly. *Additional* beef production in the developed countries is likely to occur largely on feedlots and therefore will require close to 10 pounds of grain for each added pound of beef produced.

Hogs and chickens are more efficient converters of grain into meat than cattle. In contrast to beef, pork and poultry in modern agricultural systems are produced almost entirely with feed concentrates. It takes about 4 pounds of grain to produce a pound of pork. Because of advances in breeding techniques and in the mixing of high-protein fish and oilseed meals with grains in feed rations, the efficiency of intensive broiler-chicken production in the United States has increased dramatically over the past few decades, to the point where scarcely 2 pounds of grain are now required to produce a pound of chicken meat. Turkeys are less efficient converters, requiring 4 pounds of grain for every pound of meat.

If the average U.S. citizen were to reduce his consumption of beef, pork, and poultry by 10 per cent in the next year, 12 million tons or more of grain would become available for purposes other than livestock production. If, over a multiyear period, consumption of these products were to stabilize instead of continuing to grow, as is currently projected, the annual savings of grain would be very large indeed. Even a modest shift from beef consumption to poultry would mean a very measurable reduction in grain requirements. Similar considerations, of course, apply to other nations where meat consumption is high and increasing.

An additional factor that complicates analysis of the pressures that rising meat consumption places on food resources is the varying efficiency with which livestock is produced in different nations. For example, livestock production in the Soviet Union is far less efficient than in the United States, requiring far more grain to produce a pound of meat, because of less efficient breeds, less sophisticated management practices, and a shortage of high-protein feedstuffs. Within the next decade, it is likely that total per capita grain use in the Soviet Union will actually surpass that in the United States—but the average Soviet citizen may be eating little more than half the meat consumed by the average American. If the Soviets were to attempt to increase meat consumption to U.S. levels without first substantially improving their production efficiency, they would place an extremely heavy burden on world grain supplies.

If the world's affluent minority continues to expand its consumption of livestock products, it will be outbidding the world's poor majority for food in two ways. Scarce agricultural resources and the grains and high-protein feeds they produce will increasingly be used to meet high-income consumer demands rather than direct human needs. Furthermore, the prices of available livestock products and other proteins will be pushed even farther beyond the reach of those who already most desperately need additional protein in their diets.

Eliminating Waste

The wastage of food today takes many forms, including overeating, overserving, and spoilage due to poor planning. A major cause of waste in the United States, Europe, the Soviet Union, and Japan is related to the shift of a large part of the blue-collar labor force to less strenuous white-collar work. The food needs of individuals experiencing this shift decline sharply, but their consumption habits generally change gradually if at all. The result is that many are overweight. There is an urgent need to adjust food intake so that it more closely matches food needs—both to safeguard health and to decrease food waste.

A great deal of food waste also results from mistaken or deliberate serving of oversize portions. This is partly the result of the practice of providing uniform servings for people of all sizes in various institutional situations such as restaurants. Most restaurants offer only two sizes of servings—one for adults and one for children—and some not even that. There is much to be said for having three sizes of servings. We simply have reached the point where we need to recognize that a 110-pound person does not need as much food as a 190-pound person. (But a 110-pound adult does require more food than a six-year-old child.) It should not be beyond the capacity of restaurants and other institutions to make these adjustments, which would result in an immediate major savings of food already produced.

Another important source of wastage is excess fat, especially characteristic of the beef and pork sold in the United States. Much of this fat is removed in the kitchen as the meat is prepared for cooking, and a great deal more once it reaches the plate. It makes no sense to waste significant amounts of resources on the production of fat in a society that no longer prizes or needs it. Unfortunately, our grading systems for meat still put a premium on excessive fat content. For beef to be labeled "choice" grade in the United States, for example, a high content of unused fat must be present—which is generally produced through extra grain feeding. This needs to be altered. The pork industry has made some progress in this area by shifting away from lard-type hogs to leaner, bacon-type hogs. Parallel efforts should be introduced by the beef industry as well. A similar form of waste continues to be encouraged within the milk industry, whose pricing system still rewards farmers for producing milk with a high fat content.

If those in the most affluent countries were to simplify their diets and reduce waste, the future over-all claims of these countries on the world's agricultural resources would be greatly diminished, freeing food resources and holding food prices lower for that still large segment of low-income, undernourished people in the world. Within the United States, population growth is slowing and could stabilize before many more years pass. A halt to growth in per capita food intake would permit over-all food consumption to stabilize or even decline. In West Germany, population growth stopped a few years ago. If the average German also begins to simplify his diet for the reasons outlined above, Germany's claims on world food resources will actually decline. Over time, moderate alterations in the eating habits of those in the more affluent nations could have an important cumulative effect, reducing the pressures of affluence on scarce world food resources.

15.

HUNGER AND UNEMPLOYMENT: MUTUAL SOLUTIONS?

Today most of the world's unexploited food-production potential is located in the poor countries, yet hunger remains widespread among their populations, and food production has been hard put to keep pace with population growth. At the same time, unemployment in these countries is rising to crisis proportions, leaving growing numbers without the means to improve their livelihood. For many people in the developing countries, economic and nutritional insecurity in turn provide a powerful incentive to have large families.

These difficult problems constitute the core of the development crisis, yet it is clear that the traditional view of "development," emphasizing an industrial-urban orientation and the expansion of total economic output with little regard for rural development and equity, has not done enough to solve them. Despite unparalleled economic growth rates in most developing countries throughout the 'sixties, much of mankind continues to live in desperate poverty. Growth in GNP has often failed to bring significant improvement to the lives of the poorest half of the population. In many countries, unemployment and income disparities continue to rise despite growth in output, and squalid urban squatter settlements continue to mushroom as the jobless pour in from countryside to city. The growth in food production has lagged far behind its potential rate, while a substantial part of the population remains unemployed, economically unproductive, and hence too poor to purchase an adequate diet even when food is available.

Improving the income and nutritional levels of the very poor, reducing unemployment and rural-urban migration, increasing the motivation for smaller families among those with the higher birth rates, and increasing global food output substantially in the coming years—all these urgent needs point in a common direction. Development policies need to be aimed at upgrading the well-being of the poor, not through charity, but by increasing opportunities for them to participate in productive activities.

UNEMPLOYMENT: TRENDS AND CAUSES

As we enter the final quarter of the twentieth century, the continually expanding number of people without jobs is becoming one of the world's gravest social ills. In many developing countries, entrants into the job market outnumber new jobs being created by two to one, creating levels of unemployment and underemployment far greater than any the rich countries have ever experienced. The population explosion that began in the poor countries at least fifteen or twenty years ago resulted in an almost immediate demand for food, but, since it takes time for infants to grow up, there was a grace period of fifteen or twenty years in the employment situation. In the mid-'seventies, however, this grace period is ending. In Latin America, for example, the number of unemployed tripled in the fifteen years from 1950 to 1965, climbing from 2.9 million to 8.8 million. The visible unemployment rate went from less than 6 per cent to over 11 per cent during this period. Available data indicate that the ranks of the unemployed are continuing to swell at an alarming rate.

Adding to an already dismal prospect, the classical definition of the unemployed—those seeking work at the prevailing wage rates —greatly understates the extent of unemployment because it does not measure hidden unemployment or underemployment. According to Eric Thorbecke, who has examined the employment situation in Latin America in considerable detail:

> If one considers unemployment as the ratio of available but unused labor hours to the total available labor hours, which is one way of measuring both unemployment and underemployment, the magni-

tude and the seriousness of the problem are magnified. For one continent, Latin America, this technique revealed unemployment equivalent rates ranging from 20 per cent in some countries to over 50 per cent in others. For the region as a whole it was 26 per cent. This was based on data for 1960.*

If the same data were available for 1970, they would undoubtedly show a much higher unemployment equivalent.

During the 'seventies, India's labor force is projected to increase from 210 million to 273 million. Already plagued with widespread unemployment and underemployment, it is now confronted with 100,000 entrants into the labor force *each week*. Asian economist Harry T. Oshima estimates that at least 15 per cent of the labor force is unemployed in Pakistan, Sri Lanka, Malaysia, and the Philippines. One third of Bangladesh's available manpower may be unemployed. Indonesia's working-age population is growing by an estimated 1.8 million annually; one fourth of the nation's potential labor force may now be unemployed.

Looking at the developing nations as a whole, the International Labor Office (ILO) estimates that 24.7 per cent of the total labor force was either unemployed or underemployed in 1970. The comparable figure for 1980 is expected to rise to 29.5 per cent. Among the most alarming socio-economic projections to the end of the century are those of growth in the labor force. Between 1970 and the end of the century, the labor force in the less developed nations is projected by the ILO to expand by 91 per cent, nearly doubling within the span of a single generation. Projected labor-force growth for the more developed regions during this period is 33 per cent (see Table 15–1).

In the less developed nations, the employment crisis has been particularly conspicuous in the form of urban unemployment. People with little hope of a meaningful life in the rural areas are moving on a massive scale to the cities, where they frequently are idle or subsist on whatever casual work can be found. Populations of urban centers in Africa, Asia, and Latin America are growing at 5 to 8 per cent yearly, almost regardless of the existing degree of

---

* Erik Thorbecke, "Unemployment and Underemployment in the Developing World," paper presented at Columbia University Conference on International Economic Development, February, 1970, p. 11.

TABLE 15-1. PROJECTED GROWTH IN WORLD LABOR
FORCE, 1970-2000.

	1970	1980	1990	2000	1970-2000 (per cent change)
		(millions)			
More Developed Nations					
Economically active population: total	488	542	592	649	+33
In agriculture	101	75	49	22	—88
Other	387	467	543	627	+62
Less Developed Regions					
Economically active population: total	1,011	1,239	1,547	1,933	+91
In agriculture	669	725	786	842	+26
Other	342	514	761	1,091	+219

SOURCE: International Labor Office.

urbanization. Urban centers with growth rates of 5 per cent double in size in fourteen years; those growing at 8 per cent yearly double in nine years and quadruple in eighteen years.

In the past, many development experts have emphasized the need for large-scale industrialization—almost always urban in nature—to absorb the growth in the national labor force. Consistent with this emphasis has been a view of agriculture as an inefficient, low-potential repository of surplus labor for the growing "modern" sector of industry and services. The past three decades, however, have demonstrated the futility often implicit in such an approach.

In most developing nations no conceivable rate of growth in the manufacturing sector will provide enough jobs to absorb all the new potential workers, even if it is optimistically assumed that new industries will utilize highly labor-intensive techniques. Moreover, recent research findings have confirmed the conclusion that attacking unemployment and poverty primarily by upgrading urban conditions and employment levels often merely increases the flood to the cities, as a result of making urban centers more attractive than the countryside. Finally, urban-oriented economic growth in a context of rural agrarian stagnation will generally create serious food-supply problems for a poor nation. The need to spend scarce foreign exchange on food imports, domestic inflation, and a constrained over-all economic growth rate are often the consequences of agricultural stagnation in developing nations.

In order to reduce migration to the overburdened cities, increase national and world food supplies, and provide the opportunity for a decent income for the billions who do remain in the countryside, the encouragement of labor-creating agricultural development must assume priority in most development programs. In coming decades, a majority of the people in the developing world will earn their livelihood through agriculture—or they will earn no livelihood at all. Today, roughly 70 per cent of the people in the developing world live in rural areas. Demographic projections by the World Bank indicate that more than half the developing world's population will still be living in the countryside by the year 2000, despite persistently high rates of migration to the cities.

Unrealized Agronomic Potential

Ironically, although the developing countries as a group now face difficult problems of food supply, they also constitute the world's greatest reservoir of untapped food-production potential. In some developing countries, the introduction of new high-yielding seeds and other required inputs has raised per-acre yields substantially. But some of the advances of the last decade appear very dramatic only because yields were extremely low in the first place.

Today, rice yields per acre in India and Nigeria still average only one third those of Japan, and corn yields in Thailand and Brazil are less than one third those in the United States. Very large increases in food production are possible in many developing countries—and, as we have noted, at far lower cost in additional fertilizer and energy resources than in the agriculturally advanced nations. If yield levels in India were raised to levels approaching those in the United States, for example, India's total grain production, now about 100 million tons, could easily double. If rice farmers in Bangladesh attained Japanese yield levels, rice production would more than triple, jumping from 12 million to 39 million tons.

The crises in food production and employment facing the developing world are closely intertwined; exploitation of the tremendous agronomic potential in those countries can simultaneously do much to provide the vast numbers of new jobs that will be required there in the coming decades. With appropriate government policies, idle manpower can be harnessed for the intensive cultivation of farmlands—the key to higher food production in the developing world.

A People-oriented Development Strategy

It will not be enough, however, merely to encourage the development of agricultural productivity. In theory, productivity can be increased within a framework of large, highly mechanized landholdings or in one of intensively worked smallholder farms. But development of the first type only exacerbates unemployment, poverty, and rural-urban migration. The poor may be unable to buy or produce the food necessary for an adequate diet, not to mention the political and social consequences of such a development pattern. By contrast, developing efficient small farms can help spread the benefits of growth throughout a much larger portion of the population. A wider distribution of benefits will, in turn, establish the groundwork for checking rapid population growth—which amplifies the intensity of both the food problem and the employment problem—by reducing the insecurities that provide an important motivation for large families among the poor.

Furthermore, a generation of experience shows that in most poor nations small, intensively worked farms actually produce *more* per acre than large farms. This is particularly true where the Green Revolution varieties, which thrive with extremely careful land preparation, planting, weeding, and water control, are utilized. Per-acre yields in India on the average farm of less than 5 acres are more than 40 per cent greater than those on farms of more than 50 acres. In Taiwan, where farmers with small holdings have been provided with supporting services and inputs, farms of less than 2.5 acres provide considerably higher yields than farms of more than 5 acres. In Mexico, government-distributed *ejidos* and private small-holdings are more productive than large private farms. Similar evidence is available from a large variety of developing nations. It has been shown that government policies that promote smallholder, labor-intensive agriculture can at the same time provide higher incomes for the destitute rural masses and increase food production dramatically.

Of course, it is not added labor by itself that makes for higher productivity. Often labor can be used intensively to achieve maximum productivity only when irrigation and water-control facilities are sufficiently reliable to permit multiple cropping and efficient utilization of high-yielding seeds. Thus government or private investments to improve water supplies and control, where adequate water is available, may be a precondition for greatly intensifying the use of labor on the land with profitable results.

Whether or not the great food-producing potential of the developing world is tapped will depend on both the extent to which developing-country governments are willing to adopt the policies necessary to maximize rural development and the extent to which the economically advanced nations and international aid agencies are willing and able to provide appropriate financial and technical assistance.

Many developing-country governments continue to devote a disproportionate share of their development resources to large-scale industrial development, mechanized agriculture on large farms, and the provision of social services in a few major cities. All too many national-development plans of the past two decades have paid lip-service to the imperatives of rural development but in practice have allocated little money or attention to this relatively unglamorous sector. As long as national priorities remain skewed in this direction, little progress can be expected toward halting rural-urban migration, the spread of unemployment, and agricultural stagnation.

The development of smallholder, labor-intensive agriculture requires a major commitment of resources on the part of governments. In addition to irrigation and water-control facilities (where possible) and proper price incentives (making it profitable for a farmer to purchase and use modern inputs), several interrelated services are essential to rural agrarian progress. These services, which former Agricultural Development Council President Arthur T. Mosher has aptly called a "progressive rural structure," include a rational system of market towns where products are sold and supplies purchased, rural roads, local verification trials of improved seeds and new crops, extension services, and credit facilities. Providing such a structure for small farmers—thereby giving them access to the means for increased productivity—is an arduous task in any nation, but it is the necessary basis for any real progress in reducing unemployment and hunger.

Providing small farmers with access to the modernization process requires technical aid and economic adjustments, such as new seeds and fertilizer and a fair price for agricultural products, but it also involves profound changes in national development strategies and political and social patterns. For example, meeting the minimum needs of the rural majority for literacy and practical education and establishing a network of agricultural extension services on the required scale may necessitate a sharp drop in the funds allocated to subsidizing Western-style, urban-oriented education. Meeting the basic health-care needs of the rural majority likewise may mean less expenditure on large urban hospitals and more paramedics, midwives, and small rural clinics.

Spreading agricultural-extension services and credit more widely among farmers is likely to be much more difficult, frustrating, and expensive than concentrating development efforts among a small minority of "progressive" farmers, and it is likely to encounter strong political resistance from the more prosperous farmers who benefited from the old distribution of services and from other traditional rural elites (such as money-lenders or village leaders) whose positions depend on the persistence of rigid inequities. Reform in land ownership or tenancy regulations also is likely to meet even greater opposition from those who stand to lose from the redistribution.

Carrying out the fundamental reforms often needed to attack the problems of small-farm production, employment, and poorly distributed social services is never an easy task, and it is difficult to generalize about the requirements for success. Clearly, however, one basic prerequisite for widespread improvements in rural welfare and productivity is a national government that understands the need for a reorientation in strategy and is firmly committed to pushing through reforms. Strong initiatives to create participatory institutions at the local level, such as cooperatives or effective township associations (as in Taiwan), may help both in the provision of services to farmers and in the undermining of traditional rural political patterns that favor an elite minority.

In many poor countries rapid agricultural development will not be possible without international support to complement a strong political commitment to agrarian progress on the part of developing-country governments. Both bilateral and multilateral aid agencies can help to finance the tools, fertilizers, machinery, research, and technical advice that are necessary. Outside aid cannot substitute for a strong commitment to progress and proper allocation of resources on the part of developing countries themselves, but it can provide the government of a poor country with part of the resources it needs if development efforts are to have a chance of success.

A very encouraging recent trend has been the effort by the World Bank, under the leadership of Robert McNamara, to provide much greater attention to and assistance for the problems of small farmers, food production, and rural development. Also encouraging is the new bipartisan aid legislation passed by the U.S. Congress in 1973, which directs a larger share of the AID program to agriculture, rural development, and the basic needs of the poor majority. Agencies like these are providing valuable support for agricultural-development efforts that will help build world food supplies—but they must be provided with more ample financial resources if the deteriorating food and employment situations are to be arrested.

APPROPRIATE TECHNOLOGIES

The farm-mechanization issue is extremely complex. On the one hand, it can contribute to the efficiency required for higher output and can make available the labor necessary for multiple cropping by speeding up harvesting and seeding procedures. On the other hand, mechanization does not use resources efficiently where the most abundant resource is labor, since it does not necessarily improve yields. Further, the life of a tractor investment may be shorter than that of the traditional bullock because of the lack of spare machine parts and mechanical know-how. The solution may be to encourage *selective* mechanization and thus satisfy the requirements for efficiency while minimizing the displacement of rural labor.

The mechanization of irrigation is a case in point. Traditional methods of irrigation, using human or animal power, often do not supply enough water to meet minimum crop needs. More important in this context, however, is the fact that phenomenal savings occur when mechanized water pumping is introduced. One study of pumping costs in India found that it costs 495 rupees to pump 10 acre-inches of water by hand, assuming a 40-foot lift. With draft animals used to provide the power to operate a Persian wheel, the cost drops to 345 rupees. But the really startling gain is the decline of cost to 60 rupees with the use of a diesel engine. As more water becomes available and production is boosted, more labor is required for land preparation, planting, fertilizing, weeding, harvesting, and threshing.

Once the availability of water and fertilizer permits continuous year-round cropping, there is increased pressure to reduce the time between the ripening of one crop and the planting of the next. Dr. Lyle Schertz of the U.S. Department of Agriculture estimates that a rice farmer in Asia who uses the new varieties of seeds faces a loss of 30 pounds of grain per acre for every day that his land lies idle between crops. This is equal to the amount necessary to feed one adult for a month. With this in mind, neither governments nor farmers can afford to leave land idle. The more intensive the use of land, the more jobs are created. When multiple cropping becomes possible, labor requirements may double or even triple, depending on the number of crops.

Crop production consists of a sequence of operations distributed throughout the year. Where only human labor is available, labor scarcity at planting and harvesting times can be the principal factor limiting food production. Mechanization of selected operations can overcome labor shortages during peak periods, raising the level of farm activity throughout the year.

Taiwan provides a good example of how selective mechanization, combined with intensive land use, creates jobs. In Taiwan, some farmers are growing three and four crops a year. Seedbed preparation is hastened by the use of Japanese-style tillers, comparable to the larger garden tractors used in the United States. Use of these two-wheeled, four- to ten-horsepower tillers reduces the labor required to prepare the seedbed but increases the number of crops produced, creating more employment.

In some developing nations, particularly in parts of Africa, where unused land is still available, the widespread adoption or improved use of animal power would represent an appropriate and significant strategy for rural progress. Animal power can substitute for the drudgery of cultivation by human muscle power alone, permitting extension of the area farmed, higher yields, and increased employment and income. Acquisition and maintenance of oxen and associated equipment are relatively cheap, and the requisite management techniques are likely to be within the capacities of rural farmers. Animal power has the further advantage over tractor mechanization of creating a demand for simple products like carts and plows which can be manufactured profitably on a small scale in rural areas, thus generating additional jobs beyond the farm. When animal power is already in use, the adoption of improved plows and supplementary equipment is frequently a more economically appropriate means of technical advancement than a shift to large tractors.

The pattern of technology adopted by private farmers or government agencies is strongly affected by a variety of government policies. Overvalued exchange rates, artificially low interest rates on capital, direct subsidies (such as tax or tariff breaks) for tractors and other capital goods, and high minimum-wage laws can all promote the adoption of large-scale mechanization even where the society would reap greater benefit from more labor-intensive technologies. Removing such factor distortions can encourage the wider utilization of labor, which generally remains the most abundant factor available in the developing world.

Agrarian Reform

Because the relationship of man to land is so instrumental in defining the relationship of man to man, the issue of land reform invariably raises sensitive political and social questions. Nevertheless, where land ownership and tenancy patterns seriously inhibit rural-development efforts, the case for reform is compelling.

Such a situation exists most obviously today in large parts of Latin America, where the concentration of land ownership in a very small segment of the population is a major barrier to both agricultural progress and employment generation. Vast tracts of land continue to be owned by absentee landlords with little interest in commercial agriculture—which is one reason the Green Revolution has made little progress in the continent where it originated. In parts of Asia and elsewhere, unregulated tenancy practices leave sharecroppers with little protection from capricious, unreasonable rent hikes, which in turn reduce incentives for increased output and investment. In other countries, especially in Africa, the incentive to modernize agriculture is sometimes lacking for another reason: the arbitrary determination of land titles by a chief or headman tends to discourage long-term investment in the land.

Effective land reform can take many forms depending on local agricultural, economic, and political conditions. It may mean the expropriation of large holdings and the subsequent redistribution of parcels to formerly landless laborers and tenants. The goals of land reform also may be satisfied by strong governmental measures to control the terms of land rentals in order to ensure long-term security of tenure at fair prices for tenant farmers. In some cases, the opening up of new areas for settlement and the granting of titles to those who did not previously own land may serve as an alternative to other kinds of land reform. This pattern is of course politically less painful. In many countries, however, it is no longer an open alternative, and in those where it is an option, it generally requires heavy capital investment by the state over a long period of time.

Where it is accompanied by the necessary supporting services for farmers, effective land reform tends to increase per-acre labor inputs substantially. Farmers who feel confident that they personally will benefit from yield increases are much more likely to spend time during slack seasons enhancing the land by constructing buildings, fences, irrigation and drainage facilities, and other improvements, which in turn permit greater use of yield-raising labor during the crop seasons. Farmers with a secure position on the land are also much more likely to save and make the long-term capital investment in tubewells or low-lift pumps, improved plows, or power tillers, which accelerate yields and labor utilization.

Over time, land reform nearly always spurs increases in farm productivity per acre for the same reasons it promotes intensive use of labor. Some nations, including Mexico, Bolivia, Cuba, and Iraq, have experienced an initial drop in the marketed farm output in the years immediately following land reform. This is not surprising; the unavoidable disruptions associated with the process of redistributing or resettling land are not conducive to immediate production expansion. Many who find themselves owners of land for the first time lack even rudimentary management skills and consequently may be heavily dependent at first on government subsidies and services.

But such problems are hardly a reason to oppose land reform where it is needed. Instead, they illustrate the need for government actions to ensure the availability to the small farmer of extension advice, credit, and other necessary services. Giving the smallholder farmer access to such services for the first time may entail a political commitment equal to that required by the land-reform measure itself; without such access, however, the desired effects of the reform may be blunted. Even in nations where land tenancy is not an obstacle to rural progress, there remains a need for such broad agrarian reform—for redesigning rural institutions and government services to meet the needs of smaller farmers.

Considerable evidence supports the assertion that, over the longer term, land reform results in increased agricultural productivity. Surveying yields before and after land reforms in a variety of nations, Peter Dorner and Donald Kanel conclude: "The evidence available on post-reform experiences—in Mexico, Bolivia, Chile, Japan, Taiwan, Egypt—shows that although in some cases there was an initial drop, average productivity per unit of land increased rather substantially after these reforms. All cases involved a reduction in the average size of farms."[*]

* Peter Dorner and Donald Kanel, "The Economic Case for Land Reform: Employment, Income Distribution, and Production," in *Land Reform in Latin America: Issues and Cases* (Madison: University of Wisconsin Press, 1971), p. 54.

By aiding the development of small-farm agriculture, land reform also increases the contribution of agriculture to integrated rural development and national economic growth. Productive small farms in turn create market demand for the consumer goods and tools necessary for the growth of national industries. Small farmers struggling to attain a decent standard of living are much less likely than wealthy large landowners to spend a high proportion of their income on luxury imports.

RURAL PUBLIC WORKS

In many poor nations, considerable labor remains idle or underutilized during the off seasons between harvest and planting, while there remains a great need to create the agricultural infrastructure —market roads; flood control, irrigation, and drainage schemes; terraces; reforestation programs; and rural electrification—to permit productive employment of this same wasted human potential. With the proper infrastructure and intensive use of labor, the land in such areas could be used to provide considerably more food for both the rural and the growing urban populations. Mobilizing unused rural manpower for the labor-intensive construction or repair of necessary infrastructure not only can create temporary employment for the otherwise unemployed but also can provide a basis for the productive *long-term* employment of previously idle labor without a continuing need for government-financed projects. Irrigation and drainage projects, for example, not only increase yields per harvest but can also make possible multiple cropping and the resulting multiplication of labor use and food production.

An effective rural-works program may have other less quantifiable but equally valuable results. People seemingly left out of the development process can become active participants in a project with visible returns to their own welfare—an intangible benefit of inestimable value. The bringing together of large numbers of rural laborers also gives the local or national government an excellent opportunity to supply schooling in literacy, agricultural science, family planning, or nutrition as well as on-the-job training connected with the construction projects themselves.

The use of rural public-works schemes to provide employment

and carry out needed construction projects is not a new idea. More than 6,000 years ago, the peoples of Egypt constructed an impressive network of dikes and canals to control the flood of the Nile; these cooperative labor projects preceded the era of the great Egyptian dynasties whose more dramatic public-works projects we now regard with such awe. Twentieth-century agricultural-development efforts in the Tigris and Euphrates valleys have been directed at least partly toward restoring the irrigation systems first constructed 5,000 years ago. Well-organized labor crews have been improving the productivity of farmland in China for more than a thousand years. Since World War II, several nations in Asia and North Africa have undertaken major public-works programs, and local efforts of lesser scale have been carried out in numerous other developing nations.

In China, improved water supplies and water control have been the prerequisites of agricultural progress for many centuries, since a large portion of the cultivated land is extremely vulnerable to frequent droughts, floods, and waterlogging. Over the last millennium, untold numbers of small-scale public-works projects have been carried out during slack seasons; such valuable improvements as canals, drainage systems, wells, small dams, and terraces were constructed with few mechanical aids. Effective water control permitted considerable expansion of the area planted to highly productive wet rice rather than dryland crops, particularly in the country's southern regions, and also greatly increased the area suitable for double cropping—which represented a major advance. Yet China's recent experience with labor-intensive rural construction programs has not been entirely positive. Many of the irrigation projects built in the late 'fifties, during the Great Leap Forward, turned out to be inadequate to withstand major droughts or flooding. However, since that period such projects have been gradually improved and have resulted in a steady increase in the area of dependable irrigation.

The FAO estimates that 25 billion man-days of labor are being expended in China annually in irrigation, water conservation, reforestation, and other land-improvement schemes during the slack seasons. Labor-intensive improvements in water storage and conservation significantly reduced the negative effects of a serious drought in China in 1972. The experience of China with the use of labor in rural areas clearly deserves far more careful examination by other nations, most of which have not yet exploited the potential gains of labor mobilization to improve agricultural productivity to the same extent.

Rural public-works programs often have considerable potential as means of utilizing idle manpower to build the future productive and employment potential of rural regions. Such projects cannot, however, eliminate the need for proper government policies in a variety of other areas. Faulty government policies on land tenure, credit, or capital subsidies can undermine the desired impact of rural construction by enriching those who already are well off rather than the target group of rural poor.

Since a successful rural-development program may imply a redistribution of income as well as other political and social consequences that are threatening to rural elites, a strong national political commitment to rural progress is an absolute prerequisite of a successful rural-works program. John W. Thomas of Harvard University, who has studied rural-works programs in several countries, has observed that without high-level, strong political support, there is no chance that public works programs will have the reform-type benefits which are usually considered part of their purpose. Attempts to utilize a works program for purely political ends or tolerance of a high level of corruption in project management—both of which helped undermine the initial success of East Pakistan's works scheme in the late 'sixties—will inevitably weaken or even destroy the effectiveness of rural-development efforts.

SUMMARY

The encouragement of labor-intensive agricultural modernization in the developing countries, with a special emphasis on the smaller farms where most of the very poor live, and the provision of such basic services as education, health, and farm credit to the poor majority are all basic elements of the strategy needed to help solve both food-supply and employment problems. Contrary to the belief of many economists and government officials, such a "people-oriented" strategy need not impede over-all economic growth. Indeed, idle manpower constitutes a valuable but wasted resource. Put to work to produce food and other needed consumer goods, it can accelerate economic growth as well as ensure more widespread distribution of its benefits among the population.

In many countries, adopting the policies outlined here to help meet employment, food-production, and population goals will require major changes in the way in which power is exercised. Such changes will not be easy. Established interests in any country naturally resist reforms aimed at removing much of their power. Effective land-reform programs require a shift in power from landlord to tenant. Effective low-cost health systems that reach an entire population require changes in doctors' professional attitudes and standards to permit widespread use of less costly, but also less qualified, paramedics.

We know how difficult such adjustments are in a wealthy, modern society like the United States; Americans are still at odds over the "hows" and "whys" of full employment and national health-care policies. Yet if leaders in developing countries pursue economic growth without reforming existing political, economic, and social structures, the ultimate result will be failure to reach national goals.

The need for a reorientation of development strategies in most poor countries transcends such particular concerns as food output and employment. Providing greater access to the development process among the rural masses is the only hope of giving a vast share of mankind a productive, dignified role in society and allowing hundreds of millions an opportunity to fulfill their human potential and aspirations. That this will simultaneously help to meet world food needs (keeping food prices lower for everyone) and set the stage for a slowing of population growth is a further incentive for pursuing such a strategy.

16.

ALLEVIATING INSECURITY:
SPECIAL MEASURES

Following calls for an emergency international conference to consider the world food situation—notably by the 1973 Algiers Conference of Non-Aligned Nations and U.S. Secretary of State Henry Kissinger—the United Nations determined to hold a World Food Conference in Rome in November, 1974, to test the political commitment of nations to working toward potential solutions. A single conference convened on short notice can hardly be expected to work out detailed global responses to the problems threatening our collective welfare. It does, however, provide an opportunity to lay the groundwork for cooperative efforts to reverse the ominous trends that are now coming into view.

Underlying all the issues considered at the Conference will be the twin imperatives of rapidly increasing world food production, with special emphasis on the progress of the small farms of the developing world, and of reducing growth in the global demand for food by slowing population growth everywhere and simplifying diets among the more affluent. These goals, and the need to reduce future food insecurity and associated economic instability call for several key policy measures. A new international approach to food reserves, for example, is now essential if wild gyrations in world food prices are to be controlled. The evolution of such a system will require a firm political commitment on the part of governments in both food-exporting and food-importing nations. New international guidelines are also needed to cover the responsibilities of food-exporting nations in times of scarcity and to improve the international sharing of information on national harvests and import needs. Future food-aid needs—and means of meeting them—will also have to be considered at the conference. Finally, a renewed commitment by governments to help meet critical agricultural-research needs, through both international and national efforts, is called for.

A Food Reserve

World food production varies with fluctuations in weather; world food consumption needs continue to rise rather steadily regardless of price and supply trends. Under these circumstances, production and prices are likely to fluctuate violently, to the detriment of both farmers and consumers, unless sufficient reserve stocks are available to cushion the market from supply changes.

The prospects of frequently tight food supplies and low reserves call for the creation of a new internationally managed system of food reserves, to be built up in times of relative abundance and drawn down in times of acute scarcity. This can help support prices for producers during the inevitable periods when supply exceeds immediate world demand and to restrain price increases for consumers during times of scarcity. In effect, the stability that surplus American agricultural capacity has provided for a generation can be restored at least partially by a world food-reserve system. Clearly such a system is in the best interests of all nations. Clearly also the world community has a basic humanitarian interest in seeing to it that famine does not occur in the densely populated low-income countries following poor crop years. The affluent nations may be less able to provide this assurance in the future if the current system of autonomous, nationally oriented food planning is allowed to continue without modification.

In 1973, A. H. Boerma, Director-General of the U.N. Food and Agriculture Organization (FAO), proposed the creation of a new system of internationally coordinated national food-reserve policies. Under the FAO plan, all nations—both exporters and importers— would hold agreed minimum levels of food stocks. Governments would consult regularly to review the food situation, evaluate the adequacy of existing stocks, and recommend necessary actions.

The plan received preliminary international approval at the
FAO's biannual conference in November, 1973. If it is to be implemented effectively, the United States must give it strong political
and economic support at the World Food Conference in November, 1974, and thereafter. In the past, the United States has provided the world with safe reserve levels largely as a side benefit of
its domestic farm-income program. As we have noted, in the
current seller's market for foodstuffs these reserves—both large
grain stocks and idled cropland—have been reduced substantially.
In these conditions, it would be highly unrealistic to expect the
United States alone to bear the considerable expense of building
grain reserves large enough to ensure world security. The FAO
plan has the advantage of spreading responsibility for reserve
maintenance among both the exporting and the importing nations
of the world.

Under any world-reserve plan, special measures will be necessary to help poor nations establish storage facilities and build up
needed reserves. Such measures might include concessional grain
sales to help the *poorest* nations build up reserve stocks, and a new
source of concessional assistance, perhaps in the form of an ear-
marked expansion of the World Bank's soft-loan program or of a
special fund within the FAO.

But spreading responsibility for reserve-stock management more
widely among nations does not absolve the United States and
other leading exporters from the responsibility of maintaining
reserve stocks. There has been formidable resistance in some
quarters of the U.S. government to public involvement in reserve
management—a practice recently ended by the Nixon Administration. Citing the problems of farm programs in previous decades,
when the government found itself saddled with massive surpluses
that helped to depress farm prices and were very costly to store,
some highly placed officials have suggested that all U.S. reserves
should be held in private commercial hands.

The events of the last two years, however, have demonstrated
the dangerous and economically disruptive consequences—in the
domestic as well as the world economy—of not establishing careful
reserve management. Sudden supply and price changes have had a
crippling impact on the U.S. livestock, baking, and canning indus-

tries, as well as on efforts to manage the national economy and bring inflation under control. Unexpected export controls on soybeans and other high-protein feeds and the threat of such controls for many other commodities (including grains and fertilizers) have not only disrupted normal commercial relations but also threatened the very fabric of the emerging international economic order.

The changing world food situation calls for a U.S. government policy decision to ensure that both governmental and private reserve stocks are built to adequate levels when the opportunity is there. In order to reduce farmers' fears that the presence of large reserves will be used to hold prices to unreasonably low levels, it will also be necessary to guarantee fair farm-price levels. However, food reserves are too important to the national interest to be left entirely in the hands of private traders, whose priorities are necessarily not identical with the national welfare. The United States may no longer have the desire or the ability to hold reserve stocks for the world, but both domestic needs and continuing international responsibilities require new care in reserve planning. The precise reserves needed and the price levels at which government stocks are built up or drawn down will have to be determined through careful analysis of market conditions, climatic risks, and progress in stock-building in other nations.

ASSURED ACCESS TO FOOD SUPPLIES

Since food scarcity is likely to be a frequent problem in the years ahead, careful consideration also must be given to the establishment of international standards to govern the conditions under which important food suppliers are permitted to withhold supplies as well as to provide some assurance of access to needed food supplies for importing nations. Either revision of present arrangements under the General Agreement on Tariffs and Trade or the creation of new international rules in another forum could define the circumstances in which principal suppliers would be justified in restricting exports and could provide for automatic international consultation and action in the event of international food shortages. The establishment of such international guidelines on access to food—an area in which the United States predominates—would set an important precedent of great potential value in finding solutions for problems of access to *non*food resources.

Greater assurance of access to food supplies for importing nations should be linked to participation in a new world system of information-sharing and reserve management. This would help avoid a repeat performance of the Soviet Union's covert buying up of a sizable share of the exportable U.S. wheat supplies in 1972, to the detriment of consumers throughout the world. More open sharing of basic data on harvests and reserve stocks, especially by the Soviet Union and China (which have held most such information secret), would permit potential supplier nations to plan their own production and trade policies far more efficiently.

But the principal exporting nations must also recognize an obligation not to impose restrictions on commercial food exports when world supplies become tight and world prices begin to rise. If major food-exporting nations attempt to isolate their own populations from world market trends, the chances of building a cooperative world trading system with long-term benefits for all nations will be greatly reduced. International conflict and competition for access to needed foodstuffs is bound to spill over into other areas where economic and political cooperation is needed—and the world's low-income groups, as usual, are likely to suffer the most.

CRITICAL FOOD NEEDS

Designing appropriate world food-aid policies for an era of frequent food scarcity and higher prices presents many difficult dilemmas. The net effect of long-term concessional sales of food on recipient nations has not always been wholly positive. The ready availability of food aid has permitted governments to postpone difficult agricultural reforms. At times food aid has depressed farm prices, discouraging rather than encouraging the expansion of agricultural output. When accompanied by appropriate recipient-government economic policies, however, food aid can be as valuable as any other resource transfer, and some countries, including Israel and Pakistan, have made highly valuable use of PL 480 food in their national agricultural-development plans. An additional problem with long-term concessional sales has been the possible disruption of commercial export markets of third countries, even though the FAO has hammered out detailed procedures for keeping such effects to a minimum.

When supplies were abundant and inexpensive, large food-aid programs were initiated with little serious analysis of the costs and benefits. When supplies are scarce, however, the direct costs of food aid to the donors become apparent. It is now necessary to identify those functions that food aid can perform best and those for which it is absolutely essential, and then to devise the institutional means that can most efficiently meet these specific needs.

International food aid is most clearly necessary, and most unambiguously beneficial, when populations are threatened with famine due to poor harvests, natural calamities, or other causes. Any proposal for food aid in an era of scarcity must see emergency food relief as the number-one priority and must aim to strengthen the international capacity to respond to emergencies with adequate amounts of food—even at times when supplies are tight in the more affluent nations. The international community should seriously consider recent proposals to create a permanent international disaster-relief agency. The resulting systematic international development of expertise in identifying potential food needs early, mobilizing adequate resources, and delivering food quickly to stricken areas would be an important step forward in a basic area of international responsibility now handled on a relatively haphazard basis. A further possibility would be the establishment of a sizable emergency food-reserve stock under the control of such an international body, with the foodstuffs available for release only to meet emergency needs.

A long-term food-relief effort of growing proportions is likely to be necessary for the drought-stricken nations of West Africa and probably Ethiopia as well, until very fundamental ecological and economic recovery occurs. It is certain that in future years other emergency food needs will arise in other regions. The global capacity to respond quickly and adequately when famine threatens must be systematically improved now, before a convergence of unfortunate events once again tragically underscores the failure to do so.

Food aid also has an essential and continuing role to play in an equally important if less conspicuous area of emergency relief. Unhappily, the global prevalence of malnutrition is likely to rise, not diminish, in the years immediately ahead. Projects like those of the international voluntary agencies, the WFP, and many other agencies within the developing countries—all of which use food grants to help meet directly the nutritional needs of those who have no means of purchasing adequate food supplies—deserve expansion rather than the contraction that has occurred.

Such programs, of course, cannot meet the nutritional needs of more than a fraction of those who are in danger, but they can make an important difference for tens or even hundreds of millions. Even in the affluent United States, by mid-1974 one of every thirteen residents was receiving federal food stamps under a program intended to make more adequate food purchases possible. Among the low-income groups in the developing world, few can hope to purchase an adequate diet in the foreseeable future without some form of assistance.

Given the limited resources available, food programs in the developing countries need to be focused directly on the most vulnerable groups—pregnant women, nursing mothers, and infants. Inadequate nutrition in the final months of pregnancy and during the early years of life can cause permanent physical and mental debilitation. The voluntary agencies have gradually been shifting priorities away from school lunch programs (which perform a useful role but are less urgent than programs aimed at the most vulnerable groups) toward programs for maternal and infant nutrition. However, school feeding programs are still the most prevalent type of nutrition project, and the pace of change needs to be hastened.

If programs to improve nutrition among vulnerable groups are to be administered effectively, the donors—principally the United States, but also other developed nations that give mainly through the WFP—will have to consider entering multiyear commitments in terms of actual commodity quantities rather than dollar value. Otherwise there will surely be a repetition of the events of 1973, when the food available to such programs was cut severely just at the time when the need for it was at a peak.

CONCESSIONAL FOOD SALES?

Clearly food aid is no panacea for eliminating hunger and malnutrition, and it cannot be a substitute for agricultural progress, economic development, and slowing population growth in the food-short nations. But in the immediate circumstances of serious global economic disruption, there is a need for a special program of concessional grain sales.

Concessional food sales have a crucial role to play in helping to avert a major catastrophe among the poorest quarter of the world's population. A new coordinated world program—led by the United States but also involving Canada, Australia, and possibly the EEC—to provide substantial levels of grain on soft terms to the nations hardest hit by recent energy, food, and fertilizer price rises will be needed during the next few years if a major economic setback in these countries is to be avoided. Indeed, if the shortage of fertilizers in Asia cuts indigenous production as severely as current developments suggest, only a concerted international effort can forestall a disaster of catastrophic proportions.

Such a program would not have to be viewed as a permanent food-aid effort; rather, the need is for emergency action to tide over the nations most severely affected by the jarring economic shocks of the 1972–74 period until fertilizer and food production can resume an upward trend and the necessary economic adjustments to new world commodity market conditions can take place.

The question of concessional food sales over the long term yields no easy answers. As noted earlier, many economists have serious doubts about the effect of continuing large-scale food-aid programs on progress toward the essential goal of increased food production within the developing countries. Furthermore, the psychological effect of a state of chronic dependency is not likely to produce a healthy relationship of respect and cooperation between the nations involved on both sides of the transfer.

These considerations are tempered, however, by the fact that when a real food-import need exists in a developing country, any softening of the terms of the sales will represent a real resource transfer, saving valuable foreign exchange for other purposes. And if a developing country is in serious economic trouble and simply lacks the foreign-exchange capability to buy needed food on the commercial market, concessional sales may be the only alternative to widespread malnutrition and starvation, or even economic and political collapse.

Food for Development

One important way to maximize the long-term benefits of food sold on concessional terms or of food grants to recipient nations is to tie at least a substantial share of the aid to programs that mobilize manpower and resources for the construction of needed agricultural infrastructure. The most direct utilization of food aid in this fashion is in rural public-works projects, which take advantage of idle manpower in the slack seasons between harvest and planting for the labor-intensive construction of roads, irrigation and drainage channels, and other facilities needed to spur agricultural output.

For example, the very successful works program in East Pakistan (now Bangladesh) during the early 'sixties was financed largely through the sale of wheat supplied by the United States. Workers in Morocco and Tunisia have received PL 480 wheat and semolina as part of their wages in the long-standing rural-construction programs in those nations. On a smaller scale than the public-works schemes in several countries are the "food for work" projects organized by the international voluntary agencies, the WFP, and governments in numerous developing countries, from Ghana to Brazil. Under these projects, many of which have relied heavily on U.S. grants under PL 480, the donated food is usually provided as wages to local residents, who supply the labor to build a needed school, a farm-to-market road, or some other facility important to the economic welfare of the community. The national or local governments, for their part, generally supply the building materials and engineering expertise required by the projects.

Even when food aid is not used directly in rural construction programs, it can be tied to food-production efforts. One possible approach is to earmark the local proceeds from the sale of food received on concessional terms from abroad for needed investments in the agricultural sector—as in water control, small-farmer credit, and extension services.

AGRICULTURAL RESEARCH NEEDS

Current research efforts to raise per-acre yields and protein content of food crops deserve strong support from governments and private funders. And in the United States, the unfortunate downward trend in the federal agricultural research budget needs to be reversed. Maintaining a given rate of growth in yields will require a steadily expanding research budget.

Higher-yielding, higher-protein varieties of such dryland crops as sorghum and millet are desperately needed in areas that are too dry to take advantage of the new wheats and rices. Higher-yielding varieties of protein-rich pulses are also needed if the current disturbing tendency for many developing nations to reduce pulse acreage in favor of relatively high-yielding but low-protein grain is to be reversed. Little is known about the potential of agriculture in the tropical regions, where research breakthroughs might open up new areas to food production. The possibilities of highly productive multiple cropping remain unknown in many regions for want of effective research. Cassava varieties with higher yields and protein content are sorely needed in the tropics. New methods also must be devised to achieve a further expansion of grain yields in the more advanced nations. And this is by no means the end of the long list of critical research needs in the field of agricultural production.

A very encouraging recent development with special benefit for the developing nations was the formation in 1971 of the Consultative Group on International Agricultural Research. With headquarters at the World Bank in Washington, the Consultative Group is actively supported by the FAO, the Ford and Rockefeller Foundations, the World Bank, the U.S. Agency for International Development, and several other bilateral aid agencies, foundations, and international organizations. The Consultative Group is examining developing-country research needs on a systematic global basis and channeling financial support to priority areas. It is coordinating the research efforts and funding of six key research centers in different geographic regions and varied climates: the International Wheat and Maize Improvement Center (CIMMYT) in Mexico; the International Rice Research Institute (IRRI) in the Philippines; the International Center for Tropical Agriculture (CIAT) in Colombia; the International Potato Center (CIP) in Peru; the International Crops Research Institute for the Semi-Arid Tropics (ICRISAT) in India; and the International Institute of Tropical Agriculture (IITA) in Nigeria. In 1974, the various donors allocated more than $32 million to these centers and others just getting under way, including livestock and animal disease centers in Africa.

The Consultative Group represents the creation of a global agricultural-research strategy. It is helping to rectify a serious deficiency of the past: the overconcentration of research efforts on the problems of temperate-zone agriculture in the developed nations, which often had little relevance for the needs of most developing nations. It deserves continuing strong support, and donors should be prepared to increase their contributions when new needs are identified.

There is a strong feeling among research scientists working in this field that the existing centers and the Consultative Group can handle the main research to be done and that few, if any, additional international centers need to be created. The already established institutes focus on the major crops—rice, wheat, corn, sorghum, beans—and on livestock. It is now time to focus attention on systems within the individual developing countries that can provide the services and inputs farmers need to utilize the new technologies.

Equally important is the strengthening of local agronomic research facilities within the developing nations. Improved varieties must be adapted not only to national environmental conditions but also to the varying conditions within nations. Although a number of countries have made significant progress toward building indigenous research capabilities, the gap between needs and existing facilities is still very large. The FAO estimates that developing-country agricultural-research efforts need to be raised from their current level of $250 million annually to $1 billion a year. Clearly the developed countries will have to help meet a substantial portion of this critical need. Contributions to developing-country agricultural research from oil-exporting countries with large capital surpluses would also perform a valuable international service.

With global demand for high-quality protein rising rapidly, an especially strong need has emerged for a breakthrough in soybean yields per acre. Now that there is little new land available for expanding the area planted to this crucial crop in the world's two major soybean-producing countries, the inability to raise yields substantially is an ominous cloud in the world food economy. The possibility of creating a joint Sino-American soybean research institute has great potential value. China, where the soybean originated, has the most diverse available collection of germ plasm—a vital asset in an expanded soybean research effort. The United States, on the other hand, has already invested a great deal of effort in devising better farming practices and in making the soybean plant more productive. The critical importance of the soybean to both economies—not to mention mankind as a whole—argues for the pooling of germ plasm and the coordination of research efforts in an all-out effort to raise yields.

PART FIVE

Toward Century's End

17.

COMPLEXITY, CHANGE, LEADERSHIP

Efforts to cope with food scarcity cannot be viewed in isolation. They are part of a broader effort to create a workable world order in an age of resource scarcity, worsening inflation, and growing interdependence among nations. The changes required are not trivial, and they will not come easily. The risk is that the dimensions and the urgency of the unfolding world food problem will not be recognized and confronted soon enough.

FUTURE FOOD PROSPECTS

An assessment of future food-production prospects is an incredibly complex undertaking. One must be at once an agronomist, an economist, an ecologist, a meteorologist, and a political scientist to begin to understand the scope of the problem. This difficulty is reflected in the poor record compiled during the early 'seventies by those who attempted to forecast changes in the world food economy. Very few anticipated the reversal in the oceanic fish catch. The mass Soviet grain purchase in 1972 took the world almost completely by surprise. No one expected the doubling of world wheat, rice, feed grain, and soybean prices of the 1972–74 period. The U.S. Department of Agriculture, with one of the finest economic-analysis units available, projected a 3 per cent annual rate of food-price inflation early in 1973; the rate turned out to be closer to 20 per cent. Few foresaw the possibility that the vast acreage of idled U.S. cropland would be called back into use within a two-year period—and even fewer foresaw that it might not suffice to overcome scarcity and return food prices to a more "normal" level. The slack that has existed in the world food economy since the end of World War II has now disappeared, at least temporarily.

Food-production prospects are clouded by the scarcity of all the basic inputs—land, water, energy, and fertilizer. Farmers everywhere are faced with rising costs for these essential resources. With most good farmland in the world already under cultivation, additional land is becoming more costly and less productive. Most of the easy irrigation projects have already been undertaken. Farmers in much of the world are confronted not only with higher fertilizer costs as the cost of energy rises but also with lessening returns on fertilizer use. The amount of grain produced with each additional ton of fertilizer used is beginning to diminish at the global level, largely because of the high levels of use in such areas as North America, Western Europe, and Japan. Each additional million tons of fertilizer applied by the world's farmers now adds less food than was added by the preceding million tons.

Energy prices have tripled over the past two years; yet we know that further increases in agricultural yields will require enormous additional amounts of energy to fuel tractors and irrigation pumps, and to manufacture fertilizer. As we have noted, Professor David Pimentel and his colleagues at Cornell University have calculated that, if the entire world were to move toward the energy-intensive form of agriculture and the diet prevalent in the United States, known world reserves of petroleum would be exhausted by agriculture alone within twenty-nine years. There is, of course, no realistic prospect that this will occur, but the calculation does illustrate how severe the energy constraint on food production could become in the years ahead.

One of the most disquieting developments on the food front is the unanticipated downward trend in the world fish catch during the early 'seventies following twenty years of continuous growth. There is a very real prospect that the world catch of table-grade fish may not expand much more, and, in the absence of a cooperative global approach to the management of oceanic fisheries and control of the swelling flow of pollutants, it may decline even further. Here the problem is not merely the possibility of diminishing returns on investment in additional fishing capacity but the prospect of *negative* returns. Additional investment in fishing fleets now contributes to overfishing and actually reduces the catch in many fisheries.

If the world fish catch fails to resume its upward trend, the pressure on supplies will become intense. Large countries such as the Soviet Union and Japan, which have come to depend heavily on fish, will be forced to substitute poultry, pork, or beef if they are to maintain animal-protein intake. This in turn will require them to import vast additional quantities of feed grains, putting even greater pressure on the world's exportable cereal supplies.

Assessing the adequacy of future food production depends on the answers to many questions that are at this juncture essentially unanswerable. At what point will the trend in rising yields per acre in the advanced countries tend to level off? The quarter-century now ending was marked by rapid growth in per-acre yields in virtually all industrial societies. Corn yields in the United States have nearly tripled since World War II. But is it likely that they will triple again over the next quarter-century? What about dryland agriculture in such areas as the Great Plains of North America, Australia, and the Soviet Union? Are substantial increases in prospect there, or will they come slowly and grudgingly? And what about the likelihood of rapidly increasing rice yields? No major producing country, not even Japan, has yet succeeded in achieving a rate of increase in rice yields remotely approaching that of corn in the United States or wheat in northwestern Europe.

One of the principal keys to future food-production prospects is the combination of technology from the industrial countries with the capital and flared natural gas of the Middle East to produce abundant supplies of moderately priced fertilizer. The Middle East has the raw materials and the capital to become the dominant supplier of comparatively cheap nitrogen fertilizer for the rest of the world. Whether or not it will do so depends very much on international political relationships. Probably no other single factor can affect food-production prospects over the next decade as much as the outcome of this question.

The political decision taken by the Soviet leadership in 1972 to offset crop shortfalls by imports rather than by belt-tightening has had important consequences for stability in the world food economy, for a shortfall in the crop of a vast nation with highly erratic weather can easily exceed the normal year-to-year growth in world food output. The Soviet purchase of 28 million tons of grain following its poor crop in the summer of 1972 virtually matched the 30-million-ton annual growth in world grain output.

In assessing future food prospects it is also essential to separate myth from reality. Many view the vast interior of Brazil as a potential source of almost unlimited food production, but available soil maps show only a very small percentage of arable land in the Brazilian interior. The fact is that even if Brazil were to double its food output, the resulting increase would not equal even one year's growth in world demand. Even while Brazil's leaders are talking of the need for further population growth, its cereal deficit grows larger, putting additional pressure on the world's exportable supplies. By 1973 Brazil's deficit had become the largest in the Western Hemisphere. This is not to say that Brazil may not someday be a net exporter of cereals, as it now is of soybeans, but its potential must not be overestimated.

When many populous developing countries were in serious trouble on the food front as population growth began to outstrip food output during the mid-'sixties, they were temporarily rescued from their predicament by the Green Revolution. Production increases due to these new seeds are presenting heavily populated countries with a very brief opportunity to slow population growth, an opportunity that few governments have yet moved vigorously to exploit. If the demographic brakes are not applied soon, they will face an increasingly bleak future, for there is no new food-production breakthrough in prospect comparable to the Green Revolution.

One of the most ominous trends on the world food horizon is the ecological undermining of food-producing systems. The scale and rapidity of this ecological deterioration has no precedent. The initial southward movement of the Sahara affected only the six sparsely populated countries on the desert's immediate southern fringe, countries containing collectively about 22 million people, but as it continues, it is beginning to affect several more populous countries, including Nigeria, with 59 million people, and Ethiopia, with 28 million. More than 100 million people, equal to half the population of North America, are now threatened by the Sahara.

On the Indian subcontinent the overgrazing and deforestation resulting from overpopulation are contributing to two problems: expansion of the Thar Desert in northwestern India and an increase in the frequency and severity of flooding. To date there had been no detailed analysis of this situation. Available evidence, fragmentary though it is, suggests that it is deteriorating, in all probability at an accelerating rate.

These ecological trends are well established and rather predictable. Another question of even greater importance is whether the monsoon belt may be shifting southward in Africa and Asia, as some meteorologists now believe may be the case. If this is so, the resulting reduction in food output will confront the world with a much more serious threat than any we have so far mentioned.

World agriculture also faces critical capital shortages as the requirements to achieve a given increase in output rise. This is particularly apparent with fertilizer. The new fertilizer production capacity required to meet projected growth in world demand over the next ten years must equal the total created to date. Stated otherwise, the outlays for new plant capacity over the next decade must equal those of the several decades since the industry began.

On the plus side, there is still a very substantial potential for raising yields in many developing countries, assuming that the requisite inputs of water, energy, and fertilizer are available to realize this potential. The new high-yielding dwarf wheats and rices underlying the Green Revolution are early maturing and have more flexible planting dates, thus expanding the opportunity for multiple cropping (again, assuming that additional inputs are forthcoming). New opportunities may also exist for double cropping in temperate-zone countries. Historically, little attention has been paid to this potential, simply because overproduction has been a problem in the past generation, during which the technology, especially the intensive use of chemical fertilizer, has made double cropping feasible. With food supplies now much tighter, the combination of a winter grain crop such as wheat and a summer crop such as soybeans could become an important source of additional output in the immediate future in such locales as the southern portion of the U.S. corn belt.

Also on the hopeful side is the fact that some governments have demonstrated that they *can* achieve rapid gains in food output. We know that farmers respond to economic incentives. Some governments have also demonstrated that they can put the brakes on population growth. A handful of developing countries, possibly including China, have already matched the remarkable reduction in birth rates in Japan between 1948 and 1955.

The adequacy of future food production may be influenced more than anything else by the extent to which we can slow growth in population. If food output can expand rapidly enough to meet the growth in demand as now projected, it will do so only with a steadily rising price level—a level beyond that which the poorest segment of mankind can afford. Unless future growth in population and food demand slows well below the rate currently projected, painfully high food prices seem inevitable in the future. In the absence of a massive supplemental food-distribution program, reaching the literally hundreds of millions in the world's lowest income group for whom the cost of enough food to survive is gradually climbing out of reach, death rates will inevitably rise, again becoming the ultimate check on population growth.

"FOURTH WORLD" FOCUS

Since World War II, the poor or less developed countries of Asia, Africa, and Latin America have been referred to collectively as the Third World. Today, however, this term is losing its usefulness. Asia, Africa, and Latin America are no longer an unrelieved mass of abject poverty. Many countries have achieved remarkable progress on both the economic and the social fronts.

If development is judged by social indicators, East Asia, with nearly a billion people, has actually progressed quite far. This group of countries, making up half of Asia, includes China, Korea, Taiwan, Hong Kong, Singapore, and, of course, Japan. Several Latin American countries have achieved rather high average consumption levels, but a basic problem plaguing these societies is the grossly uneven distribution of income and wealth. Brazil and Mexico, for example, are raising average living levels impressively, although large elements within these two countries remain desperately poor. Moreover, if the price of oil remains high, the likelihood of a dramatic improvement in social and economic well-being also is good for the 250 million people living in oil-exporting countries, which include some of the more populous countries: Iran, Algeria, Nigeria, Venezuela, and Indonesia.

This leaves about forty countries with 900 million people, or one fourth of the world's population, in which average per capita income is still less than $150 per year. This population is concentrated in the Indian subcontinent, in sub-Saharan Africa, and in pockets within Latin America, such as northeastern Brazil. The countries in this category not only have the lowest incomes but also are resource-poor. At a time of rapidly rising world energy and food prices, they are facing an acute crisis. Many simply do not have the foreign exchange required to cover their import needs.

This is the group of countries most severely affected by the sharp increases in energy, fertilizer, and food prices of the 1972–74 period. Without assistance, they cannot afford enough of these basic commodities; therefore they face a substantial real decline in consumption. For millions, perhaps tens of millions, consumption levels may fall below survival levels. As of mid-1974, there already are indications that the twenty-year trend of declining death rates has been reversed in a number of countries in Central America, sub-Saharan Africa, and in the Indian subcontinent. Faced with a scarcity of resources and, in many cases, the ecological undermining of food systems, this "Fourth World" group of countries desperately needs help from the international community.

In these Fourth World countries, even a minimal expenditure to establish family-planning clinics and improve food production will pay enormous dividends in human well-being. These nations desperately need capital inputs to help exploit their as yet unrealized agronomic potential for expanding food production and to combine with their one abundant resource—labor. If producing more food can create more jobs, productive employment in the countryside will not only improve nutrition and raise incomes but also slow urban migration, preventing the cities from being completely overwhelmed. It will also help create a social climate of progress in which birth rates will begin to fall voluntarily.

REORDERING PRIORITIES

In an age of increasingly severe ecological stresses and resource scarcities and of resulting economic and political instability, the time has come to re-examine threats to human security and well-being—to redefine security or, more precisely, new sources of insecurity. It is becoming more and more difficult to justify the current scale of U.S. and global military expenditures. The U.S. involvement in Southeast Asia is a sad reminder of the limitations on what the world's leading military power can do against even a tiny nation such as North Vietnam. The relative impotence of a vast array of military armaments is also evident in the U.S. relationship with Ecuador. Ecuador has blatantly violated existing international regulations on offshore boundaries, seizing some fifty-six U.S. tuna trawlers in a twelve-month period and fining them $2.3 million. The United States could not even threaten to intervene in this situation, for the simple reason that intervention by the U.S. Navy would have cost U.S. investors billions of dollars in Latin America, and because a denial of access to vital raw materials in Latin America, such as copper, tin, and oil, would have jeopardized U.S. economic security.

The Soviet Union finds itself in a similar predicament. Given their dependence on imports of technology, not to mention huge quantities of grain and soybeans from the United States, Soviet leaders would be exceedingly unwise to consider attacking their major supplier. No other country or combination of countries has the capacity to meet future Soviet food-import needs.

Moreover, rapidly accumulating evidence suggests that the threats to man's future security and well-being are not so much the traditional ones of international conflict and invasion by a foreign power but, rather, emerging economic and ecological instabilities. Continuing population growth may endanger man's future even more than nuclear war—suggesting the need for a massive commitment of resources to move the world away from its present demographic path. What is now essential is a commitment to bringing population growth to a halt at a much lower level and much earlier than was previously projected. At the same time, educational programs and economic incentives are needed to encourage the more affluent to reduce their per capita claims on the earth's scarce food-producing resources.

Current circumstances strongly suggest the need to channel far more resources into agricultural production in the developing countries. Energy scarcity and food scarcity are closely related. Unless energy can become more abundant in developing countries, it will be virtually impossible for these countries to increase food supplies at an acceptable rate. This means, among other things, reducing the frivolous use of energy in affluent countries in order to free scarce fossil-fuel supplies to expand food production in the developing countries. Huge, gas-guzzling autos in the United States and other affluent societies, soaking up a disproportionately large share of the world's available energy, may be a greater threat to future global security than many commonly recognized dangers. Such societies must now reduce their dependence on the grossly inefficient large automobile by substituting smaller ones, developing efficient mass-transit systems, and increasing opportunities for bicycle transportation.

If the international community seriously desires to achieve nutritionally adequate diets for all, to cope with food-price inflation, and to maintain some semblance of economic and political stability, the need to modify severely the projected growth in the world demand for food cannot be ignored. An all-out effort must be made both to slow population growth and to avoid excess per capita food consumption, particularly where it becomes detrimental to human health.

Every person added to the world's population today, regardless of where, puts some additional pressure on the earth's resources of land, fresh water, and energy. If the person is added to the population of the industrial countries, then the pressure on the global supply of these resources may be three, four, or five times as great as when the person is added in a less developed country. The combined effect of these growing pressures is that man is in serious trouble in his efforts to ensure adequate food supplies. The signs are ominous. The urgency of checking population growth everywhere and of moving toward stability as rapidly as possible cannot be overemphasized.

A global strategy to cope with the new problems now confronting mankind brings into focus certain areas that need much more investment than they are now receiving. Slowing population growth quickly requires a massive immediate effort to satisfy basic social needs—including assured food supplies, literacy, reduced infant mortality, and access to at least rudimentary health services. Although availability of family-planning services alone cannot be expected to solve population problems, it will be essential. The evidence of 40 million induced abortions around the world each year attests to the gap between the need and the availability of family-planning services. The U.N. Fund for Population Activities estimates that it would take about $2 billion per year to make family-planning services universally available in the developing countries. Even if the cost were twice as much, it would be a trivial investment compared to the potential deterioration in human security and well-being—not only our own, but that of generations to come.

THE MORAL DIMENSION

Although world food output has expanded impressively over the past generation, population growth so far has absorbed all but a fraction of the increase. Hundreds of millions of the world's people still do not have enough food to fully realize their genetic potential as human beings. In a situation of global food scarcity, if some of us consume more, others must of necessity consume less. The issue that some of us are forced to confront in a world where we are dependent on common resources of energy and fertilizer to produce food is whether we can realize *our* full humanity if we continue to overconsume in full knowledge that we are thereby contributing to the premature death of fellow human beings. Former Chancellor Willy Brandt of West Germany summed up this point effectively in his first address before the U.N. General Assembly in the fall of

1973: "Morally it makes no difference whether a man is killed in war or is condemned to starve to death by the indifference of others."

Altruism is a hallmark of civilized society. But in a world transformed from a collection of relatively independent, isolated nation-states to one of complex interdependence, reliant on the sharing of often scarce resources, our concept of altruism must be adjusted. It is no longer merely a matter of alms-giving but of abstaining from excessive consumption when that consumption jeopardizes the very survival of human beings elsewhere in the world. For a man with only one crust of bread, a second crust may ensure survival, but for one with a loaf of bread, an additional crust is of marginal value. What is at issue in the global politics of food scarcity is who will get the additional crust—affluent consumers in the United States and the Soviet Union, who do not need it, or those on the brink of survival in the Indian subcontinent and in the sub-Saharan countries of Africa.

Both conventional wisdom and economics have long held that the more the rich countries consume, the greater the markets will be for products of the developing countries. This is still true in some situations, but only to a degree. If the supply of a given resource cannot be expanded easily, continuing growth in consumption in the affluent countries will drive the price beyond the reach of the poor countries.

Our intent here is not to suggest that all affluent Americans, Russians, Europeans, or Japanese should abandon their automobiles or abstain from eating meat; it is to urge those who are more affluent to re-examine the link between their consumption of material goods and their own well-being. We need to ask whether a 20 per cent increase in income indeed brings a 20 per cent increase in well-being, a 10 per cent increase, or any increase at all. It has been said that there are two sources of unhappiness: not getting what we want, and getting it. Many of us may be in a situation where the only real satisfaction can come from trying to improve the lot of the world's most seriously deprived: those living in the Fourth World. Indeed, this could be the new moral and social frontier for mankind.

THE CHALLENGE TO LEADERSHIP

At a time of rapid change and growing complexity of problems, there is a premium on leadership at all levels. The more rapid the change and the greater the complexity of problems at both the national and the international levels, the greater the need for leadership. The answer to Robert Heilbroner's question, "Is there hope for man?"* hinges on whether the necessary leadership, both intellectual and political, is forthcoming.

The pressures that make leadership so necessary at the same time make it much more difficult for decision-makers to reach intelligent, responsible decisions. Such decisions require adequate information and analysis. In the population field, for example, one of the great bottlenecks continues to be the fact that so few leaders understand the dynamics of population growth. Not two national political leaders in a hundred are aware that a 3 per cent annual rate of population growth will result in a nineteenfold increase in a century.

Even when they understand the facts, decision-makers may not be prepared to act. One of the most difficult international political issues ahead derives from the shift in the nature of the world's food reserve from excess stocks and idled cropland to expanding herds of cattle and hogs and flocks of poultry. At a time of international food emergency it is much more difficult politically to tap the latter reserve by slaughtering back herds than simply to ship surplus stocks of grain abroad; leaders in rich countries may not be able to take this step in the absence of assurance by the political leaders of countries with rapid population growth that they will simultaneously make an all-out effort to reduce birth rates quickly and dramatically. This *quid pro quo* eventually may become an important part of any solution to the emerging global food crisis.

Additional political obstacles include the difference between the time horizons of office-holders and those of the problems they confront; bureaucracies traditionally are unable to change direction as rapidly as is necessary. Moreover, when the problems to be handled are large and complex, there is often a tendency to confuse

*Robert Heilbroner, *An Inquiry into the Human Prospect* (New York: W. W. Norton, 1974).

symptoms with causes. The result is often treatment of the symptoms and neglect of the causes. There is likewise a dangerous tendency to confuse triggering events with long-term trends. The massive 1972 Soviet wheat purchase in the United States, for example, was a triggering event which merely brought the changing relationship between long-term global food supply and demand trends into sharp focus—yet some have ascribed global food scarcity to that single event.

There is an age-old temptation to leave the difficult task of problem solution—in this field as in others—to someone else. The churches want to leave it to business, business wants to leave it to political leaders, and many political leaders prefer to follow rather than lead. The problems the world faces today are of such immense proportions that individuals in all walks of life will have to participate in solving them. If we are to change behavior, we must have information on the circumstances that make it necessary to do so, whether these are the ecological undermining of major food systems or worsening inflation resulting from excessive consumption. Widespread changes in behavior will occur only if the communications media play a central role; unless they take on this task on a large scale, there is little hope that we can change direction short of a global catastrophe.

We delude ourselves if we think the years ahead will be easy. At best they will be traumatic, and they could be catastrophic. The issues we have outlined will place great stress on the international political fabric. The crucial question is whether we can create a workable order for an increasingly interdependent world. This will require of our generation a level of leadership, understanding, and generosity of spirit that few past generations have been called upon to supply.

SELECTED READINGS

2. History and Geography of Malnutrition

Berg, Alan. *The Nutrition Factor: Its Role in Development.* Washington, D.C.: Brookings Institution, 1973.

Energy and Protein Requirements. Report of the Joint FAO/WHO *Ad Hoc* Expert Committee. Rome, FAO, 1973.

Lives in Peril: Protein and the Child. Rome: FAO, on behalf of the Protein Advisory Group, 1970.

Masefield, Geoffrey Bussell. *Famine: Its Prevention and Relief.* London: Oxford University Press, 1963.

Sauer, Carl O. *Agricultural Origins and Dispersals,* Cambridge, Mass.: MIT Press, 1969.

3. Population and Affluence

Organization for Economic Cooperation and Development. *Food Consumption Statistics, 1955–1971.* Paris, 1973.

————. *Meat Balances in OECD Member Countries, 1959–1972.* Paris, 1974.

4. Ecological Undermining of Food Systems

Brown, Lester R. "Human Food Production as a Process in the Biosphere," *Scientific American,* 233 (September, 1970): 160–70.

Brown, Lester R., and Gail W. Finsterbusch. *Man and His Environment: Food.* New York: Harper and Row, 1972.

Council on Environmental Quality. *Integrated Pest Management.* Washington, D.C., November, 1972.

Curry-Lindahl, Kai. *Conservation for Survival: An Ecological Strategy.* New York: William Morrow, 1972.

————. *Let Them Live: A Worldwide Survey of Animals Threatened With Extinction.* New York: William Morrow, 1972.

EHRLICH, PAUL R., and ANNE H. EHRLICH. *Population, Resources, Environment: Issues in Human Ecology.* Rev. ed. San Francisco: W. H. Freeman, 1972.

FARVAR, M. T., and J. P. MILTON, eds. *The Careless Technology: Ecology and International Development.* New York: Doubleday, Natural History Press, 1972.

Inadvertent Climate Modification: Report of the Study of Man's Impact on Climate (SMIC). Cambridge, Mass.: MIT Press, 1971.

OECD, Environment Directorate. *Scientific Fundamentals of the Eutrophication of Lakes and Flowing Waters, with Particular Reference to Nitrogen and Phosphorus as Factors in Eutrophication.* Paris: OECD, 1971.

Report of the Secretary's Commission on Pesticides and Their Relationship to Environmental Health, Parts I and II. Washington, D.C.: U.S. Department of Health, Education and Welfare, December, 1969.

U.S. Agency for International Development, Office of Science and Technology. *Desert Encroachment on Arable Lands: Significance, Causes, and Control.* TA/OST 72-10, Washington, D.C., August, 1972.

WARD, BARBARA, and RENÉ DUBOS. *Only One Earth: The Care and Maintenance of a Small Planet.* New York: W. W. Norton, 1972.

5.   GROWING GLOBAL FOOD INSECURITY

ALEXANDER, TOM. "Ominous Changes in the World's Weather," *Fortune,* February, 1974.

BROWN, LESTER R. "The Next Crisis? Food." *Foreign Policy,* No. 13, Winter, 1973–74.

BRYSON, REID A. "World Food Prospects and Climatic Change." Testimony before Committee on Agriculture, U.S. Senate, October 18, 1973.

COCHRANE, WILLARD W. *Feast or Famine: The Uncertain World of Food and Its Policy Implications for the United States.* Washington, D.C., National Planning Association, Report No. 36, February, 1974.

SCHERTZ, LYLE P. "World Food: Prices and the Poor," *Foreign Affairs,* Vol. 52, No. 3, April 1974.

SIMON, PAUL, and ARTHUR SIMON. *The Politics of World Hunger.* New York: Harper's Magazine Press, 1973.

6. LAND FOR FOOD

BROWN, LESTER R. *Man, Land and Food.* U.S. Department of Agriculture, Economic Research Service, Foreign Agriculture Report No. 11, November, 1963.

DALRYMPLE, DANA G. *Survey of Multiple Cropping in Less Developed Nations.* Washington, D.C., U.S. Department of Agriculture, Foreign Economic Development Service, FEDR-12, October, 1971.

President's Science Advisory Committee. *The World Food Problem.* Report of the Panel on the World Food Supply. 3 vols. Washington, D.C.: U.S. Government Printing Office, 1967.

WITTWER, S. H. "Maximum Production Capacity of Food Crops," *BioScience,* 24, No. 4 (April, 1974): 216–24.

7. WATER AND BREAD

ADDISON, HERBERT. *Land, Water and Food.* 2d Rev. Ed. London: Chapman and Hall, 1961.

BRADLEY, CHARLES C. "Human Water Needs and Water Use in America," *Science,* Vol. 138, October 26, 1962.

CLAWSON, MARION, *et al.* "Desalted Sea Water for Agriculture: Is It Economic?" *Science,* Vol. 166, June 6, 1969.

FAO. *The Environmental Aspects of Water Resources Development and Management with Suggestions for Action,* presented to U.N. Conference on the Human Environment, Stockholm, 1972, August 17, 1971.

FURON, RAYMOND. *The Problem of Water: A World Study.* Trans. PAUL BARNES. New York: American Elsevier Publishing, 1967.

National Academy of Sciences. *Weather and Climate Modification: Problems and Progress.* Washington, D.C., 1973.

8. ENERGY AND AGRICULTURE

GRANT, JAMES P. "Energy Shock and the Development Prospect," in JAMES W. HOWE, ed., *The U.S. and the Development World: Agenda for Action, 1974.* New York: Praeger Publishers, 1974.

HIRST, ERIC. "Food-Related Energy Requirements," *Science,* Vol. 184, April 12, 1974.

PIMENTEL, DAVID, *et al.* "Food Production and the Energy Crisis." *Science,* Vol. 182, November 2, 1973.

STEINHART, CAROL E., and JOHN S. STEINHART. *Energy: Sources, Use, and Role in Human Affairs.* North Scituate, Mass.: Duxbury Press, 1974.

————. "Energy Use in the U.S. Food System." *Science,* Vol. 184, April 19, 1974.

9. THE ROLE OF FERTILIZER

EWELL, RAYMOND. Population-Food-Fertilizer Relationships, 1953–85. Testimony before Select Committee on Nutrition, U.S. Senate, June 19–21, 1974.

FAO. *Annual Fertilizer Review, 1972.* Rome: 1973.

SLACK, A. V. *Defense Against Famine: The Role of the Fertilizer Industry.* New York: Doubleday, 1970.

Tennessee Valley Authority. *World Fertilizer Market Review and Outlook.* Muscle Shoals, Ala.: National Fertilizer Development Center, 1974.

U.S. and World Fertilizer Outlook, prepared for the use of the Committee on Agriculture and Forestry, U.S. Senate, 93d Congress, 2d Session, March 21, 1974.

10. THE GREEN REVOLUTION

BROWN, LESTER R. *Seeds of Change: The Green Revolution and Development in the 1970s.* New York: Praeger, 1970.

DALRYMPLE, DANA G. *Development and Spread of High Yielding Varieties of Wheat and Rice in the Less Developed Nations.* U.S. Department of Agriculture, Foreign Economic Development Report 95, July, 1974.

FALCON, WALTER P. "The Green Revolution: Generations of Problems." *American Journal of Agricultural Economics,* December, 1970.

FRANKEL, FRANCINE. *India's Green Revolution: Economic Gains and Political Costs.* Princeton, N.J.: Princeton University Press, 1971.

PALMER, INGRID. *The New Rice in Monsoon Asia.* Geneva: U.N. Research Institute for Social Development, 1974.

11. DEEP TROUBLE IN OCEANIC FISHERIES

CHRISTY, FRANCIS T., JR. *Alternative Arrangements for Marine Fisheries: An Overview.* Washington, D.C., Resources for the Future, RFF/PISFA Paper 1, May, 1973.

HOLT, S. J. "The Food Resources of the Ocean." *Scientific American,* 221, No. 3 (September, 1969): 178–94.

IDYLL, C. P. "The Anchovy Crisis." *Scientific American.* 228, No. 6, (June, 1973): 22–29.

————. *The Sea Against Hunger.* New York: Thomas Y. Crowell, 1970.

JARRIN, EDGARDO MERCADO. "Utilizing Sea Resources for Human and Social Welfare." *Pacific Community,* 3, No. 2 (January, 1972): 302–12.

MACINTYRE, FERRIN, and R. W. HOLMES. "Ocean Pollution," in WILLIAM W. MURDOCH, ed., *Environment: Resources, Pollution and Society.* Stamford, Conn.: Sinauer Associates, 1971.

PILLAY, T. V. R. "The Role of Aquaculture in Fishery Development and Management," FAO Technical Conference on Fishery Management and Development, Vancouver, Canada, February 13–23, 1973.

12. NON-CONVENTIONAL FOOD SOURCES

ALTSCHUL, AARON M., ed. *New Protein Foods, Vol. 1A: Technology.* New York and London: Academic Press, 1974.

BERG, ALAN. "Industry's Struggle with World Malnutrition," *Harvard Business Review,* January–February, 1972.

ORR, ELIZABETH. *The Use of Protein-Rich Foods for the Relief of Malnutrition in Developing Countries: An Analysis of Experience.* London: Tropical Products Institute, August, 1972.

SCRIMSHAW, NEVIN S., ed. *Single Cell Protein II.* Cambridge, Mass.: MIT Press, 1974.

TSEN, CHO C., ed. *Triticale: First Man-Made Cereal.* Saint Paul, Minn.: American Association of Cereal Chemists, 1974.

U.S. Agency for International Development, Bureau for Technical Assistance, Office of Agriculture. *Increasing Food Production with Emphasis on High Protein Crops,* Washington, D.C.: March, 1973.

13. PUTTING ON THE DEMOGRAPHIC BRAKES

BERELSON, BERNARD, ed. "World Population: Status Report 1974; A Guide for the Concerned Citizen." Population Council, *Reports on Population/Family Planning,* January, 1974.

BROWN, LESTER R. *In the Human Interest: A Strategy to Stabilize World Population.* Washington, D.C.: W. W. Norton, 1974.

FREJKA, TOMAS. *The Future of Population Growth: Alternative Paths to Equilibrium.* New York: John Wiley & Sons, Population Council Book, 1973.

KOCHER, JAMES E. *Rural Development, Income Distribution, and Fertility Decline.* New York: Population Council, 1973.

McDONALD, J. CORBETT. *Unmet Needs in Family Planning.* London: International Planned Parenthood Federation, 1973.

MORAES, DOM. *A Matter of People.* New York: Praeger Publishers, 1974.

NORTMAN, DOROTHY, assisted by Ellen Hofstatter. "Population and Family Planning: A Factbook." Population Council, *Reports on Population/Family Planning,* September, 1973.

RICH, WILLIAM. *Smaller Families Through Social and Economic Progress,* Monograph No. 7. Washington, D.C.: Overseas Development Council, 1973.

14. SIMPLIFYING DIETS

EWALD, ELLEN BUSHMAN. *Recipes for a Small Planet.* New York: Ballantine Books, 1973.

HEWITT, JEAN. *The New York Times Natural Foods Cookbook.* New York: Quadrangle Books, 1971.

LAPPE, FRANCIS MOORE. *Diet for a Small Planet.* New York: Ballantine Books, 1971.

MAYER, JEAN. *U.S. Nutrition Policies in the Seventies.* San Francisco: W. H. Freeman, 1973.

15. HUNGER AND UNEMPLOYMENT

DORNER, PETER. *Land Reform and Economic Development.* Baltimore: Penguin Books, 1972.

EICHER, C. K., T. ZALLA, J. E. KOCHER, and F. WINCH. *Employment Generation in African Agriculture.* East Lansing: Michigan State University, Institute on International Agriculture, Research Report No. 9, July, 1970.

GRANT, JAMES P. *Growth from Below: A People-Oriented Development Strategy.* Washington, D.C.: Overseas Development Council, Development Paper 16, December, 1973.

JOHNSTON, BRUCE F., and PETER KILBY. *Agricultural Strategies, Rural-Urban Interactions and the Expansion of Income Opportunities.* Paris: OECD Development Centre, January, 1973.

LEWIS, JOHN P. "The Public Works Approach to Low-End Poverty Problems: The New Potentialities of an Old Answer," *Journal of Development Planning,* No. 5. United Nations, 1973.

MCNAMARA, ROBERT S. *One Hundred Countries, Two Billion People: The Dimensions of Development.* New York: Praeger, 1973.

MOSHER, ARTHUR T. *Creating a Progressive Rural Structure.* New York: Agricultural Development Council, 1969.

OWENS, EDGAR, and SHAW, ROBERT D'A. *Development Reconsidered.* Lexington, Mass.: Lexington Books, 1972.

SHAW, ROBERT D'A. *Jobs and Agricultural Development.* Washington, D.C.: Overseas Development Council, Monograph No. 3, 1970.

THOMAS, JOHN WOODWARD. "Employment Creating Public Works Programs: Observations on Political and Social Dimensions," in EDGAR EDWARDS, ed., *Employment in Developing Countries.* New York: Columbia University Press, forthcoming.

TODARO, MICHAEL P. "Income Expectations, Rural-Urban Migration and Employment in Africa," *International Labour Review,* 104, No. 5 (November, 1971): 387–413.

16. ALLEVIATING INSECURITY

FAO. *Proposal by the Director General on International Action to Assume Adequate Basic Food Stocks.* Romé, FAO Council, 11–22 June, 1973.

JOSLING, TIMOTHY. *An International Grain Reserve Policy.* London and Washington: British-North American Committee, July, 1973.

SHEETS, HAL, and ROGER MORRIS. *Disaster in the Desert: Failures of International Relief in the West African Drought.* Washington, D.C.: Humanitarian Policy Studies, Carnegie Endowment for International Peace, 1974.

THOMPSON, LOUIS M. *Weather Variability and the Need for a Food Reserve.* Ames, Iowa: Iowa State University, CAED Report 26, 1966.

INDEX